Donald Sinclair
1968.

SEÑOR KON-TIKI

SEÑOR KON-TIKI

by

ARNOLD JACOBY

ILLUSTRATED

London

GEORGE ALLEN & UNWIN LTD

RUSKIN HOUSE   MUSEUM STREET

Translated from SEÑOR KON-TIKI. Boken om Thor Heyerdahl
© J. W. Cappelens Forlag A/S 1965

PRINTED IN GREAT BRITAIN
in 12 point Bembo type
BY C. TINLING & CO. LTD.
LIVERPOOL, LONDON AND PRESCOT

FOREWORD

THE old sundial above the Italian *piazza* of Colla Micheri showed nine o'clock. The gable of the slate roof above it still threw a shadow across the weathered motto I knew so well. Which could be roughly translated:

'Can I tell you the time? Of course I can:

It is time to work, for an honest man.'

Nearer to the village church a young couple were hesitantly pushing at the heavy oak gate leading into Thor Heyerdahl's estate, hoping to get a glimpse inside. As I passed by I heard the girl say, 'I wonder what he's really like, this Señor Kon-Tiki?'

It struck me that the man himself, Thor Heyerdahl as a person, perhaps remained half obscured by the shadow of his world-famous enterprise: Kon-Tiki. It could be that I was the one who knew his intimate story best. We were boyhood friends and I had enjoyed his confidence throughout the years.

It would be fun to tell the story of why a water-frightened land-lubber ventured into the stormy Pacific on a raft; of why a man who suffered from fear of heights became a parachutist; of why an idealistic dreamer who would never hurt a sparrow had to combat sharks and submarines, bears and alligators; of why a man who despised most modern inventions had to become a radio expert; of why a man who was publicly accused of being a dilettante, an adventurer and not a scholar received the highest scientific awards from all over the world; of why a man who knew nothing about film-making won an Oscar; and of why an amateur writer one day woke up to find his book a runaway best seller, translated into more languages than any other book besides the Bible.

The remark of the curious young girl had kindled an idea in my mind. Yes, the story ought to be told. I pushed open the gate and let the couple inside.

1. Thor Heyerdahl, at seven years of age, dreamed of a home in the South Seas and drew this picture.
2. (*next page*) Thor and his mother outside No. 7 Stengaten.

CONTENTS

	page
FOREWORD	7
PART I: RETURN TO NATURE	
1. Number 7 Stengaten	15
2. The Quietest Boy in the Class	21
3. The Plan	33
4. In Search of Paradise	44
PART II: THE TEMPERING YEARS	
5. The Riddle of Bella Coola	69
6. The Ball Gang	82
7. Little Norway	97
8. I-Group	110
9. Out of the Doldrums	117
10. Murmansk Convoy	122
11. Back to the Finnmark Front	135
PART III: THROUGH THE STORM	
12. Burning all Bridges	145
13. The *Kon-Tiki* Odyssey	162
14. Kon-Tiki Fever	178
15. Cold Shoulders	196
16. The Bewitched Islands	218
17. The Road to Tiahuanaco	228
18. The Navel of the World	238
19. A Change of Wind	265
20. An Italian Village	277
INDEX	283

3. (*previous page*) Father giving Thor his first riding lesson.
4. (*previous page*) Thor and the author as students.
5. Inside an igloo in the high mountains. Thor, his cousin Gunnar Nissen, and Kazan the husky.
6. Winter holidays were spent roaming in the wilderness where no trees grow because of the climate.

ILLUSTRATIONS

between pages

1. Drawing by Thor Heyerdahl at age seven
2. Thor and his mother
3. Thor's first riding lesson
4. Thor and the author as students
5. Inside an igloo in the high mountains
6. Thor on a winter holiday   *8 and 9*

7. Chief Teriieroo of Tahiti and his wife
8. Going ashore on the island of Fatu Hiva
9. The Heyerdahl's first home in the Omoa Valley
10. The Ouia Valley   *40 and 41*

11. Wild pigs near the hut
12. Strange ruins in the Ouia Valley
13. The former cannibal Tei Tetua
14. Heyerdahl and his wife living in a cave on a desolate coral beach
15. Thor at the start of a career as an author   *72 and 73*

16. Thor Heyerdahl and little Thor
17. Thor and Moose-skin Tent journey into the forests of British Columbia
18. The cave city of 'Spring House' in Mesa Verde
19. The I-Group
20. Thor as a soldier with his mascot 'Peik'
21. Thor and his son 'Bamse'   *104 and 105*

22-3. Parachute training
24. Liaison officers Rörholt, Heyerdahl and Stabell in Finnmark
25. Capt Rörholt and Lt Heyerdahl planning radio links and the dropping of supplies
26. Lt Heyerdahl in the field
27. Enemy devastation on the Finnmark front
28. An Allied man-of-war in the convoy to Murmansk   *136 and 137*

29. Drawings of balsa rafts which sailed along the coasts of the Inca Empire
30. Cutting balsa logs for the raft
31. Herman and a native preparing food on drifting logs
32. The *Kon-Tiki* raft
33. Killed sharks aboard the *Kon-Tiki*
34. Inside the bamboo cabin of the raft   *168 and 169*

ILLUSTRATIONS

between pages

35. Thor and Torstein with a dolphin
36. Shipwreck on a reef in Polynesia
37. The crew of the *Kon-Tiki* wades ashore
38. The *Kon-Tiki* crew back in Europe
39. Yvonne and Thor in the Hound Tor Inn on Dartmoor
40. Queues for the *Kon-Tiki* film
41. Knut Haugland guides distinguished visitors round the Kon-Tiki Museum   200 and 201

42. Thor with Princess Margaret
43. Thor Heyerdahl receives the Vega Medal from the King of Sweden
44. Yvonne meets jungle Indians in the interior of Brazil
45. Dancing witch doctors at the Araguaia River
46. Thor Jr, Thor, Yvonne and Anette   232 and 233

47. The giant statues of Easter Island had subterranean bodies
48. Natives raise a fallen statue on Easter Island
49. Stone gods hidden in the soil on Easter Island
50. Father Sebastian, uncrowned king of Easter Island
51. Yvonne at home in Oslo   264 and 265

52. Queen Elizabeth II and Prince Philip visit the *Kon-Tiki*, escorted by Thor Heyerdahl
53. Thor's three daughters outside the tower at Colla Micheri
54. Thor at work
55. The village of Colla Micheri
56. Thor Heyerdahl and Arnold Jacoby   280 and 281

PART ONE

RETURN TO NATURE

Chapter 1

NUMBER 7 STENGATEN

PERHAPS it was a toy boat, made of wood, which led to my intimate acquaintance with the village of Colla Micheri of later years.

It was the spring of 1927. In the handicraft workshop of the school at Larvik, Norway, we had opened the windows to the south, where the poplars stood decked in sparkling green. I was standing sandpapering a model sailboat. The wood had a beautiful grain, and I had certainly been successful with the design and lines. I was looking forward to giving it a trial on the water.

Then suddenly he was standing at my side—that fair-haired, good-looking, modest boy who had been in our class for nearly a year before we had really come to understand him. Now he took the boat from me, twisted and turned it about, holding it close to his eyes. Then he asked if he might have it. This rather took me aback, but I felt generous.

'Yes,' I said, 'please take it. I can easily make another.'

I have seldom seen anyone so delighted with such a trifle.

This toy boat began a friendship that has lasted ever since. We discovered that we had much in common. Both of us enjoyed hiking through the woods and mountains; both of us regarded school as a necessary evil. We could go into fits of laughter over jokes no one else understood, and could philosophize together beyond all reality. One day I went with him to his home, and gradually I penetrated into his little world of home and family, and his greater world of imagination.

Today I know that his childhood world of imagination was to become a reality. To explain how it all came about, let me begin from the beginning.

Number 7 Stengaten was a long, low, wooden house almost as old as Larvik itself, the little coastal town at the entrance of the Oslo Fjord. A dignified and beautiful house, covered with a cloak of wild vine and full of antique furniture and works of art, it stood at the top of Stengaten, a street running down to the centre of the town and beyond to the harbour; and it commanded a wide view across the sea.

On October 6, 1914 a champagne cork popped to the ceiling in Number 7. A baby boy had arrived in the world, a wonderful event for his parents, no longer young, and both with children by former marriages. When the confinement was over satisfactorily, the father sat by the mother's bed and drank a toast with her to the health and happiness of the boy, named Thor after himself.

The family of Thor Heyerdahl senior, born in 1869, had come from the great forests near the Swedish frontier. On the early death of his father, Heyerdahl senior had inherited a considerable fortune which enabled him to acquire a good education. After studying at a technical school in Trondheim he took up brewing in Germany, and married the daughter of the owner of a brewery in Worms. In 1892 he returned to his own country, and two years later used the greater part of his legacy to buy a brewery in Larvik. To this town, still wrapped in dreams of its former importance as a port in the days of the clipper ships, Heyerdahl was a breath of fresh air. Thanks to a masculine charm so strong that everyone was affected by it, he soon won friends and popularity. There was something lively and inspiring about him; whenever he entered a room he filled it with life, and when he departed he left a void behind him. He was a lover of mankind, frank and extroverted, with a constant twinkle in his eyes.

It was soon evident that Heyerdahl was not only a competent brewer but also a brilliant businessman. On the other hand his marriage, by which there were three children, turned out so badly that it ended in divorce.

His second wife, Alison (*née* Lyng), whom he met in Oslo, was born in Trondheim in 1873, the daughter of a prosperous merchant. When she was only six her mother died. She had been in poor health and had grown tired of life, hoping only that God would soon call her away from this vale of tears. This attitude aroused in Alison a wild antagonism towards Him who was to take her mother from her.

After her mother's death Alison lived a restless and disturbed life, sometimes with puritanical aunts, sometimes with her uncle, a cheerful and broad-minded man. It would have been surprising if such different environments had not created contradictions in the child's mind. A sensitive girl with artistic leanings and interests, she was at the same time quick and sharp. She began to wonder about much that she saw and heard; she compared her uncle's gay attitude to life with the stern outlook of her aunts; and as time went by there grew in her a deep dislike of prudishness and affectation.

These opinions were much strengthened by a stay in England, where she came across the teachings of Darwin. After a year of liberty and social engagements, she returned home burning with enthusiasm for Darwinism and with two trunks full of lingerie. At home she continued to live a free life, with parties at night and long morning horseback rides. By the time she met Heyerdahl and married him she had two broken marriages behind her, with one child by the first and three by the second.

Heyerdahl's break with his first wife and his subsequent marriage to Alison caused shocked comment in a town where divorce was almost unknown, yet this mattered little to them. He had his business to look after, while she was fully occupied with tapestry-weaving, work in museums, and antique-collecting. Neither paid any attention to local gossip, preferring to make their own friends—friends with broad views and cultural tastes. Their marriage, however, became more and more difficult.

In circles in which he was known, opinion of Heyerdahl differed widely and was remarkably positive. Business people regarded him as a capable and honest man, energetic and full of ideas. His workmen looked up to him as a generous, easygoing, and sympathetic employer. His friends enjoyed his humour and wit. The leading people of the town said he was a frivolous social lion. But some—a small minority who knew him in his serious moments—maintained that behind his mask of smiles and irreverence they could trace an undercurrent of religion. Perhaps the sum of all these estimates gave the truest picture of the man. But there is no doubt about one thing: among his efficient and virile qualities there were weak points.

By comparison, Fru Alison, as tall and stately as a woman of the Norse sagas, had developed into a strong-minded and richly gifted character, rejecting all faith in Christianity. Her turbulent emotional life was curbed by the firmness of her resolution. Seldom or never had she any doubt as to what was right or wrong, a conviction bound to lead in the end to a certain intolerance of others, including her husband.

Whatever the conflicts between husband and wife, they were in complete agreement that the boy should get the best care they could give him.

The children of Fru Alison's previous marriages—Leif Bruun by the first, and Tulli, Jacob, and Ingrid Matheson by the second—all left home during Thor's early years, so he grew up as an only child. From the very first his mother took charge of his upbringing with a determination rare in those days. He received every attention from her, but not in the form of tenderness and warmth. She rarely showed him any affection, for she found it difficult to express her feelings; but she was constantly on her guard for possible dangers. Punctuality and strict attention to rules were important elements in young Thor's upbringing. He had to go to bed earlier than other children of his age, and he was wakened at a definite time every morning. Cleanliness was a virtue—he heard that at all times of the day. To drink from someone else's glass, or to use another person's fork and spoon, was strictly forbidden. He was given only what was considered the most wholesome food. His mother thought goats' milk was more nourishing than cows' milk, so she bought two goats and kept them down in the brewery stables in the centre of town. This naturally attracted the attention of the children in the neighbourhood and greatly astonished their elders who had never heard of such a thing. But Thor had all the goats' milk he could swallow.

Inevitably, he was overprotected and guarded more than was good for him, which showed a curious inconsistency in Fru Alison's methods: while wishing to make her boy a strong healthy, and upright man—a man unlike all the others she had known—she tried to keep him a child as long as possible.

Association with the other children on Stengaten was kept to a minimum, and during his early boyhood Thor was almost exclusively with adults, in particular with his nurse Laura. White-haired and wrinkled, Laura was his guardian angel. If neither his father nor mother was available she was there looking after him, reading to him, or hitching up her skirts and playing football with him. It is she who is also associated with his memories of the Manor pond and the hill to the south of it.

Some hundred yards from their house, between tall poplars and fir trees, lay a picturesque pond forming part of an estate that had belonged to Count Gyldenlöve, the Danish viceroy in Norway. It had been constructed to supply water to the mansion and to the big fountains in the park. When Heyerdahl had settled in Larvik he had bought both the pond and the hill; these became a living storybook for little Thor. He went there nearly every day with Laura and made determined efforts to reach the top of the hill by the old, moss-grown flight of stone steps that led to it. It was a difficult climb, but he was resolved to get up, and up he got. In the hollows at the top grew moss and short windswept grass; here he could lie for hours on his stomach, watching the insect life in the primaeval forest in the grass.

For the most part Thor played by himself, with toys selected by his mother to encourage his interest in nature and primitive life: models of prehistoric animals; stuffed monkeys, giraffes, elephants, and crocodiles; African and Indian dolls; books about animals, and books with pictures of the South Sea islands. When he was five years old his mother took him with her to the museum of the Royal Science Society in Trondheim, an experience that made a great impression on him, leading him within a year or two to form a collection of his own.

Without companions of his own age, Thor was driven more and more into the habit of daydreaming. Many an evening, when his parents believed he was asleep, he was sitting by the window in his bedroom. Beneath him lay the terraced garden and, farther below, an entangled pattern of white wooden houses with fascinating little backyards where other children were still playing. At the foot of the hill the two long quays of the harbour projected like signposts toward a world he knew only from books. From the quay to the left, ships pulled out into the fjord at regular times. He could hear the ships' bells as if they were ringing in his own room. One day he would be on board. One day he too would travel away. Out of the mouth of the fjord, where the sky so strangely melted into the sea, romance lay waiting.

These daydreams were happy, but in fact Thor was a lonely boy. If only he had had a brother or sister to share his room, and with whom to exchange secrets and dreams during the silent hours when the house had gone to sleep! To this day he can see his big room in the old house, white and bare, with his mother's bed in an alcove off the wall farthest from his own bed. As he lay there trying to sleep, fear often came stealing in from all sides. In the autumn and winter, storms howled in from the sea, through the narrow alleys below, and on to the exposed house on top of the hill. The incessant beating of the halyard against the flagpole outside the window was particularly frightening, for Thor had an eerie feeling that it had been beating that way on the autumn night when he had been born in this very room.

In the sleeping hours the house, too, was alive with sounds. The most friendly was the creaking of the staircase, for it nearly always meant that soon his father would appear, a smile on his face, an inaudible 'hush' on his lips. Their private hour had come. His father would sit down on the edge of the bed to hear a softly spoken 'Lord's Prayer'. Then, in a cheerful low voice, he would talk to the boy of this after-life, which, although no one knew its nature, was certainly more beautiful than life on earth. If Thor prayed, he said, he would receive help in need. At such times the boy experienced a feeling of intimate contact; he and his father were sharing a secret.

But then, all of a sudden, his mother might be standing at the door.

'Why do you tell the boy these things?'

Then his father would get up and leave without a word, and Thor was alone, confused and unhappy because something of real value had been broken. Because of his admiration for his wife, Heyerdahl always gave way to her in the upbringing of their child, nor did he openly oppose her atheistic views. She strove to get young Thor to see the absurdity of the Christian faith and its naïve account of the creation, and she coolly proclaimed that when a person died it meant burial in the ground and nothing more. Heyerdahl himself was not particularly religious, yet he felt that death was not the end, that the goodness and beauty in this world must have a divine origin and a deeper meaning. So for several years he never quite abandoned his guerilla tactics in the contest for his son's soul.

Naturally enough these strongly conflicting views gave Thor much to ponder about. His meditations on life and death found expression in a series of naïve drawings of God and the Devil. These fantasies continued into his schooldays, but his mother's view, which was very clear and logical, influenced him for a number of years.

The friction between the parents apparently increased as time went by, yet it cannot have been very noticeable to Thor in his childhood.

The atmosphere in Number 7 Stengaten was usually bright and cheerful, with parties and frequent visitors from out of town. Heyerdahl always tried to create laughter and happiness around him, and while Fru Alison's sense of humour was more sarcastic than tolerant, she could see the amusing side of many daily events.

Then there were the holidays. Unlike other families in Larvik, the Heyerdahls had no sailingboat and no cottage on the seashore. Instead they had a cluster of picturesque log cabins at Uglevika (Owl's Creek), by a remote lake on the family's estate in the deep forests on the Swedish border. They also had roomy log cabins in two widely separated areas of the mountain highlands of Norway's interior. Heyerdahl liked best his cabin at the popular mountain resort at Ustaoset, where there were plenty of people about and much to do. As in most others matters, Fru Alison had another preference and took the boy to their isolated summer cabin at Hornsjö, a lofty hill farm enclosure in the mountains high above Lillehammer, a small town and resort on Lake Mjösa, some eighty miles from Oslo. At Hornsjö she had just what she liked best—fresh air under a wide expanse of sky, and endlessly rolling mountain plateaux covered by heather, creeping juniper, and dwarf birch, with a view of sparkling lakes and deep forest-covered valleys; and far away on the horizon the rugged range of Jotunheimen and Rondane, capped with almost eternal snow and ice.

Thor was only five when he first went to Hornsjö.

Chapter 2

THE QUIETEST BOY IN THE CLASS

SCHOOL began badly. Against regulations, his mother insisted that he should begin in the second form. Since he was not only the youngest, but also the smallest in the class, he suffered a sense of inferiority. He was silent and timid; in play periods he stood watching his schoolmates at their games. Nor was his respect for the school increased by Fru Alison's radical opinions on education and the stern demands she made upon the teachers. Several times—and there was certainly good reason for it—she complained to the inspector that one of them was a complete imbecile. The only result was that the staff came to look upon her as a dangerous woman. They acquiesced every time she asked for an extension of the boy's holidays, and always excused him when he wished to accompany her on her travels, collecting antiques, studying natural history, and visiting the zoological museum in Oslo, which were her main interests in life. He missed classes so frequently that he fell behind in his lessons and had to have private tutoring.

The tutor was a young woman and her choice was a fortunate one. In the beginning the two of them fought continually, but soon she became his friend as well as his teacher, making school work easier and more appealing to him.

It was in drawing and natural history that Thor showed unusual talent. In drawing he displayed a rich imagination and a sense of humour. One of his drawings came into the hands of a journalist and appeared in the local paper. In natural history he had almost unbelievable knowledge for a boy of his age. He knew the Latin names of the rarest animals, and often caused some embarrassment to his mentors, as when he brought a cuttlefish into the classroom, and asked the teacher to tell the class all she knew about it. She saved herself by saying:

'Today we have something else to do. We can talk about that thing tomorrow.'

That evening she read everything she could find about cuttlefish.

Schooling provided new advantages. Now Thor was able to write and illustrate stories of his own about children who left home for tropical countries and islands. Reading soon became a passion with him. He read the usual boys' adventure stories of the period, but of much greater interest to him were the illustrated books about foreign lands and peoples. When he had to stay in bed with a cold, he took with him *Living Races of Mankind* and two or three thick reference books, one of them with coloured pictures of Polynesians in canoes—pictures that stamped themselves indelibly in his mind. Popular scientific works about modern and prehistoric animals presented a world that he explored more and more deeply, until there was no dividing line between it and his own real life.

His fascination with this subject and the daily influence of his mother led him early to decide upon his future career. When other boys dreamed of becoming airplane pilots, bus drivers, or policemen, Thor always said he would be 'the sort of man who studies animals'. Even before he was seven years old he started a biological collection in his study. I well remember this cosy retreat with its white furniture and a bright red woollen cover on the sofa. Here he kept his glass-topped cases of butterflies and other insects, adding further interesting specimens as time went by. Some of the more exotic ones were brought back by his father from abroad, where he went either on business or to take the cure at some health resort for his stomach trouble.

During Thor's first year at school his young teacher managed slowly to give her difficult and rather spoilt pupil greater self-confidence, even if he did not always feel quite on a level with the other boys. With this came the demand for more liberality at home. His parents now allowed him greater freedom in the choice of his friends, receiving his schoolmates kindly when they came to the house. Soon he was playing every day with the boys on Stengaten and speaking two languages: polished speech at home, and in the street the broad dialect of the local children.

Suddenly, this shy 'mummy's darling' became the leader of the gang on Stengaten. Perhaps it was his talent for leadership asserting itself, but his hobbies and resourcefulness played a great part. Nor was it unimportant that his father was the owner of a brewery, a man with a kind heart—and with the key to an inexhaustible supply of lemonade. Stengaten soon grew into a larger world of other streets and alleys, with new possibilities for play and mischief.

All the pranks were not equally amusing. Thor could not swim. Once he fell through the ice on the Manor pond and nearly drowned before his friends could rescue him. Another time he went with the gang to Kirkebukten (Church Bay), a gloomy cleft in the mountain south of the

town church. Thor, who had had a fear of water since his close call in
the pond, would not go swimming with the others; he joined them
afterwards in a game and, in his excitement, slipped off a narrow bridge
and fell into the sea. Paralysed with fright his friends watched him
splashing wildly. Then one of them rushed off to the nearest bathing hut
for a life belt. Thor had already been under twice before the boys hauled
him up.

Two tragedies at this time increased still more his fear of water. A
schoolmate of the same age, the son of the head watchman in the brewery,
was lost in Kirkebukten. Then one evening a distraught woman threw
her newborn child from Church Rock. Full of morbid curiosity, Thor
hurried there with the other boys; but when he stood and looked down
at the dark waves washing the seaweed at the foot of the cliff, he was
overcome by a fear that came from another and a nameless world.
Without a word to his companions he turned away from the yawning
abyss and ran the long way home until he stood behind locked doors.
From then on, the depths of the sea were to him like the gate of death,
and the sea with its quiet rollers became a dreadful power, a living creature
that with invisible hands drew its helpless victims down below.

His father tried in vain to teach him to swim, enticing him with five-
and ten-kroner notes, a lot of money for a boy at that time, and he paid a
professional teacher to help, but all to no avail.

When storms are raging, the people of Larvik still mention with horror
the night of November 2, 1922. On that night, a few weeks after Thor's
eighth birthday, a storm swept like a hurricane over the town. At about
half-past one in the morning there were shouts of 'Fire! Fire! The town
is burning!' Awakened by the storm, the cries of terrified people, and the
red glare that danced across the walls of his room, Thor jumped out of
bed and ran to the window.

Up from the post office, in the centre part of the old town, a flickering
pillar of fire rose to the sky, and every squall swept the flames and the
rain of sparks in over the wooden buildings in the vicinity of Stengaten.
Stifling black smoke was pouring over the housetops, and the bitter smell
of burning forced its way in through the window. Blazing fragments of
wood sailed through the air and fell on the neighbouring roofs. A violent
gust of wind dragged the door of Number 5 Stengaten from its hinges,
lifted it in the air, and flung it across the street. Soon fire began to break
out in the roof directly below Thor's window, and quickly spread to
another building.

And then at last his mother was standing in the doorway. Thor must dress at once, for the town was burning down. But first of all Thor must go to the lavatory, an unbroken rule when he got up. While the tempest and the fire broke into the surrounding houses, the boy sat in deadly terror on the seat and heard the servants, Laura and Helga, fetching blankets and food, and his parents preparing to seek refuge in the great vaults beneath the old brewery. Fortunately this did not become necessary. Aided by the townspeople, the firemen finally gained control of the conflagration.

This wild autumn night remained in Thor's mind ever afterwards like the night of Judgement Day.

'He's got plenty of spunk, but he talks like a little child.'

Thor had been driven in a hurry to the hospital with appendicitis. On the operating table he had made the doctors promise to preserve his appendix in alcohol; it would be a valuable addition to his biological collection. As he fell under the anaesthetic he heard these words spoken by the nurse, who, after the operation, gave him his appendix in a test-tube. But her words remained like a severe wound.

While he had been under the anaesthetic, he had had an experience that was to have a great effect on his future view of life. Although he could not hear, feel, see, or move a finger in spite of all his struggles, his real self was alive, but independent of its mortal frame. He was panic-stricken that he might not get back into his own body, and all the time he saw before him a pattern of rotating circles, none of which crossed another, and yet there was no room in between. For months afterwards he pondered over this strange experience, and twice it was all repeated as a nightmare in his sleep. Each time he was amazed at the ingenious simplicity of the system of circles that was geometrically impossible to the conscious mind, and each time he was determined to remember how it was done when he woke up—but always in vain.

These wrestlings with the subconscious were of far greater importance to Thor than to other boys of his age. They left him convinced that his father was right; the spirit's existence was independent of the body, and another reality was experienced by a spirit freed from the senses. Even if he shared his mother's views on the Church and dogmas, he was never really an atheist afterwards. For long periods he might forget this certainty of reality behind earthly life, but every time it really mattered it was there as an inward source of strength.

'He's got plenty of spunk, but he talks like a little child.'

These words bore out his suspicion that he was less grown-up than he ought to be at his age. At school he drew into himself still further, and it was difficult to get him to go to any party where he might possibly meet girls or strange boys. He had to be lured into most activities. To help him become more confident his parents arranged for dancing lessons, but these were no more successful than the attempts to teach him to swim.

His self-confidence was not increased by the discovery that he was short-sighted. There was talk of wearing glasses, but Thor was firmly opposed to this, imagining he could hear the children making fun of him. Great, then, was his delight when the doctor said he should do without them; there was nothing wrong with his eyes, but the muscles were weakened by too much reading and all his work with tiny biological specimens. Nevertheless this shortsightedness remained a handicap in work and play. He was in constant fear that his schoolmates might discover his sight was bad, and he missed a good many lessons that were written on the blackboard. Then he discovered a trick that helped him, not only then but also in later life. He found that if he pressed his little fingers gently on the corners of his eyes he could see almost normally, and that if he rested his head on his hands no one noticed anything odd about his position. But not all the difficulties could be overcome in this way, and the weakness worried him a great deal, and prevented him from mixing freely with others.

His father saw more clearly than his mother that if the boy was to grow into a man something must be done. He took him for long trips through field and forest, in summer on foot, in winter on skis, looking for the tracks of animals. He also tried to arouse his interest in shooting and hunting, but very little came of it; Thor was too fond of animals for that.

Between the ages of ten and twelve Thor continued to add to his collection: shells, dried starfish, and crabs from the shore; freshwater insects from the Manor pond; snakes and other reptiles from the fields and woods around Larvik, carefully preserved in jars of formaldehyde and alcohol. Once, after spending a whole day in search of good specimens, he walked nearly five miles back to his home with a poisonous adder held by its tail at arm's length, constantly changing hands from fatigue, and shaking the snake's head down every time it tried to curve up to strike at his arm or chest.

Thor had not forgotten the Royal Science Society in his mother's native town and his many visits to the zoological museum in Oslo. There was no such museum in Larvik, in his opinion a great deficiency of the town. Now he planned to realize an old dream. He would build a museum and call it the Animal House.

Already he had chosen a site. In the courtyard at the rear of his house was a long, red-painted wooden building, the former stables of the old brewery. At the far end was a room that was seldom used and seemed ideal for his purpose. When the walls had been covered with tongue and groove, he transferred his collection from the house. Then, on the floor along one of the walls, he laid a sloping bank of sand on which he arranged all kinds of shells, sea-urchins, and starfish in a natural setting of driftwood and seaweed.

His father continued to help him all he could. Early one morning he took him down to the harbour where the trawlers were coming in with their night's catch. Thor senior, who had a way of his own with people, fell into conversation with the fishermen, and from then on they always put aside for the boy anything unusual they caught in the trawl. In this way the museum grew from day to day.

Thor turned then to the construction of an aquarium among the hazel trees in a secluded corner of the terraced garden. He got hold of some packing cases, filled them with earth and turf, then sunk large jars and other containers into them which he filled with water from the ponds in the town wood. Next, he carefully placed some stones in the jars and returned with his friends to the ponds where they sat for hours, waiting for anything to swim their way. Great was their delight each time they caught a giant water-beetle, a newt, or a frog, which they moved to the aquarium and did all in their power to keep thriving. Besides this, they embellished the cases with grasses and flowers, so that everything might be as true to nature as possible. When the tenants began to multiply, the boys took great interest in their development.

When the aquarium was no longer new and exciting, Thor and his friends transferred their attention to nonaquatic creatures. They hunted around the gardens, lifting stones and extracting beetles of various kinds, centipedes, and anything else that attracted them. These they collected in earth-filled, glass-covered cases where they studied them and tried to find out how they lived.

Children from other parts of the town came in to look around. This led to occasional visits by the general public, and one day some teachers of natural history arrived in a body with all their pupils, and admired the museum. A project had been realized. For all its modest pretensions, the Animal House had become a town museum.

In the autumn of 1928 Thor and I entered the secondary school together. Thor was still only a moderately bright pupil. He did best in mathematics; he liked the clear logic of equations, and geometrical problems were to him a sort of game. But in natural history he no longer showed the same interest he had at the primary school. The advanced study of plants proved disappointing, for flowers were no longer delightful works of the Creator, but objects to be classified according to the shape of their petals and the number of their stamens. Their scent and beauty ceased to be valuable qualities; they were cut to pieces, analysed, and thrown away. Zoology was treated in much the same way, though we were taught a little about the animals' way of life.

On the whole, school struck Thor as remote from life and unrealistic. He found it hard to concentrate on work in the classroom. On the slightest provocation his thoughts were elsewhere. His pencil was in-cessantly conjuring up palm trees and weird animals on the covers of his books.

At sports he was a complete failure. He detested football, and if we went swimming, he always sat on the shore and looked on. This was perhaps the reason why a true friendship developed between us. Certainly I could play football and swim, but my main interests were music and poetry. And we both had an open eye for the beauties and wonders of nature. Thor had his Manor pond. I had a water barrel. My father owned a nursery and in one of his hothouses was a large oak barrel where he stored water for his plants. As a little boy I often hung over the edge of the barrel, staring into the depths of a green watery world. Tiny water creatures of the strangest forms paddled and darted about and, occasionally, shiny bubbles rose to the surface like a message from a hidden monster at the bottom. Apart from ourselves, no one in the class could be fascinated by the repulsive life in an old water barrel so long as there were football fields about.

Thor's father, however, did not give up his efforts to encourage the boy's interest in some form of sports. In a corner of the yard he erected two high poles with a crossbar at the top. A climbing rope, a pole, and rings were rigged up, and it soon became apparent that Thor could per-form exercises that none of the rest of us could manage. He could hang for a long time by one hand, his arm bent at the elbow; more than that, he could hang the same way by a single finger. He began to get really toughened. Without moving a muscle on his face, he could strike the edge of a table with his knuckles with great force, a feat we were not at all eager to imitate.

There now moved into the neighbourhood two brothers who lived and breathed for athletics, particularly cross-country running or skiing, depending on the time of year. They were good-natured boys, and gave Thor sympathy and encouragement. They induced him to join them in training runs and ski trips, even persuading him at length to take part with them in minor competitions with other local boys. If it was a question of running a long way for a long time, there were few to equal Thor, but he was never interested in results. He entered these races merely for the training, to become strong and tough. If he felt like a rest in the middle of a race he would take one. And if he saw animal tracks he would cut right away from the course and follow the spoor. The results of two such cross-country competitions are still on record. In one, Thor came in fourth, which was last. In the other, he was fourth out of five, but only because one boy had lost his way!

The _höy-fjell_—the open moors of the lofty Norwegian inland mountains —gradually became to Thor the symbol of freedom. At Hornsjö he spent his summer holidays year after year. Here the mountain plateau, nearly three thousand feet above sea level, was a boundless playground with adventures waiting for him everywhere. The true Norway—his Norway —was the moors where the last rugged trunks of pine, fir, and birch stopped and handed over the barren soil to windswept dwarf birch and juniper, wild flowers, rocks clothed with grey, green, and yellow lichen, and isolated groups of hill farms or shepherds' huts, with grey, weathered log walls and roofs of turf on which the grass still grew. There were jagged peaks, far away in a blue haze and, deep in a kind of underworld below, thickly forested valleys with sparkling strips of rivers. Here on the _höy-fjell_ the goats played about on the rocks, the cow-bells tinkled, the small birds twittered, and now and then wild gusts of wind wafted the scent of flowers through the sun-warmed air. This was his kingdom.

One day, when Thor and his mother were on a long hike in the mountains, they came upon a tumbledown log hut in a mountain glen to the east of Hornsjö. It had recently become the home of Ola Björneby, a weather-beaten mountain wolf, remarkably cheerful in view of the circumstances that had brought him there. He came from a lumber town in eastern Norway, the son of a wealthy landowner who had lost all his money. Ola could not bear the thought of staying in his former surroundings under these conditions, so he packed his few possessions in a knapsack and went into the wilderness to live as a hermit by hunting and fishing.

The hut, which Ola had borrowed from a shepherd, had an earth floor. On one side the space between the ground and the bottom log was so wide that sheep could get through. On some stones in a corner of the shack stood an iron pot. This was his kitchen. The only other furniture was a homemade table and a couple of stools. Beneath a heap of blankets and hides on a bunk close under the roof, Ola slept all the year round.

Both Thor and his mother were fascinated by this strange man. To Thor he seemed a reincarnation of the Tarzan of his childhood, to Fru Alison an amusing mixture of Pan, Peer Gynt, and Mowgli, with his countless stories about animals. He told them of his lonely life in the wilderness, and showed them how he carved lovely bowls and cups from curiously-shaped knurs of wood.

As their friendship grew, Thor, at the age of fourteen, was allowed to join Ola during the summer and be his helper. Now he was able to see how a cultured man could so acclimatize himself to the wilderness that he was perfectly at home there, just as much as a hare or an elk. For the first time in his life Thor had to work hard, carrying heavy loads of wood, hay, fish, and game, and he would not show signs of fatigue, even if sometimes he was ready to drop. If they had been fishing all night, they slept all day on a flat rock at the edge of the marsh.

In the time he spent with Ola Björneby, Thor learned about tracks in the grass, about what can be read from a tuft of fur caught up in a tree, and of how to live in the wilds in all weather and under every condition. He often said later that his lessons from Björneby were among the most important in the whole of his upbringing.

To Thor, Larvik could never compare with the *höy-fjell*. Hornsjö meant summer, light, and liberty. Larvik meant winter, darkness, and going to school. I had never been to the *höy-fjell*. Like the rest of our friends I spent the summer holidays by the sea, and while I was reading and daydreaming on the beach, Thor was involved in real adventures.

I have a vivid recollection of a discussion we had when we returned from our holidays one year. Thor thought the reading of fiction was a poor substitute for reality; he wanted to experience life for himself, in close contact with nature, to set out on journeys of discovery to strange and distant lands. My argument was that there was nothing more to discover.

'Africa', I said, 'is no longer the dark continent. Australia was drawn on the map years and years ago. Only the Amazon has still a certain number of twilit spots, but it's not an undiscovered country.'

'It's not only in geography that we can make discoveries', said Thor. 'There are still many great challenges in the world, among other things the mystery of Easter Island.'

Those were his very words.

A subject that filled his thoughts more and more was the difference between modern and primitive life. His freedom on the *höy-fjell*, his half-religious worship of nature, caused him to doubt whether civilization was a blessing to mankind. Was it a worthy form of life? This question became at last the most important of all problems for him. He talked continually on the theme of returning to nature. Modern man, he said, had his brains stuffed full, not so much of his own experience as of opinions and impressions derived from books, newspapers, magazines, radio, and motion pictures. The result was an over-loaded brain and reduced powers of observation. Primitive man, on the other hand, was an extrovert and alert, with keen instincts and all his senses alive.

But, Thor admitted, the problem was extremely complicated and many-sided. The drawbacks of civilization were not discernible unless seen from the outside. We were incompetent to judge the virtues and defects of our own way of living. To decide, one would need some standard of comparison. Civilization might be compared with a house full of people who had never been outside the building. None of them knew what their house looked like, although they lived in it. It was necessary to go outside to see the house as it really was. This was precisely what he wanted to do.

I noticed Thor showed a certain hesitation about the future. Perhaps he would not find it possible to settle down doing zoological research. Perhaps he would be the man who went out-of-doors to try to see what no one else had looked for.

More than once since he had sat by Fru Alison's bed and drunk a toast to their newborn son, Heyerdahl had said that that occasion had been the happiest day of his life. As Thor grew older he realized more and more that there was something wrong between his parents. During secondary school he steadily saw less of his father, who was constantly on trips abroad. At the age of sixty Heyerdahl decided to retire from active business and left Larvik, ostensibly to take a holiday at Ustaoset. He did not return home as long as Fru Alison lived there. Without informing the boy, the parents had quietly decided to separate. For his sake there was no divorce, and he was given every opportunity to see his father.

The gay atmosphere in the old house was gone, and the shy boy living with his mother seemed as reserved as ever. Few discovered his keen sense of humour until the variety show that was put on by the seniors before graduation. Thor wrote the main sketch and played its leading part: the famous Professor Piccard, who ascended to the heavens in a beer barrel. For Thor to act before a large audience was unheard of. Yet he did it, and showed surprising talent as a comedian. The local papers outdid themselves in praise. We knew how hard it must have been for him, but to Thor his performance was of far greater importance than anyone guessed at the time. To him it was a baptism of fire. From then on he was a full-fledged member of our group.

To celebrate our success in the finals, ours and other schools in neighbouring towns ran a number of gala evenings. Although Thor joined in these with new confidence, he was as shy as ever in the presence of the opposite sex.

'Thor doesn't care for girls', his mother would say time and time again. 'The only thing that interests him is zoology.'

Of course he was interested in girls, but he was terrified of being left alone with one. Certainly they had begun to take an interest in *him*. Often one would take him under her wing at a dance and make it plain to him that if he was a gentleman he would escort her home. He could not refuse, but he always managed to send me a distress signal and—tactless idiot as I must have seemed—I went with them. On one occasion I even had to feign deafness as we passed my home and the girl said:

'But surely that's your house, isn't it, Arnold?'

When these disappointed young women had been brought safely into port, we could be ourselves once more, strolling the streets filled with the scent of lilac and talking in capital letters of the Glories of Nature and the Follies of Civilization. Thor continually dreamed about what a good time mankind must have had while still living in full harmony with nature, before any civilization had begun to take shape. He turned our ruined society inside out and asked what pure and natural pleasures modern life had to offer.

'We are building a sort of Tower of Babel,' he would say, 'which serves no purpose but to complicate existence. When we really create any benefits, it is merely to compensate for civilization's deficiencies.'

He would point to factories in the east. In a few short hours their chimneys would again start spewing out poisonous smoke and fumes. For most of the year the workmen went to their jobs by electric light early in the morning, and came out, grim-faced when the lights of the town were again lit in the afternoon. He compared these people with Ola Björneby, in his mountain home, bursting with health and happiness. If, said Thor, he could be sure that his views were the right ones, he would return to nature and accept the consequences. But first he must find a girl who was willing to carry out the experiment with him. She must be simple and natural. She must not use lipstick or nail polish, for it was mad to want to improve what nature herself had created. She must be strong too, and have a rock-like faith in the experiment. Did I think such a girl existed?

'Yes, I think so,' was my reply, 'but where and how are you going to find her?'

One evening, at a dance in a neighbouring town, Thor disappeared. I found him again later in a quiet corner, and he was not alone. She was tall and slender as a Nordic birch, and her name was Liv—Liv Coucheron Torp. Afterward, in high spirits, he told me that a miracle had happened: He had found the right person, the only one who would be able to carry out the experiment. Mutual friends had brought them together. As Thor could not dance he had to hit on something to hold her attention and he had suggested a walk down to the beach. There they had sat talking. He thought her a miracle in more ways than one, and before he could consider its full implications he blurted out the question:

'What do you think about returning to nature?'

At that moment he could have bitten off his tongue and spat it out into the sea.

She sat quite still for several seconds before she turned to him and said seriously:

'It would have to be complete.'

Could he have heard correctly? They agreed to meet at the next dance, but she did not appear. He was miserable, so we decided to help him. One of us managed to borrow his father's car, in which we drove off in force to Brevik, her hometown. There we sat for a long time outside her house, like detectives on a job. None of us had the courage to go up and ring the front doorbell, least of all Thor, who now had sunk into uncertainty. Eventually, we drove home with our mission unaccomplished. For days afterwards Thor was consumed with the desire to find out why she had not kept the date. When a boy told him with ill-concealed relish that Liv had another friend, Thor could not and would not believe it, but Liv did not turn up at any of the later festivities. Then the season ended and our schooldays were over.

Chapter 3

THE PLAN

FRU ALISON moved with Thor to Oslo when he entered the University in the autumn of 1933. She took a flat on the top floor of a house in the western district of the city, furnishing it with all her beautiful antiques from Number 7 Stengaten, to which Thor's father now returned.

More than a year passed before I met Thor again, but we kept in touch with each other through frequent letters. In one of them he told me that Liv was studying economics at the university. He had seen her with a man who seemed so sophisticated he knew he had no chance in that quarter. It was easy to read between the lines that he did not intend to do anything to renew their acquaintance, yet found it difficult to forget her.

He began his studies at the Faculty of Zoology under Professors Kristine Bonnevie and Hjalmar Broch.

'I was at once fascinated', wrote Professor Broch of their first meeting, 'by his clear-cut face, which suggested determination—there was such sparkling liveliness in his eyes, his questions so concise and to the point, and his range of expressions revealed a quick grasp and appreciation of everything that was said. A resolute, almost set expression of his mouth suggested that if this fellow started on a project he would hardly give up until he had reached his aim. That was how the young student Thor Heyerdahl looked as a freshman.'

Although Thor developed a high regard for his professors, he was disappointed by their approach to the subject. He had hoped to be taught about the living unity of nature, the interplay between an animal and its surroundings. However, he thought highly of the training in scientific argument and method. He was also willing to admit that dissection and the use of the microscope were necessary in order to understand the functions of organisms, but he felt that the scrutiny of intestines played too large a part at the expense of the knowledge of living habits in animal geography. In his opinion the microscope in the laboratory should be supplemented by the telescope in the field. His fellow students have since told me that even if Thor showed only moderate interest in the lecture hall, he was the keenest of them on field trips and the one who always came back with interesting discoveries.

Thor's letters during this period were full of enthusiastic references to his latest acquisition: Kazan, a large Greenland husky, which his mother allowed him to keep in the apartment. Kazan, he wrote, could easily carry a thirty-pound pack in the summer, and draw a hundred pounds on a sledge over any kind of terrain in winter. On the level he could pull two men and a full load.

In the summer Thor often climbed the mountains alone with Kazan, each carrying his own pack. Once, in the exceedingly precipitous mountains above the valley of Sunndalsöra, they followed a narrow trail with a vertical drop of nearly three thousand feet down to the farmland below. At one point there was a break in the path and a few iron bars had been driven at right angles into the rock to bridge the gap. While he was standing on the bars, enjoying the view with Kazan in his arms, he looked straight down and was suddenly seized by so violent a dizzy spell that it was only with great difficulty that he reached safety on the other side. He had to spend the night on a shelf high above the abyss, tortured by a vertigo that was to threaten him for many years to come.

In the winter, he generally had another companion besides Kazan: either his cousin Gunnar Nissen or a childhood friend, Erik Hesselberg. With skis and dog sledge they always headed for the wildest mountain regions. On calm starry nights they slept in reindeerskin sleeping bags in the open, preferably where there was the finest view. On the top of a windswept knoll where the wind had exposed the hard-frozen green heather, they would lie under the tremendous arch of the sky; and when the disk of the sun rolled up across the white horizon, after a prelude of colours which they had never seen anything to equal, they could feel the joy of living run like a warm current through them.

But the winter weather on the mountains is changeable, and they could seldom lie under the open sky. In bad weather they made themselves a hut of branches down below the tree line, under the snow-laden boughs of a fir. It was pleasant to lie and meditate amid the fresh scent of pine needles while the wind moaned through the tree tops and the snow piled itself up like an extra blanket on the lower part of their sleeping bags. Kazan often slept outside in the open, but if the weather got too bad he shook off the dry snow and lay down close to the men in their fir-branch shelter.

It was only on their climbs to the *höy-fjell* regions that they found sheltering trees. As a rule they wandered high above the tree line. For that reason they carried a small tent and used their skis as tent poles. However, they soon learned that a tent was vulnerable and sometimes dangerous during the snowstorms on the mountain. One night in the clearest moonlight, Thor and Erik, on skis and with the dog sledge, tried to cross the top of Glittertind, Norway's highest mountain, covered by a permanent glacier. They had climbed to an altitude of more than six thousand feet when a storm began to blow up and black clouds swallowed up the moon and half the sky. It began to snow, and violent gusts of wind whipped up an extra flurry of snow from the glacier. With the aid of a pocket flashlight they managed to put up their little tent in a hollow sheltered by rock, while the wind tugged and tore at it. Covered with snow they crept in with Kazan under the canvas.

Outside, the storm was howling across the glacier and piling heaps of snow on the roof of the tent, forcing it down on their faces. The warmth of their bodies inside their sleeping bags and the icy air in the tent created an intermediate area around their faces and necks, where the temperature was almost exactly at melting point, and water gradually penetrated to their bodies.

Next morning the snow was even worse and the wind threatened to split the canvas when they tried to shake off the mass of snow. The place appeared to be so unsafe that they did not dare stay there any longer. Buffeted by the pressure of the wind, they fastened their frozen equipment on the sledge. They should have returned to the valley, but the cliffs were not to be trifled with when they did not know their exact position, and to see anything at all in the blizzard was impossible.

So they climbed slowly towards the top. There they would know where they were, and could navigate more easily by compass. They knew that to the right of them was a precipice of more than a thousand feet, but they also had to avoid bearing too far to the left, for there other abysses lay in wait for them. Before the storm had begun they had seen treacherous cornices of hardpacked snow jutting out in mid air along the edge of the precipice. If they were to step on one of these it would break off and carry them to the bottom. Every move had to be carefully thought out. To get a firmer footing they took off their skis and tied them to the sledge.

Everything was white snow flakes in a wild flight towards an invisible background of glacier and clouds. All that could be seen were the faint shapes of each other and of the dog and sledge, looking as if they were floating between heaven and earth. Kazan was leading with the sledge, which Thor held firmly with a rope. Every time they thought by the state of the wind that the precipice was close, they threw out balls of brown wrapping paper into the shapeless, ghostly world, to see if they rolled farther up the glacier or disappeared down into an invisible void.

When they reached the first ridge they calculated their true position. Now they had come to the gable of the topmost roof of Norway. Here there was only a very sharp ridge flanked by two precipices leading to the main peak of Glittertind, on which they knew stood a small hut cut down in the ice and anchored with steel cables. But it would be a tightrope dance in such weather—an act of madness to attempt it. Instead, they unharnessed Kazan and sat on the sledge, Thor with compass in hand. They set a course and coasted down from the summit, braking as hard as they could with their legs.

After many upsets in the snow they finally ended up in a side valley to the west, where there was some shelter against the worst of the storm. Here they put up the frozen tent for one more night. It took the whole of the next day to get the dog and sledge up a steep mountainside and across a lower ridge below the peak of Glittertind. From this point they came down to the birch-covered slopes of Visdal and then to the tourist hut at Spiterstulen. There they heard that the route they had traversed had been followed only once before in the winter, and then without a dog or a sledge.

This outing nearly cost Erik his feet. On a moonless night they went on to Tyin Lake and followed the frozen lake southwards in a biting cold wind. In a curve of the hill they found a sheltered camping place. They had not been really dry since those days on Glittertind, and when Erik was preparing to go into his sleeping bag he could not take off his boots. They were frozen to his double pair of heavy socks, and the socks to his toes. He took out both bootlaces and crawling down into his bag with his boots on, tried to get his toes loose. Finally he managed to loosen them from his socks. His toes had become two rows of ivory-white piano keys which he showed off by hammering with them on the lid of the cooking pot. The next day his feet were so swollen that he had to wear his socks outside his boots. There was no alternative but to go down into the valley and get medical treatment.

In these combats with nature Thor felt at ease; but on his return to Oslo his feeling of confidence and satisfaction soon disappeared. The traffic, the noise, the great city growing up all around him as if to crush him, the streets getting narrower and narrower, and he himself was just an ordinary little man in a crowd, lost in the great hall of the university, full of sombre, restless human beings. What was all this by comparison with standing on the top of Stor-Ronden and looking down into the wildest ravines of Rondane, with half Norway seeming to lie within sight?

His disappointment with the study of zoology, his contempt for life in the city, the uncertain future at that time for all young people, strengthened his mistrust of the modern age. What had been a retreat or a way of escape in his schooldays had assumed the shape of a resolution: to return to nature. Although his object was to withdraw permanently from civilization, he knew that when he made the attempt it might prove unsuccessful. He must have a plausible explanation both for his departure and for his possible return. Nor could he shock his parents by telling them that perhaps they would never see him again. He would only say that he was going to travel somewhere, perhaps to a South Sea island, to carry out zoological studies. If the experiment failed, he would at least be able to come home with some scientific results.

As a part of his plan he took geography under Professor Werenskiold as an extra subject. He read everything he could about tropical regions, and after thorough and prolonged study, decided that the Marquesas, the isolated group of French islands in the Polynesian archipelago, were best suited for his purpose. At the time of their discovery, about a hundred thousand natives had been living on these islands. The diseases and other miseries which the Europeans had brought with them had reduced the population to two thousand, which suggested that plenty of land and food must now be available.

Oddly enough, it was just at this time that Thor came across Bjarne Kroepelien, a prominent Oslo businessman, who had lived on Tahiti and had later accumulated the world's largest private collection of literature on Polynesia. When he heard of Thor's expedition he opened his home to him. Thor was able to come and go like a son of the house and to use the library whenever he wished. Here he found an enormous quantity of useful material for study, far more than he had dreamed of finding in all the university libraries in Scandinavia put together. Finally he knew so much about the animal life in the Marquesas group that he delivered a lecture on the subject at the university.

He also discussed the scientific part of his plan with his professors. What could he do on the South Sea islands to get a profitable return out of the expedition, apart from making a valuable collection of insects, snails, or marine fauna? They agreed that the most interesting subjects for study were perhaps the problems of the origin and isolation of animal life on desert islands in the ocean. How had these different species arrived there? Where did they come from? And how had they been affected by their environment?

Professor Bonnevie was keen that Thor should also devote some time and effort to the land snails. On the Marquesas there were a number of mountain-locked valleys effectively isolated from one another. The species of snail that moved very little would find it difficult to cross the high mountain ridges, and would therefore, in all probability, have developed various subspecies in the different valleys and the different altitudes. This was a subject with great possibilities for study.

Professor Broch was strongly in favour of Thor's studying also the stray domestic animals on these islands. The natives already had pigs and poultry —and rats—when the Europeans had arrived with cattle, goats, horses, donkeys, cats, and dogs, all of which had multiplied. As the natives had died, sometimes whole villages at a time, the domestic animals had wandered out into the wilds, and now, after many generations, they might be counted as wild animals. This too was an interesting course of study.

When the objectives had been settled, and the island of Fatu Hiva chosen as a centre of activity, both professors wrote their recommendations.

All this time Thor was conducting a secret and determined search for a companion on the expedition—not a fellow student to help him with the zoological work, but a girl to help him find his way back to Paradise. It was no longer a boy's dream of 'the Great Love'; it was primarily a link in his secret plan, and he did not doubt for one moment that he would grow to love anyone who could completely fulfil his requirements.

At one time he thought that if such a girl existed he must look among country people. On a walking tour he came across a candidate, a blonde lass from Gudbrandsdal. She was pretty, athletic, and natural, and not at all uninterested in the young biologist. He finally disclosed his plan to her, and she was excited over the idea of going with him. However, when she later moved to Oslo to study, she was greatly impressed by just those sides of urban life that Thor despised. She began to use makeup and polish her nails, and Thor immediately wrote her off. It was clear that she hadn't grasped the whole idea.

It now occurred to him that he would be more likely to find his companion among town dwellers. Some city girl ought to realize how hollow and unnatural a life she was leading. He came across her holidaying in the mountains: a ballet dancer with blood-red nails, scarlet lips, and cigarette holder. Something always happened to Thor when he got to the mountains; he at once became master of the situation. Now he felt quite sure of himself, and it was not long before the dancer came under his influence. She soon stopped smoking and gave up cosmetics, and when they had discussed the plan, neither of them doubted that she was the right girl.

After the holidays they met in Oslo, where Thor did not produce so favourable an impression; he seemed rather worried and unsure of himself, certainly not on a par with several other suitors. He also heard that the woman of his choice had boasted that soon she would be the queen of a South Sea island. It was clear that she had not understood his idea any better than the country girl. In the end he gracefully retired.

Then, in 1935, he ran across Liv at the University. They immediately became friends again. When Thor asked her if she remembered anything of their discussion on the beach, she replied that she had never been able to forget it and was still ready to join him in his plan. The matter was settled, he thought.

They began to make preparations for the experiment. Without telling Fru Alison their secret, they stayed with her and other guests that summer at Hornsjö, and tried to live as primitive a life as possible. If they went for a walk, Liv had to follow Thor's example and harden her feet by going barefooted over rocks and heather. On the island in the lake below the hut they cooked trout on hot stones and roasted potatoes in the ashes.

When Christmas holidays came, Thor left for the rugged Trollheimen Mountains with his cousin Gunnar Nissen. Kazan drew their supplies, and they slept in igloos built in Eskimo fashion from cut blocks of packed drift-snow. When descending to the lowlands to catch a train for Oslo, they found letters awaiting them in a country post office. One was from Liv who had decided that the experiment was silly and bound to fail. It could never be more than a beautiful dream, she wrote. Her father had now sent her money for a further period of study at the university and she thought it was wrong to disappoint him.

Such a lack of trust made Thor feel as if he had been betrayed. Instead of taking the train to Oslo with Gunnar he turned back to go with Kazan across the mountainous plateau known as Dovrefjell and on to the highest part of Gudbrandsdal, a distance of about a hundred miles through trackless mountain country. He had no set purpose, his one desire was to be alone in the wilderness with the elements until he had worked off some of his annoyance and disappointment.

There are not many hours of daylight in the Norwegian mountains at that time of the year. He had not been on the Dovrefjell long before a terrific storm broke out. It was in this storm that a group of people perished in this very region, but Thor was used to the mountains and well-equipped. Instead of turning back he continued across the plateau. The violence of the storm steadily increased until it blew so hard that it was impossible to walk upright. In order to make any progress Thor had to lean against the wind with the whole weight of his body.

'This is the thing to turn a boy into a man. . . . This is the thing to turn a boy into a man. . . .'

Thor repeated these words to himself as he fought his way ahead inch by inch. It was as if he were settling accounts with his own childhood. Crossing a lake his skis got wet. When they became so coated with ice that it was almost impossible to manipulate them, every step became a triumph.

'This is the thing to turn a boy into a man.'

A blizzard started, so heavy and with such force that he could hardly see his skis. He had to test every step, at the same time keeping Kazan to heel. He moved carefully down a steep slope covered with loose snow, then stopped and waited for Kazan. He did not come, and when Thor tried to shout, the storm drowned his cries. No Kazan, no tent, no sleeping bag, no food—an alarming prospect. Then a bundle came tumbling through the blinding snow. It was Kazan, still with the sledge in tow, its runners in the air and the supplies beneath it, an incredible performance for a single dog under such conditions.

Further progress was out of the question, and so was getting the tent up. All Thor could do was slide into his sleeping bag, pull Kazan with him under the folded tent, and allow the snow to cover them. He drew the dog close beside him so that they could keep one another warm. He had to lift the canvas to push off the snow every time it got so heavy it was difficult to breathe, and there was no sleep for him that night. When the weather improved a little they went on through the storm.

Hour after hour they struggled forward. Thor's watch had stopped and he was far from certain where he was. At times he thought he heard a train in the distance, but it was impossible to say from which direction the sound came. When he had crossed the Dovre plateau and drawn near to the birch woods on the other side, the storm was still raging. He tried to find a motor road or a railroad track, but it was hopeless as everything lay buried under the fresh snow.

As night fell the wind slackened. He managed to get the tent set up, supported with some firm stems of birch, and by the time he crept into his sleeping bag he was completely exhausted. He hoped that the next day he would be able to get as far as some house in the valley.

He had hardly settled down when he heard a train whistling in the distance. This time he knew he was not mistaken. Tomorrow he would find the track left by the snowplough and follow it until he reached a station. He closed his eyes and was on the point of dropping off to sleep when he heard the train whistle again, this time much nearer. He began

7. Chief Teriieroo of Tahiti and his wife.

8. (*next page*) Going ashore on the South Sea island of Fatu Hiva—a farewell to civilization.

to feel uneasy. Suppose he had pitched his camp in the middle of the track? Again the whistle, sharp and threatening. Then he heard the train puffing. It was coming straight for him. His first thought was to get out of the sleeping bag and the tent and run for his life, but a voice within him said that wherever he ran might be just as bad; he might run straight into the giant engine thundering through the drifts. 'You don't know where you are in relation to the tracks', said the voice. 'Lie quiet, lie quiet.' Now the noise rose to a climax, and the snow shook beneath him. The next moment the train rushed past so close that the tent was nearly buried under the white cascades from the plough. The next day he found that there was only a couple of yards between them.

He followed the tracks until he saw the railway junction of Dombaas, lying in the frost haze down in the valley. From there he caught a train back to Oslo, all the bitterness and disappointment drained out of him.

How could he blame Liv? How could he expect her to give up her life and go with him into the unknown? He told himself, accepting it philosophically, that even she was not the right girl. So what now? The question was resolved by Liv, who told him soon afterwards that she could not desert him and would go with him to Fatu Hiva after all.

Fru Alison had to be told. Not at all sure about how she would take it, Thor began the difficult conversation by pointing out that zoological studies at the University were so arranged that the lecture series were repeated after three and a half years, and there would be little new to learn, except laboratory work. If, he said, he was to go in for graduate work, it would be a decided advantage to travel abroad and collect material first hand. He would like, therefore, to break off his studies and go on a research expedition to the South Seas.

To his great delight his mother gave the plan her enthusiastic support. She, who had always thought primarily of Thor's health and security, could suddenly set aside all such considerations in favour of an idea that appealed to her. Perhaps she now saw her dreams coming true in the person of this young idealist.

The eagerness she displayed gave Thor the courage to go one step further. He hinted that he would like to try to live like a Stone Age man, under the most primitive conditions. This, too, she understood. She thought it might be an interesting experiment. But there was obviously something or other that disturbed her about letting her young son go to a South Sea island. Thor took the last step and told her that he was thinking

9. (*previous page*) The Heyerdahls' first home in the Omoa Valley where early morning is always the loveliest part of the day.
10. The Ouia Valley hidden and forgotten behind high mountains and deep jungle.

of taking Liv with him. To his surprise Fru Alison's doubts vanished. With a nice, decent girl she knew, life in the South Seas seemed safer! From then on she gave him all the encouragement and support she could. She never understood that the young couple would not return if the experiment succeeded.

One great obstacle had been removed. An even greater one remained: to get his father's consent. The whole thing depended upon him. Unless he gave his approval and added to it a considerable sum of money for the expedition, it would be difficult if not impossible to put the plan into practice.

With recommendations from Professors Bonnevie and Broch, Liv and Thor went to Uglevika (Owl's Creek), where Heyerdahl was then staying. They talked to him for three days about trivialities without getting a chance to bring up the real object of their visit. It was not until they were in the car on the way back to the station that Thor summoned up enough courage to mention that he wanted to go on a scientific expedition to the South Seas and that both his professors supported the plan. Taken by surprise his father agreed with it in principle, but raised certain questions of detail. Among other things, he considered that it would be too much of a risk to travel alone to such a desolate place. Here Thor saw his chance to approach the most awkward matter of all.

'Would you feel easier if I got someone to go with me?'

'Yes, it would undoubtedly be better. Whom are you thinking of?'

'Liv.'

'What! Are you mad, boy?'

The reaction was so violent that Thor almost regretted that he had spoken. His father went on to say that it was extremely irresponsible to get married long before one could support a wife. What was worse was to take her away to an unknown life among savages, far removed from civilized habits. Then he stopped speaking and was silent for a moment or two before suddenly saying with a sly twinkle in his eyes,

'I must talk this over with your mother.'

A new problem for Thor. Heyerdahl had not seen his wife since their separation, and his strongest desire was to meet her again although she had been vigorously opposed. Thor's only chance now was to induce her to act against her principles. As soon as he got home he laid his cards on the table and told her that everything now depended on her. Could she persuade his father to put up the money for the expedition? After serious consideration she said she was willing to help him. Knowing what this must have cost her, he was filled with gratitude.

It was an unforgettable moment when he saw his parents together again.

They were sitting by the hearth in his mother's flat, drinking wine and chatting with one another as in the old days. They first discussed the plan as a whole and reached full agreement. Then his father asked Fru Alison:

'But what do you think about Thor's plan to marry and take his young wife with him to the South Sea islands?'

'I think it is a splendid idea,' she answered immediately.

Heyerdahl sat openmouthed. He had never expected this. It had been his dearest wish to meet Alison again, so that they might part as friends, and what he now wanted most of all was to remain on good terms with her. So he had no alternative but to give in. He said he was ready to pay for the trip out to the Pacific islands and back.

It was worse for Liv. She had not mentioned the idea of marriage to her parents, or told them about the projected expedition, and she was extremely reluctant to do so. But she had gone so far that it was difficult to draw back. She therefore wrote a letter, saying approximately:

'Dear Mother and Father, I have met a young man called Thor Heyerdahl. He wants me to marry him and I have said yes, and I have thought of terminating my studies to go with him to the Marquesas Islands.'

This came as a bolt from the blue. When her father had read the letter several times, he went quickly across to the bookcase, took out a volume of an old encyclopaedia and opened it at M. There he found that the Marquesas were a very remote group of islands in the Pacific, where cannibalism and immorality flourished. In a rage he shut the book and accused his wife of having seriously neglected their daughter's upbringing. He then sent Liv a letter in which he expressed his opinion in no uncertain terms.

When Heyerdahl heard of this he rallied at once to the young people's side. He went with them to Liv's home and met her parents. In the course of a few minutes he charmed them both to such an extent that they listened calmly and with interest to what he had to say. He assured them that his son was an honourable boy who was perfectly sincere about his proposal, and that he—Heyerdahl—would finance the whole project. Soon he made them so completely confident that they gave Liv their blessing. All difficulties had been removed. The marriage took place in Brevik on Christmas Eve, 1936.

I had not heard from Thor for a long time when he wrote asking me to collect those of his friends who were still living in Larvik for a farewell party in Number 7 Stengaten. On the day following this happy reunion, he and Liv took the first train away from civilization.

Chapter 4

IN SEARCH OF PARADISE

THE savagely beautiful island of Fatu Hiva, as well as the entire Marquesas group to which it belonged, was far beyond any European, American, or Australian shipping lines, so the young couple had to go first to Tahiti. They travelled on a French liner, taking with them a letter of introduction from Bjarne Kroepelien to his friend the Tahitian chief, Teriieroo a Teriierooiterai. The chief gave them a warm welcome in his tropical bungalow in the Papenoo Valley and asked them to stay with him until he could find a native copra schooner that would take them as deck passengers to the lonely Marquesas group, just below the equator and nearly a thousand miles away.

In the Papenoo Valley they had their first education in native ways of life. They learned to eat with their fingers—everything from sweet potatoes to soup—to light a fire with two sticks, to catch crayfish with a three-pronged spear, to roast breadfruit in the embers, and to bake fish and root vegetables in the stonelined earth oven. They also learned to make tools of bamboo, bark, and different sorts of leaves.

A couple of accidents during this period nearly put an end to the adventure for Thor. One day Teriieroo taught him how to climb a coconut palm to collect the nuts. Thor struggled upwards, bow-backed in the native manner. It was terribly difficult and before he reached the top his strength gave out. He clung to the trunk, not able to move a single inch farther. He wanted to slide down, but the barbs on the trunk held him back. The alternatives were clear: either he must release his hold or he must stay up in the tree. Finally he decided to let go and trust to luck. The trip down was made with lightning speed, but parts of his clothing and skin were left behind on the trunk.

Another time, when he was catching crayfish in the Papenoo river below Teriieroo's house, he stepped on a prickly river snail and lost his balance. The next moment the current swept him down toward the mouth of the river. He struggled frantically. When he saw the ocean breakers beyond, his old fear of water completely paralysed him. But he told himself that he must keep calm; he must remember everything about learning to swim that he had heard over and over again when he was a boy. He began to use the strokes, found himself gliding smoothly through the water and was soon washed up on a sunbaked sandbank, surprised at how easy swimming had been when compelled by necessity and determination. Although waves and breakers still filled him with panic, from that day on his fear of deep water vanished. Unfortunately he had little opportunity to test himself further when they reached Fatu Hiva, since that island was without coral reefs. A heavy surf beat continuously against the coast, and sharks lay in wait outside.

Practically everyone with whom they spoke in Tahiti advised them against landing on Fatu Hiva. The white people laughed at their plan and regarded them as completely insane. They talked of sullen natives who only a short time before had been cannibals, of leprosy, elephantiasis, and other unpleasant diseases. But Thor and Liv were not to be dissuaded. Only under pressure did they consent to take with them a machete and a cooking pot.

'When we learn to do without them', said Thor. 'We must give them away', and Liv agreed.

They would not take even medicine with them. To get an honest impression of civilization as seen from the outside they must abandon its benefits as well as its evils. They planned to give away upon arrival personal belongings they had used on shipboard, and keep only the glass bottles and other equipment essential for their zoological collections.

Their stay on Tahiti culminated in a ceremony in which Teriieroo, in the presence of all his friends, adopted them as his children, naming them 'Mr and Mrs Blue Sky'.

They sailed on the little copra schooner *Tereora*, commanded by Captain Brander. This is how Thor describes their arrival in the Marquesas:[1]

'Then, one day, they rose with the morning sun, the islands we had dreamed about. Steep, rugged, and menacing, the mountain masses hurled themselves upward, soaring high above the ocean. Tumbling, frothing, thundering, the sea beat wildly against these unexpected obstacles in a world of water. From the distance the islands seemed far from hospitable. They resembled dark ruins of gigantic castles, with wisps of cloud sailing round their towers like smoke. But they were magnificently beautiful.

'As one island rose from the sea another sank and disappeared, for there was a great distance between the islands in the group. The Pacific stretched between them in varied tints of blue. But the sea round each individual

[1] *Paa Jakt efter Paradiset (In Search of Paradise)*, published in Oslo, 1938.

island was green as grass, due to the micro-organisms that lived upon what the perpetual succession of waves broke from the brittle rocks of the islands. Shoals of fish were also attracted to this green pasture with dolphins in pursuit of them. Swarms of seabirds followed our boat and plunged after the fish which struggled on the line we were towing astern.

'Then we glided closer to the shore and realized that here the Pacific reached its highest degree of fertility, putting to shame the finest of hot-houses. Deep wild gorges cutting into the central mass of the mountains continually opened before us. The jungle clothed the mountains like giant moss, then flowed down the ledges and clefts in the cliffs, to end in a chaos of luxuriant foliage in the valley, the crowns of the palm trees growing ever higher, striving to outstrip the steep precipices on either side. It seemed as if the green wealth of vegetation was reflected in the sea around, green on green. But the naked rock of mountains was red, and the sky was as blue as the ocean farther off shore.

'It was not the equatorial heat alone which created these floating hot-houses. In the interior of the island, peaks soared into the air to intercept the course of the clouds and squeeze the rain out of them before they were able to pass by. The rainwater poured down from the interior parts of the mountains in rushing torrents and rivers, through the jungle and the palm valleys and out into the green sea. And the tooth of time had played with the fragile volcanic rock. Deep caves and subterranean streams, pinnacles and grotesque carvings in the mountains turned the whole picture into a fantastic fairyland. It was here we were to be put ashore: to dive into the mysterious jungle while the *Tereora* disappeared again.

'We lay on the bouncing deck with our glasses and tried to pierce the dense woods which were to be our home. Lovely but oppressive was the impression they gave us as the schooner glided past. Empty of human life, but full of mystery. . . .'

'One feels crushed down to nothing by the jungle and the mountains', said Captain Brander. 'Better come back with us.'

They thanked him but declined. Nevertheless, they were a little uneasy when they had been actually put ashore with their luggage at the un-sheltered mouth of the narrow Omoa valley, on the western coast of Fatu Hiva, and stood alone on the beach as the lifeboat was rowed through roaring breakers back to the *Tereora*. Captain Brander waved to them. Then the schooner weighed anchor and disappeared over the horizon. They knew that a whole year would pass before the little schooner returned.

Up in the shade of the palm trees a crowd of natives stood and stared, dressed in rags or merely in loincloths. One withered old crone came up to Liv, licked a finger and rubbed the saliva on her face. Liv stood dumb with fear while the woman carefully examined her finger, then laughed a toothless laugh. The white colour was genuine. The natives had never seen white women on board the schooner, and no white man had ever mentioned that there were white women to be found at home.

The first night was a nightmare. They slept in the village down by the sea, in a corrugated iron shed as hot as a baker's oven. Next morning they moved up the Omoa valley to a remote plateau, which a half-breed pointed out to them as the place of residence of the last king, near the only spring in the valley. Here they would be a good distance away from the natives and the danger of infection. That morning some of them were bathing in the river with their clothes on, while others drank the same water just below. The islanders were well acquainted with imported European diseases, but had no knowledge of modern medicine or the causes of infection.

To Thor and Liv on their plateau, life before them looked bright and paradisal. They were surrounded by beauty and plenty. The forest was thick with fruit trees: banana plants of seven different kinds, orange trees, lemon bushes, coconut palms, breadfruit trees, and paw-paw and mango with their ruddy, yellow, tasty fruit. Among the trees grew abandoned coffee plants, and vanilla plants climbed like lovely creepers up the stems of the palms. This really had to be Paradise.

Here thousands of human beings had once lived. Fifty years ago only seven hundred were left. Now the last wretched remnants, a hundred in all, had huddled together in the village down by the sea.

This ancient 'palace plateau', high up in the valley, was the property of an elderly man whose name was Ioane. Thor and Liv were able to rent all its glories for the equivalent in francs of fifty kroner (about £2 10s) a year, with a right to build a hut and gather all the fruit they could eat. Thor started at once to clear the site with the machete that Chief Teriieroo had persuaded him to bring with him, and at nightfall Liv roasted her first breadfruit in the heap of embers from the fire. They slept in a little portable tent.

During the clearing of the site the next day they uncovered old stone terraces and remains of utensils, a heavy stone seat and a sleeping platform, as well as rare fruit trees and a pretty bush with red flowers. All these they left undisturbed. After three days the site was cleared. But when they began to build a hut on the old terrace with bamboo and palm leaves, Ioane arrived and protested vigorously. He explained by words and signs that the hut would wither away, the rain would pour through the roof, wild horses would trample down the walls, mosquitoes, ants, and poisonous giant centipedes would torment them, and clothing and furniture would be ruined. For seventeen and a half francs a day he and some of his friends would set up a proper Polynesian hut. So it was arranged. Walls, floor, and bed were plaited from split bamboo and lashed together with strips of bark from the hibiscus tree. The bamboo door and window shutter were hinged with oxhide, and the roof was thatched with plaited leaves of the coconut palm.

While the work on the hut was proceeding, Thor made a great hit as a magician. His microscope terrified the natives; it turned a tiny mosquito into a monster. They were tremendously impressed by the telescope. A magnifying shaving mirror made them roar with laughter. But the greatest success was the zip on the tent. With it, Liv and Thor could entertain a crowd for a whole evening. The natives were also impressed when Thor pushed a wad of cotton soaked in naphtha through the sparse teeth of one of the men and cured him of toothache.

Talking with the islanders was anything but easy. From the very first evening, Thor and Liv had written down a number of words which they thought might be useful. These they tried to learn by heart, but as the word for 'ugly' was *aoehakanahau*, and seventeen and a half francs, the daily wage, was *etoutemonieuatevasodiso*, it took time to memorize them. The worst thing was when they inadvertently exchanged a couple of vowels, the word acquired a totally different meaning. Nevertheless, they eventually picked up enough of the language to carry on simple conversations.

At length, the hut stood finished, as green and fresh as if it had grown out of the jungle ground. Now the natives began to troop up with presents of food—poultry, fish and roast wild pig in such quantities that much of it hung on the walls of the hut until it rotted. Before long Thor and Liv discovered the reason for this unending flow of gifts. For each item the natives brought, they expected something in return. This was their custom.

Seizing the opportunity to dispose of their personal belongings, they opened their boxes and everything was eagerly grabbed, including, to Thor's disappointment his wristwatch. For years he had looked forward to the day he could smash his watch—that symbol of civilization's hectic tempo and man's slavery to time, but this pleasure was now denied him. When the suitcases were empty the traffic up the Omoa valley came to an end.

To realize their goal, the young couple had taken two tremendous leaps—first, from the Christmas-decked streets of a Norwegian winter to summer in the primaeval forest of a tropical island; second, from the twentieth-century manner of life to the life of natural man before the dawn of history.

'Our days begin with a heavenly chorus of joy, after the brightly-coloured Marquesan cuckoo has awakened the choir of forest birds with his trumpet call. While the cool night wind from the mountains is still blowing through the hut and arousing us with a thrilling joy of life, the sunlight blazes like a revelation through the tops of the palm trees and on the colourful bamboo floor. The bare mountain peaks at the head of the valley, which loomed rust brown in the twilight of dawn flame out like a cock's comb in the morning sun, and all nature is suddenly turned into a festival, crowded with every kind of sun worshipper rejoicing to welcome the new day.

'We two in our green bamboo hut are happy spectators of all this harmonious combination of light, air, and music, which has gone on just like this ever since the Creator started it in the dawn of time. No human beings have had a hand in this performance. Shades seem to fall from our eyes at such a moment. When we go to wash in the spring, hidden among gigantic leaves, every drop of water spilt from our hands can sparkle like a jewel of incomparable beauty. No precious stone polished by human hands can shine with more loveliness than that pure liquid drop beneath the flame of the sun. Here—at the spring—we can bail them up by handfuls and afford to let them trickle by the thousands down toward their reflection and obliteration in the water beneath. And what about the melodious dance of the little stream, and the artistic composition of this frame of green vegetation which surrounds the living water? Can mankind create anything half so beautiful? Here the work of creation is perfect and complete, the masterpiece in which physics and chemistry, art and religion are inextricably blended, to fashion the Creator's great *perpetuum mobile*.'

The morning hours were always the most pleasant. As the day went on and the sun roasted the steaming jungle, Thor and Liv grew so drowsy that they had no energy to study animal life, to make notes or to do anything. It was as if they were completely drained of strength. In the evening the mosquitoes descended on them in dense masses. As these insects were the agents for spreading the filaria causing elephantiasis, Thor was finally forced to buy mosquito net from a half-caste who sold a very limited stock of goods in a tumble-down shack down in the village.

All the furniture they had was a couch of branches, a bamboo table, and two bamboo stools. The plates were big mother-of-pearl shells, and the cups were coconut shells. Liv refused to go on eating soup with her

D

fingers, so they made a couple of spoons out of bamboo cane. While she looked after their home, Thor would go out into the forest to find food, dressed in a flowered loincloth and armed with his machete in an oxhide sheath. One day when he returned with a load of green vegetables, Liv, sooty and her eyes watering, was standing in a cloud of smoke preparing dinner. She had a surprise for him, 'hamburgers' made out of grated coconuts and pounded breadfruit, cooked over the fire with the help of two wet sticks.

'Taste them', said Liv, handing her Tarzan a coconut shell containing some fragments of charcoal. 'I'm sorry they are burned on the outside.'

'It doesn't matter', answered Thor. 'Inside they're quite raw!'

The weeks went by, one after another, until one day they became dissatisfied. They were not really tired of their daily fare, but clearly there was something missing. That night they lay a long time chatting before going to sleep.

'Smoked salmon', said Thor.

'Roast pork with sauerkraut', replied Liv.

'Grouse with cream sauce', suggested Thor.

'Filet mignon', said Liv.

Thor dreamed that night of a three-course dinner. The next morning he went out and caught crayfish in the river.

One day when he was out in search of food, a native appeared on the bank of the stream and spoke to him. He was Pakeekee, the Protestant pastor of the island, to whom Thor had brought a letter from Chief Teriieroo in Tahiti. The chief was a devout Protestant and asked the pastor to look after the two white people, since they were his adopted children. Pakeekee did indeed look after them. For three full days and nights he feasted them in his home, where they met Tioti, the sexton, the same man Thor had cured of toothache.

'Are there many Protestants on the island?' asked Thor in the course of conversation.

The pastor thought for a while.

'No, there are mostly Catholics here. Père Victorin, who travels around the islands, paid those who became his converts such a terrible lot of sugar and rice, more than I could afford.'

'But how many Protestants are there?'

Pakeekee made a further calculation.

'One has died', he said, 'so there are now just myself and the sexton.' He gave a rather troubled laugh. 'There was one more, but he moved to Tahiti.'

On the third day of his party the pastor got up and said he had to bring the festivities to an end because it was Sunday, and he and the sexton must go to their bamboo church.

Tioti soon became their close friend. He invited them to go with him and his *vahine* (woman) to see Tahaoa, the only coral beach on the island, where no white man had ever been. The walk across the mountains was difficult and tiring, but it was well worth it. Among the snow-white sands and sparkling blocks of white coral they discovered an aquarium like none they had ever seen. Thor was wildly excited. What a marvellous community! What a picture of brightly coloured creatures, creeping, or darting and swimming, in swarming profusion!

While Thor and Liv were occupied with this romantic sight, the *vahine* 'laid the table' on a block of coral on the shore.

'Tioti drew two lemons from his trouser pockets. He squeezed out the juice onto the stone where he was sitting. A wriggling red fish with green spots was chopped to pieces with the machete. The woman kneaded the pieces in the lemon juice. The meal was then served. The sexton had already helped himself, and the noise of his swallowing was unbelievable. I stuffed a slice of the fish in my mouth and chewed and chewed. We had tasted raw fish before on Fatu Hiva. Poor Liv cautiously let the fish slide back into the water. The next course was produced. The woman had picked up some pretty large snail shells on the shore. She broke the shell with a stone, as if it were a nut, and the evicted mollusc was brutally rubbed on the stone and washed in the sea. This course was then ready to be served. I thought of oysters and ate it.

'But then came the third course. Before we realized what was happening, we each had a prickly sea urchin in our laps. "Help yourselves", said Tioti. "They are not the poisonous kind." As we pricked ourselves, we felt we needed a stomach lined with shoe leather for this sort of thing. I turned my brute over and stole a cautious glance at the sexton. Looking as if it were an everyday matter, he took his animal by its longest prickle and hit it against the rock with a smash. Inside, it was spring-green with red lumps. The sexton stuck his finger in and smacked his lips contentedly.

'Liv put her animal on the ground and said, "Be off with you!" but it was too sluggish to move. I shut my eyes, smashed the sea urchin and took a mouthful, thinking hard of sago pudding and currant jelly.

'Then we came to the fourth course. It lay crawling among the rocks, quietly hoping to get away. I have never been able to stand the sight of these long and slimy sea slugs. I thought feebly for a moment of our domestic Norwegian sausage, but it was no good!'

After they had learned to cope with the various surprises, difficulties, and dangers that Fatu Hiva had waiting for them in the mountains and jungle, they ventured out on expeditions steadily increasing in length. One day they were cutting a path with the machete through the dense network and sometimes bottomless carpet of creepers, trees, branches, and rotting tree trunks. With them were three natives who had offered to show them a curious fish. A stone fish. A very heavy shower delayed them, but at length they reached the spot.

Two stone slabs almost concealed by coffee bushes were lying close to a fallen tree trunk of enormous size. On the larger slab, its flat surface now covered with moss and lichen, was carved the outline of a curious fish, six feet in length. Carved around the fish were mysterious designs, and when Thor examined these more closely he found that some of them were partially covered by turf and soil, which suggested that more carvings were hidden from view. He and the natives then cleared the whole surface of the huge slab and found it entirely covered with strange symbols and menacing human figures with raised arms. No doubt magic had been associated with it once upon a time, for the natives became frightened and solemn.

'Tiki', they said in low voices. 'Menui tiki.' ('Gods. Many gods.')

'The forest was quiet after the rain, and just behind us hung a reddish peak of lava above the roof of the jungle, menacing and sharp as a knife. We felt as if it was watching our work and guarding the ancient secret of the stones. And at our feet the grotesque figures danced their motionless dance as if petrified by the sunshine. They had stood like this for centuries, since the time when an unknown civilization ruled the Marquesas islands. They were a mysterious people, who remain an unsolved enigma to science. Where they came from and who they were no one knows. The only traces we have are huge walls and terraces of enormous stones, left by a branch of the unknown race who once raised the colossal stone statues on Easter Island. . . . When the moon shone over the jungle we lay awake for a long time, on the couch in our bamboo hut. We thought about the dead stone figures dancing up there in the moonlight. . . . And we suspected that there were many hidden clues here in the deserted jungles of Fatu Hiva, the island which had been overlooked by science.'

Their suspicions soon became a certainty. They began to hear of remarkable discoveries made in the jungle by the natives. Many objects had been smashed and thrown into the sea because there were curses attached to them, but others were so completely taboo that the islanders did not dare to approach them. Through great effort and generous compensation Thor gradually managed to buy a number of these, things

he had not believed existed. There were grotesque stone images, ceremonial tools, ornaments made of turtle shell, teeth, and human bones,
and a complete royal robe made of human hair—all the work of a Stone
Age people who knew no other tools than stone adzes, shells, and rats'
teeth.

One morning when they were going to the terraced site of an old
temple on a mountain plateau by the sea, they were followed by a native
who was obviously spying on them. They discovered a large collection
of grinning human skulls, a treasure trove for a specialist, but the native
watched every move they made to make sure not even a tooth was
disturbed or taken away. Finally Thor wandered out into the jungle by
himself. Ignoring Liv, the spy followed him. On Fatu Hiva a man is a
human being, but a woman is merely a woman, created only to provide
food and sex. Otherwise she does not count. While the men were gone,
Liv seized the opportunity to put several skulls into a sack. When they
returned she pretended she had been picking coconuts for dinner.

On their way back home they were beckoned into the hut of Tahia-
pitiani, the beauty of the valley, who asked them to join her for a meal.
They were very reluctant to accept because they knew some of the people
in her house had infectious diseases. On the other hand, they did not wish
to alienate any of the natives, so squatting on the stone paving they took
their places with the others in a close circle around the large wooden
family bowl. They all ate fermented *poipoi* in coconut sauce, an evil-
smelling leaven made of long-buried breadfruit, the ancient staple food
of the Marquesans. It was scooped up with two fingers and sucked off
with audible sounds. And Thor, the boy who a few years before was
not allowed to drink from a glass that his mother had used, was now
dipping his fingers into the common container and gulping down the
same food as the natives did. Beside him was a man with his legs swollen
by elephantiasis, and across from him sat another with the telltale signs of
leprosy evident in one of his ears.

A native horseman came galloping along the path to their bamboo hut.
He looked ill, and shocked them by asking whether the 'plague' had
reached them. Thor shook his head.

'It's sure to come here later', said the native, and he laughed.

An infection had been spread on the island by men from a visiting
schooner and now everyone in the village was sick. Several had died,
he said, but he himself had got over it.

That day Thor and Liv did not have any appetite as they thought about
the plague coming. It duly arrived. Thor developed a sore throat, and Liv

nothing worse than summer diarrhoea. When they felt better, they laughed at how needlessly worried they had been.

The natives, however, had far less resistance to it as they discovered to their horror when their friend Tioti arrived, pale and with the light of fever in his eyes.

'Will monsieur come with me and take a photograph of Tioti's last remaining son. They have all now been taken away by the plague.'

A pall hung over the village. Funeral ceremonies were going on in most of the dark huts where the sick and dying coughing and spitting, lay right among those who had escaped so far.

It was a shocking tragedy, yet surprisingly it was forgotten very quickly by the natives who continued their carefree island life.

Liv had hidden the skulls from the temple plateau under the bed, the only hiding place in the hut. One night she pinched Thor, whispering, 'There's someone under the bed, I hear rattling!'

Thor muttered that perhaps it was cannibals and to let him sleep. But there was another noise now, loud and clear. When they looked under the bed they saw that three skulls, lying close to each other, were shaking so much their teeth were rattling. Liv started to scream. The next moment a hairy shadow dashed across the room and vanished through a gap in the plaited bamboo wall. A fruit rat. It had got into one of the skulls and had been unable to find its way out.

One morning the *Tereora* unexpectedly anchored off the island. There was rejoicing when Liv and Thor came on board, for a rumour circulating among the coral atolls to the south had said that the white couple had been demoralized by the horrors of elephantiasis, and were waiting for a ship to take them away. Captain Brander was greatly surprised that they did not wish to go back with him to Tahiti. When the *Tereora* sailed away this time, it was even longer before they would sight her again.

Some time later the sexton, Tioti, turned up at the hut one afternoon. He stood there a long time scratching his back, a thing he always did when anything had gone wrong. Finally, he told me that the little Catholic priest, Père Victorin, had arrived on the *Tereora* and was now living among his native congregation down in the village.

When he had heard of the white couple living up in the jungle, who were friendly with the Protestant pastor and his sexton, Père Victorin had become alarmed; they were surely competitive missionaries. He remembered with horror what had happened on the atoll of Takaroa. There had been 300 Christians there, a few of them Protestants, but the majority Catholics. Then a Mormon missionary had arrived and 298 had at once become Mormons, leaving the other two with a big wooden church apiece.

Tioti told Liv and Thor that on the very day of his arrival, Père Victorin had attacked them in his church. These two white people in the mountains were heretics, he said. It was not wrong to make life intolerable for them, for they must not become tempted to settle on this island forever. They must be given no gifts. If they bought anything, they must be charged the highest prices, and the goods were to be left outside their hut, for none of the faithful must enter their dwelling. It was a happy congregation that had flocked out of the church that day. The road to heaven was really easy and pleasant.

Tioti claimed that Père Victorin had acted in the same way towards him and Pakeekee, the pastor. Haii, son of Ioane, who suffered from elephantiasis, had even mixed his urine with orange beer and sent it to Pakeekee, hoping that his whole family would become infected.

This was disturbing news. The good chief Teriieroo had inadvertently involved them in a religious feud through his friendly note to the Protestant pastor, though to what extent the sexton's story was true they had no way of telling. All that night they made plans and early the next morning set off for the interior mountain range to get as far away as possible from their unknown enemy. On their way through the valley they met natives who no longer greeted them.

The days spent in the mountains proved a delightful change. The air was clean and fresh—at night time really cold—and some of their dwindling energy returned. They no longer feared dangerous infection, and the insects were not nearly as troublesome as down in the valley. On their first evening there, however, Thor turned over a stone near their camping place and found under it a poisonous giant centipede, its repulsive yellow shape twined round a dense clutch of white eggs.

After a time, however, their supplies of food began to give out. There were no fruit trees on the open mountains and they had no weapons for hunting, so they were forced to go back down into the valley. They decided to call on Père Victorin, show him a jar of rare creatures they had caught, and convince him that it was these they were collecting, not human souls.

Père Victorin was a little man who almost disappeared beneath his black cassock. He eagerly invited them in and offered them chairs. He was politeness itself and seemed to radiate goodwill, but his eyes never smiled. Thor tried to explain that they had come to Fatu Hiva for scientific reasons, but Père Victorin deftly sidetracked that topic by speaking of his own life in the Marquesas. For thirty-three years he had travelled from

island to island. He had lived as the only white man in native huts, eaten
native food, and gone among the sick and dying. His legs were swollen
with elephantiasis. He had no friends, for the Marquesans had no understanding of friendship. He had never felt any interest in plants or animals.

As he talked, Thor and Liv realized that he was lonely and unhappy.
The aim of his entire life was to gather names for the church register.
'He was like a philatelist when his collection is complete—hysterical for
fear of losing a single stamp.'

When they left the lonely man with the enormous legs, they returned
to their bamboo hut with a feeling of relief and gratitude. They had each
other, they had health, they had life, they had everything; and in such
immeasurable richness there was no room left for any enemy, least of all
the little man down in the native village who had given everything away,
including himself.

In the weeks that followed, they organized new expeditions into the
mountains or the jungle, or by dugout canoe along the precipitous coast
to reach wild glens where white men had never been and no human foot
had trod for many, many years. Once they were away for several days
with Tioti and another native guide. They visited abandoned temple
terraces, and burial vaults guarded by images carved in stone, and even
took their canoe down to a subterranean lake unknown to most of
the living natives because their forefathers had cursed the entrance and
made it taboo. When they decided to return home, they realized they had
delayed too long, and before they came in sight of the Omoa valley
night descended upon them. They now took serious notice of something
to which they had previously given just a passing thought. The sea
had each day become more rough. This evening it was particularly ugly,
and the water came almost up to the gunwale of the little canoe. They
threw the breadfruit and all the rest of their load overboard, but even
so they had to bail for dear life before the next heavy sea broke over them.
Tioti, alternately paddling and bailing, consoled them by saying that the
dugout could not sink; even if it became completely submerged they
could go on paddling without fear were it not for the sharks. Some of the
Marquesan sharks measured three times the length of the canoe, and
although they did not usually attack, there was fish blood in the dugout
and sharks could scent blood from a long distance. At long last, after a
stiff fight against the waves, the group saw lights from some of the huts
in the Omoa valley. Tioti was a capable seaman. He waited for just the
right wave, and then let the dugout be carried ashore with the spray on the
crest of a breaker.

'That was a close one', said Thor as they stood on land once more, drenched from head to foot.

'Taboo', said the sexton, thinking of the devils and gods they had offended by their curiosity.

For some time Liv and Thor continued to explore the coast and inland jungles, nearly impenetrable in places. Then they developed bad cases of boils and sores on their legs and ankles. In a few days their condition grew really serious. On Liv's feet there were three boils as big as teacups, while Thor's feet were a mass of open, many-coloured sores. If they got wet their feet swelled up like balloons, and this could not be avoided now that they were entering the rainy season. They were told they had caught the *fe-fe* disease. The boils went down after a time, but they turned into sores that did not heal.

As the weeks passed, the sores spread further, and sometimes the pain ran right up to the groin so that they had to stay in bed. The rain poured down every day. The soil in the forest turned to mud, the hut and leaf bedding grew mouldy. Everything was mildewed. The mosquitoes hatched out in enormous swarms, hanging in clouds outside the hut, hunting for human blood inside. If a gust of wind penetrated the jungle, hundreds were pressed through the mosquito net, and then the pygmy ants arrived to feed on the mosquitoes Thor and Liv managed to kill. All kinds of insects now entered the hut to escape the mud of the jungle. To keep the muck from their sores, Thor and Liv wore sneakers bought from the storekeeper in Omoa. Once when Liv slipped her foot into her shoe she let out a yell. In the toe lay a huge, hairy spider as big as a mouse— and did it bite!

Then came a plague worse than all the rest. Bamboo dust, as fine and white as flour, filled the air. It poured out of millions of tiny holes in the walls, swirled about, or lay in cakes all around. It made its way into everything; it covered Thor and Liv like snow while they slept. They breathed it into their lungs, and swallowed it in large quantities. Soon there was little that was idyllic left in the once romantic hut. The natives had swindled them thoroughly. They had built the walls with green rather than ripe and yellow bamboo, perfectly aware that eventually millions of tiny beetles would devour the hut. Then, they had reasoned in their simple fashion, they would be well paid for putting up a new one.

In spite of the pain in his feet, Thor had to hobble out into the forest to gather food, but now he was surprised to discover how little there was to be found. Banana plants and *fei*, wild, red mountain banana, edible only when cooked, had been chopped down, and the breadfruit trees were having a cropless period. They began to get hungry. When the sexton turned up on one of his rare visits with fish, they were more than delighted to see him.

They soon found out what was happening to their fruit. One day before sunrise Ioane, the landlord, was seen with a crowd of giggling *vahines* and young boys, carrying fruit away in sacks and barrows. Even the coconut palms were stripped of their nuts. Why? Surely they had enough down in the valley? In a rage Thor pursued the crowd and caught up with them down by the river.

'Ioane', he shouted, 'that fruit is mine!'

'I took it from the next lot', replied Ioane impudently.

Not long afterwards Thor caught sight of Ioane climbing down from a coconut palm right next to the hut. He was on him at once.

'We've rented this site.'

'But the coconut palm is mine!'

'You sold me the rights to both the site and the fruit.'

'The fruit but not the nuts.'

'To everything edible, including nuts. We can't live without the nuts.'

'Coconuts are not food. They are for copra, Ioane's income.'

There was nothing Thor could do but settle for the few nuts that Ioane left behind.

In the jungle, living conditions grew worse and worse. The rain continued and the mosquitoes became so bad that the natives could not gather their copra harvest. The two 'birds of Paradise' sat in the hut, waiting for a schooner. One night they heard the hoot of a steam whistle, but when they went down the next day they learned the ship had sailed past far out at sea.

When they visited Pakeekee, the pastor, and Tioti, they were warned that Haii, son of Ioane, had caught a female scorpion near the shore. Her eggs had hatched, and Haii had a box crammed full of little scorpions ready for Thor and Liv.

In the village too, conditions began to be wretched. The storekeeper's stock had long been exhausted. Everyone was waiting for a schooner with fresh supplies. Week after week went by. One month—two months—three. When the third month had passed without a visit from a ship, Père Victorin grew desperate. He felt he must get away from the island. But how? The sea was running white with foam every day, and the nearest island was a good sixty miles away. The largest craft on Fatu Hiva was an old, abandoned lifeboat, which lay, battered and worn, under a palm roof on the shore. The priest gave orders to the natives to patch it up as well as possible, and then one day he persuaded them to leave with him. Liv and Thor had to admire him in spite of everything. No doubt he was fanatical, yet he lived up to his faith and displayed a courage few could equal. They stood watching the boat as it bobbed in the troughs of the waves, finally disappearing from sight. They'd never make it!

But a week later the native rowers returned. They had landed the priest on the island of Hiva Oa, but all they had been able to bring back with them was a small bag of waterlogged flour, and they themselves were in a state of collapse.

Liv and Thor discussed the situation thoroughly. Their legs were now in dangerous condition. Even the natives avoided looking at them. There was no longer any alternative. They must take the same hazardous course as Père Victorin. The half-caste storekeeper and some of the natives, among them Ioane, were willing to go along to bring back flour and rice, for rice had become an indispensable item on Fatu Hiva.

But what about the stone images, the skulls, the ornaments, and the jars full of the creatures they had collected? They could not take them in the open boat, and if left behind they were sure to be stolen. Thor hit on a plan. Now that the priest had left, he was once more on speaking terms with the natives. He took a group of them with him to the hut, let them smell some formaldehyde and explained that the liquid turned into a poisonous vapour. They could see for themselves that it killed a centipede that could otherwise creep and crawl even when cut into pieces. With plugs of cotton up his nostrils and a bandage over his eyes, he poured formaldehyde on the floor of the hut. Then he jumped out and shut the door behind him. His collections were safer than they had ever been.

At daybreak they set off in the lifeboat, Ioane at the helm. Great quantities of bananas and *fei* were piled under the seats of the oarsmen, and a water cask and a hammer and nails to repair any planks damaged by the waves were stored in the bow. The boat lay deep in the water; the whole plan seemed completely mad.

Once clear of the breakers, Ioane crossed himself. The oarsmen, tough and muscular, sat and bowed their heads while the old man slowly recited the Polynesian prayer for those at sea. And then they set off.

As soon as they were no longer under the lee of the island, they began to feel the motion of the sea in earnest.

'Ioane was brilliant at the helm. Bent double and with clenched teeth he manoeuvred the boat to catch and ride with every crest of a wave. If one did break sideways and into the boat, he clung to the rudder with a devilish energy, never removing his eyes from the next wave driving towards him. Though the water dripped off him and the salt made his eyes smart, he held firmly to the rudder and remained on guard. He was a good captain.'

After several hours two of the oarsmen collapsed with sea-sickness, while Liv lay unconscious in the bottom of the boat, her legs swollen to a grotesque size.

Hour after hour passed. Every time the trough of a wave yawned beneath them it seemed as if it would swallow them up, but each time invisible hands carried the little craft over and beyond. Late in the day they sighted the uninhabited island of Motane. Now they could correct their course. Other islands rose up out of the sea and in the evening they caught a glimpse of their objective, Hiva Oa. But the most dangerous part— the current between the islands of Hiva Oa and Tahuata—was still ahead. Under full sail they ran into the tideway. Ioane sat with a look of dogged determination. Everything now depended on him.

The sun set while over and over again they tried to ride in on the surf. Suddenly an unusually high wave rose behind them and the next moment they were backing water for their lives. Ioane cried wildly:

'Row, row, row!'

It was too late. The boat swung sideways. Ioane lost control of the helm while the rowers abandoned their oars and dived over the gunwale. Thor grabbed Liv and got her clear of the boat as it turned over. Then everything was a whirl of water and foam and sand, until suddenly his feet struck solid ground. By this time the crew was already starting to save the boat. They did not worry about the oars and cargo; the sea itself would throw them ashore.

On Hiva Oa, the large island where Paul Gauguin spent the last years of his life, there was no doctor. But a native whose name was Terai, had learned some basic remedies in the hospital on Tahiti, and he used this slight knowledge in a masterly way. Their legs and feet were in serious danger, he said, when he saw the sores, and then he probed and cut, rubbed on ointment and removed inflamed toe nails to prevent infection of the bone. The sores stopped spreading, but it was clear it would be a long time before they were cured. Weeks passed.

Fortunately there were horses on the island, and the two patients were able to take long rides up into the hills without damage to their feet. Once Terai accompanied them. High up in the mountains he stopped his horse and pointed to the wild and fertile landscape beneath them. Far below, between the jagged ridges and peaks of former volcanoes, lay knolls covered with withered ferns and *teita* grass, like yellow islands in a sea of dark green jungle. Here and there steep cliffs descended and vanished in blue-green shadow. Viewed from this altitude the ocean seemed boundless. Far out in the haze, beyond Tahuata and Motane, rose the topmost mountain crest of Fatu Hiva.

'*C'est joli*', said Terai. 'That is what the country was like in the old days. And we were all happy. Our old king composed the national song of Tahiti. It ran, "I am happy, *tiare*[1] flower of Tahiti." That was all.'

In the isolated Puamau valley Thor saw more amazing ruins, as well as the largest stone statues in the Pacific, with the exception of Easter Island. His interest in animal life now became completely secondary. Particularly remarkable was a strange god lying prone, in the position of a swimmer, and supported by a vertical pillar out of the same rock on which were carved smaller conventional figures. But the real surprise was a relief figure of a four-legged animal with a long raised tail on both sides of the pillar. When the first Europeans arrived in the Marquesas, the only mammals they found there were the pig and the rat. Could the ancient sculptors have seen dogs or felines in other lands?

A month and a half had passed since they had come to Hiva Oa. Their sores were healed, although their legs and feet were still ugly to look at. With plenty of time to think things over they had decided to go back to Fatu Hiva and make one last attempt before admitting defeat and returning home to Norway.

When they disembarked from the native schooner that had brought them from Hiva Oa, the Omoa valley was damp and smelt of fungus. The insects were worse than the natives could ever remember. Thor and Liv found their hut had become a little jungle in itself. The supporting hibiscus post had taken root and sprouted long shoots and green leaves. Otherwise the hut was a ruin. The bamboo walls looked like rotten cardboard, and the roof was hanging in shreds. Centipedes and spiders were scurrying about in all directions. But the natives had not touched anything inside.

To stay there was out of the question. After talking it over they decided to move away from the Omoa valley to the completely isolated side of the island. That night they slept outside under the mosquito net, and the next day Thor arranged with Tioti to help them move. He was the same pleasant chap, but one of his legs was fast becoming a shapeless lump. He too had fallen victim to elephantiasis.

The eastern part of Fatu Hiva was a closed world. Tremendous mountain walls made the narrow coastal strip nearly inaccessible by land, and from the east huge ocean waves rolled in, accompanied by the easterly trade

[1] A Shrub with fragrant white flowers, of the genus *Gardenia*.

winds straight from the South American mainland. To land by canoe in the wild surf on that coast was almost impossible.

With Tioti as guide, they decided to move to Ouia, the largest of the east coast valleys and the only one possible to approach from the inland side. It was an exceedingly difficult climb down the precipitous mountain wall once they had reached the lofty water shed, but at length, quite exhausted, they came to the deep Ouia valley, which opened up into a friendly palm grove extending towards a beach of water-worn rocks.

An old man in a loincloth ran up to them from a lonely thatched hut down by the sea.

'Kaikai puaa!' he exclaimed with a broad grin.

This, meaning 'Let's eat pig', was the symbol of friendship and hospitality. They joined him for a long meal of pig roasted in an earth oven.

Old Tei Tetua and his pretty little foster daughter were the only human beings on the entire east coast. He had survived the whole of his generation, including his twelve wives.

Near him, right on the beach where the wind kept the insects away, Thor built his new home—a thatched cabin with one end open, erected on piles and reached from the ground by an outside stepladder. Around the campfire at night, old Tei proved a most interesting companion. He was the only living Marquesan islander to have eaten human flesh. He told them which were the most delicious pieces of the body and how the meat should be prepared. It was best raw, he said, or baked between stones. His father, who had been the most savage warrior in the valley, had seldom eaten anything but human flesh, preferring it when it had hung until it was high. Tei himself had eaten it only once, during a ceremony in his childhood.

Sometimes Tei would sing old folksongs, monotonous and unmelodious, but extremely interesting. Thor liked best the primaeval story of creation:

'Tiki, the god of mankind, who lives in heaven, created the earth. Then he created the waters. Then he created the fish. Then he created the birds. Then he created the fruits. Then he created the pig. When all this was finished, he created mankind—a man who was called Atea, and a woman who was called Atanoa.' To this Tei added: 'The rest these two managed by themselves.'

When Thor asked why the natives were dying out, the old man answered:

'Diseases which the double-man brought with him.'

'The double-man? What do you mean by that?'

'The first white men who came to the Marquesas were called double-men because they had two heads, two bodies and four legs.'

The natives had never seen tight-fitting clothes before. They had thought that the white men discarded one body when they undressed themselves.

In the old days, said Tei, people never died of illness. If anyone died young, it was because he fell down and broke his neck or was caught by sharks or eels in the sea. Even if one hurt oneself badly, the medicine man could often cure him. Tei remembered a native in Ouia who had broken his skull. A medicine man named Teke cleaned the wound, removed the splinters of bone, and cut away rough edges, then closed up the gaping hole with a piece of coconut shell rubbed thin, all without injuring the brain. The wound healed and the man lived for many years afterwards.

Liv and Thor discovered proof of this. Among the bones in a burial cave they found a skull showing evidence of just such an ancient trepanation. They later learned that these difficult head operations, common in ancient Peru, had been practised on several South Sea islands.

During their stay in Ouia valley, Thor was struck by an idea that led him later to embark on something that would take him half a lifetime to complete.

'That evening we were sitting, as we had so often sat before, in the moonlight down by the shore facing the sea. Wide awake and full of the romantic atmosphere around us, we allowed no impression to escape us. Our nostrils were filled with the scent of luxuriant foliage and salt air, and we listened to the wind rustling in the palm tops, when every sound was not drowned out by the great waves rolling in from the ocean. They broke in spray upon the shoal, until they were smashed into eddies of foam among the pebbles on the beach.

' "Why are there never breakers like these on the other side of the island," asked Liv.

' "This is the exposed and windy side," I replied. "The open sea comes in from this side."

'Then we settled down again and marvelled at this sea which never stopped proclaiming that it was coming this way, rolling in from the east, from the east, from the east. . . . It was thus that the waves and the light cloud formations had rolled up over the eastern horizon since the dawn of time. The first human beings to reach these islands knew perfectly well that it was so. Birds and insects knew it too, and the island's vegetation was completely dominated by this state of affairs. And we ourselves knew that far, far below the horizon, yonder in the east, where the clouds used to rise, lay the mainland coast of South America. It was four thousand miles away, and there was nothing but ocean in between.

'We stared at the drifting clouds and the heaving moonlit sea, as we listened to Tei Tetua, who sat crouched before us, gazing down into the dying embers of a small, burnt out fire.

' "Tiki", said the old fellow quietly, "he was both a god and a chief. It was Tiki who brought my ancestors to these islands on which we live. Before that we lived in a great land far beyond the sea."

'When we climbed into the bunks in our little pile-hut that night, my brain was still haunted by old Tei Tetua's account of the legendary fatherland of the islanders. The dull roar of the distant breakers sounded like a voice from antiquity, which seemed to have a message for us there in the night. I could not sleep. It felt as if time no longer existed and Tiki and his mariners were just in the act of making their first landing down there in the surf on the shore. Then a thought suddenly struck me. Those huge stone images of Tiki up in the jungle were strikingly reminiscent of similar giant statues left behind by extinct civilizations in South America.

'I felt distinctly that a roar of approval came from the breakers. And then they came slowly to rest as I fell asleep.'

The barking of dogs and loud human voices echoed one day in the forest. A number of natives had heard Tioti after his return home speaking about the pigs and all the fruit in the valley of Ouia, and they came to share this luxury. It was all right at first, but more and more natives arrived. They got drunk on orange beer, and finally managed to turn the old man against Liv and Thor.

And then one night Liv woke up when something bit her on the thigh. She yelled that the bed was crawling with insects, but Thor at once realized what it was—one single giant centipede. Where had it come from? In the morning Liv's leg was stiff. That day Thor killed two poisonous centipedes in the hut, and saw another escaping through the wooden slats in the floor.

They could stay no longer in the Ouia valley. Thor bribed a native to help them move out. Their flight up the mountainside was even more difficult than their climb down had been. The heat was like an oven. Halfway up their guide deserted them, so they had to struggle back to Omoa by themselves. Everything there was as before, damp and miserable. Their retreat continued. In a cave on Tahaoa, the desolate shore with the white coral blocks, they made their last stand.

But it was uncomfortable here too. Fruit was nearly non-existent because of the vertical mountain wall that rose close behind the shore, and they lived mostly on hermit crabs, shellfish, and what fish there were in the shallow water. The cave was unsafe due to falling stones from the mountain above them, and when the tide rose poisonous eels came up on land and twined themselves like gleaming serpents among the wet boulders near where they slept.

Finally one morning the white sails of the *Tereora* twinkled in the sunlight on the blue horizon.

PART TWO

THE TEMPERING YEARS

Chapter 5

THE RIDDLE OF BELLA COOLA

THE bamboo hut at Omoa, the house on stilts at Ouia, the cave at Tahaoa—all appeared as a distant dream to Thor as he sat, pencil in hand, in an old mountain hay barn near the family's cabin at Hornsjö. The weathered timber of the barn was cracked and covered with lichen, and it looked as if it had stood forever in that Norwegian meadow, now thick with a colourful multitude of mountain flowers. The door was wide open to the summer weather, and the table was covered with photographs and neat bundles of manuscript. The young man was recording all that had happened in his search for Paradise, and passing a merciless judgement on his experiment and on his dreams.

They had arrived back in Norway in March of that year, 1938. When I had seen them off in January, 1937, they had been ruddy-cheeked and bursting with health. Now they looked thin and pale. Did they regret their trip? No. Whether good or bad, it had been an invaluable lesson, convincing them that a complete and unconditional return to life in nature was no longer practicable. As Thor summed it up:

'There is no Paradise to be found on earth today. There are people living in great cities who are far happier than the majority of those in the South Seas. Happiness comes from within, we realize that now. Man has forsaken nature, and thus changed himself through thousands of years, while altering nature at the same time. To turn back altogether is out of the question. It is in his mind and way of life that man may find his Paradise—the ability to perceive the true values of life, which are far removed from property and riches, or from power and renown.'

They had gained a fresh store of experience and the discoveries they had made had started Thor off on a new track. As he wrote later in *Kon-Tiki*:

'I remember how I shocked my father and astonished my mother and her friends when I came back to Norway and handed over my glass jars of beetles and fish from Fatu Hiva to the University Zoological Museum.

I wanted to give up animal studies and tackle primitive peoples. The unsolved mysteries of the South Seas had fascinated me. There must be a rational solution of them, and I had made my objective the identification of the legendary hero Tiki.'

There were no breadfruit trees or coconut palms in the Norwegian forests, and Thor had a wife to support. Under no circumstances would he resort to asking help from his father. Instead he, and Liv too, began writing accounts of their adventures for newspapers and magazines, and Thor also gave a series of lectures.

Meanwhile they were looking for a house. Thor would have preferred one deep in the wild forest, without electricity and other modern conveniences, but Liv protested. In the Marquesas she had accepted all hardship with the greatest fortitude; but her faith in a paradisal existence in the wilderness was gone. Since she was expecting her first child shortly, it was desirable to have at least some of the comforts that civilization could provide. Quietly but firmly she made clear to Thor that living like a savage was now finished with as far as she was concerned.

To Thor, nature and modern society were still in the same violent conflict. He sought a compromise and managed to find a log cabin high up on the fir-covered hill overlooking Lillehammer. His mother sold her flat in Oslo and bought herself a house next to theirs.

In his new home Thor started on the task his thoughts had been wrestling with for a long time. He could not forget how the breakers always came rolling in against the east coast of Fatu Hiva, and how the clouds drifted over the island from the same direction day after day, year after year, always. He saw before him the giant stone images in the jungle, left there by an unknown people. Who were these Stone Age sculptors who came to Polynesia? Who were Tiki and his men? And where did they come from? He had found in many books the theory that they had come from the west, from the islands and continents of the sunset. But this theory was hard to reconcile with what he himself had observed and experienced, and besides, the various researchers disagreed with one another on all important points.

He now devoted his time in earnest to the study of this subject. If he was not in the cabin surrounded by photographs and manuscripts, he was off to Oslo, to the University library and to Bjarne Kroepelien's unique collection of literature on Polynesia, returning home with his suitcase full of material to go over. As he covered this mass of books he made notes of everything of interest with the most painstaking accuracy, and time after time he discovered something that completely fitted in with his own conjecture: the earliest settlers of Polynesia must have come from the east, from the ancient civilizations in South America. Other scientists had touched on this point, but they had all rejected it as impossible. He could not ignore the fact that this was not a simple problem. Although he found evidence to support his theories, he also found evidence that did not, for example, the differences in language. If the Polynesians had emigrated from South America, why were their dialects related to Malay, the tongue of the semi-continental islanders next to the coast of Asia? All the time he pursued his studies he had an uncomfortable feeling that what he had read was only half the truth and that his own solution was not fully satisfactory.

Then occurred a remarkable coincidence, one of those which, in a sense, have so often marked out Thor's way through life. Not long after September 26, 1938, when the new Thor junior came into the world, Thor delivered a radio lecture about Fatu Hiva and mentioned his discoveries of hitherto unknown petroglyphs (rock carvings). The next day he took his usual walk to buy milk at a neighbouring farm. He was met at the door by the farmer, who with a mysterious smile, invited him into the kitchen and showed him some surprising amateur snapshots. They might have been taken in Fatu Hiva—the same petroglyphs, the special kind of stone adzes, even the faces of the people. One of the men bore a striking resemblance to Thor's adopted father, chief Teriieroo of Tahiti. How could these photographs have turned up here among the far mountains of Norway?

The farmer took him into the parlour, and he introduced him to his elder brother, Iver Fougner, a sturdy, white-haired man who had heard Thor's lecture on the radio. It was he who had taken the photographs, not in Polynesia but on the Pacific coast of North America. Herr Fougner was back from America for the first time in many years. As a young man he had settled in British Columbia, where he had served for a long term as a judge among the coastal Indians of the Bella Coola valley, halfway between the United States and Alaska. When he had heard Thor's lecture he had recalled his own photographs and shown them to his brother.

The talk began over a cup of coffee. The Bella Coola Indians, explained the judge, were part of the great stock of salmon-fishing and seafaring people who had occupied all the islands and channels of the northwest coast of America before Europeans had arrived. They had become known as the Northwest Coast Indians and were unlike all other American Indians, bearing more resemblance to certain tribes of Asia and the Pacific islands.

As the conversation proceeded, Thor studied the photographs strewn over the table and became more and more astonished by all the likenesses between the people and their art and household goods of Bella Coola and Fatu Hiva. Surely this could not be put down to mere chance? In the days that followed, he constantly thought about this problem. Then it occurred to him, while considering the globe, that the valley of Bella Coola was a particularly suitable stopping place for a migration from Indonesia to Polynesia. The Philippine current from Indonesia becomes the Japan current, which leads straight towards that part of the North American coast where it turns away and joins the tradewind route down to Hawaii in Polynesia. This raised interesting possibilities. Suppose that not one but two migrations had reached the South Sea Islands—one from South America and the other from Asia by way of North America?

In great excitement Thor looked first for answers to two questions: did the Northwest Coast Indians of old understand the art of making pottery and had they been acquainted with the loom?

On all their islands, the ancient Polynesians had been without any kind of ceramic art, nor had they any knowledge of the loom, the wheel, or metalworking of any sort. This was remarkable, since knowledge of all these arts had been widespread in the coastal districts of Southeast Asia and Indonesia many centuries before the Polynesians had set sail for their present archipelago. In South America, too, weaving and pottery-making had been well known and highly developed, although iron and the wheel had been unknown in all of America until the arrival of Columbus. Some scholars had tentatively suggested that the immigrants from Asia had not been able to continue their pottery-making in Polynesia because of the absence of clay, but this idea didn't hold water. Thor had seen with his own eyes suitable clay on a number of the islands.

Filled with hopeful expectations, Thor put his theory to its first test: were the Northwest Coast Indians as ignorant of pottery as were the Polynesians? In his research he found in Dr P. E. Goddard's book, *Indians of the Northwest Coast*, the following statement: 'On the Northwest Coast pottery is entirely lacking, and clay, the material most readily modelled, is not employed in art.' Dr Goddard went on to say that the Northwest Indians, like the Polynesians, were one of the extremely few peoples in the entire Pacific area who were ignorant not only of pottery but also of the loom. On the whole of the Northwest American coast the Indians cooked their food not in pots but in stone-lined earth ovens of the Polynesian type. Further, they made their clothes from the inner bark of certain trees, which was softened in water in the Polynesian manner and beaten with the same sort of grooved mallets as were used in the South

11. Wild pigs came fearlessly close to the hut.
12. (*next page*) Strange ruins were found in the jungle of the Ouia Valley.
13. (*next page*) The former cannibal Tei Tetua who played the flute with his nose.

Sea islands. Here was a possible conclusion: that the Polynesians had come to their present island world without pottery, loom, wheel, or iron by way of the coast that differed precisely in these respects from all the rest of the region around the Pacific. They had come from the Northwest American coast to Polynesia and there displaced the original islanders who, at one time, had arrived from South America, familiar with both ceramics and weaving.

Gradually, as Thor plunged deeper into the special literature of the Northwest Coast Indians, particularly that of the Kwakiutl tribe of the central section, the pieces fell into shape in his great pattern and satisfied the countless questions that neither a direct Asian nor a South American migration could alone explain. Such remarkable similarity between the adjacent areas of the Northwest Coast Indians and the Polynesians was shown by physical types, manners and customs, bark cloth and ornaments, fishing tackle and food preparation, even utensils and products like the elbow-handled stone adzes, sea-going double canoes, totem poles, dwellings, musical instruments, stone pounders and pestles, grooved wooden mallets, war clubs and other weapons—often of types not be found anywhere else in the world—the attention had been drawn to it since the days of the very first explorers. But nobody had ever been able to come up with a satisfactory explanation for all these remarkable parallels.

If Thor was to prove his point, he couldn't sit reading in a Norwegian mountain valley. He would have to make on-the-spot investigations, dig and search within the old dwelling sites of the Northwest Coast Indians. Above all he wanted to visit the central section of this island-dotted coast, the home of the Kwakiutl tribes, who had more in common with the Polynesian islanders than any of the surrounding tribes. The Bella Coola valley was in the very heart of the Kwakiutl territory, yet it was occupied by an alien tribe who had wedged into the mountain-locked valley and probably driven the original people away from the coast.

He had to get there. But how? To me, struggling like Thor to make a living by my pen, his problem seemed insurmountable. Even the voyage there, halfway around the world, would cost him a small fortune and where would he get it? It was not possible. Or was it?

On September 1, 1939, the Germans invaded Poland. The hope of peace for all humanity was drowned in a deluge of shame, blood, and flames. In our group we had often discussed the possibility of war and it had been generally agreed that it could not happen in our enlightened age.

14. (*previous page*) Living in a cave on a desolate coral beach, the Heyerdahls were on constant look out for ships.
15. At the beginning of Thor's career as an author—first a popular travel book then a scientific manuscript.

Only Thor had disagreed, arguing that another war was certain. Modern arms had become nearly perfect, he had said, but man himself had never improved.

A couple of days after the infamous day Thor knocked on my door. He had come to say good-bye, and with him were Liv and a blue-eyed charmer not yet a year old. They were off to Bella Coola. Money shortage, war, or uncertainty were not deterring him. How had he managed it? His book, *In Search of Paradise*, published in November, 1938, had had a unanimously favourable press, yet its sales were only moderate. Even so, the income from this and his other writings and lecturing would suffice for six months' field work in Bella Coola, although not for the long journey. He knew, however, that Norwegian ships were leaving Norwegian harbours every day, just as he had seen them from his bedroom window as a boy. Thinking of those days, he remembered a visitor to Number 7 Stengaten, old Fred Olsen, whose company, the Fred Olsen Line, owned ships that ploughed every sea. He discovered they even had a regular service of cargo-and-passenger vessels to Vancouver in British Columbia, from which it was no great distance to Bella Coola.

He decided to call upon Thomas Olsen, who had taken over his father's business. He explained his plans and problems, then produced a report that he had shown no one else. It was very simple and easy to understand. Drawings showed the direction of the currents and trade winds in the Pacific, and arrows indicated the suggested routes of migration to Polynesia, the first from Peru by the Humboldt current, and the second from Southeast Asia by the Japan current via Northwest America. There were also several pages of drawings showing parallels between Polynesian and Indian petroglyphs, sculptures, weapons, and tools.

'From its original centre of isolation in Southeast Asia', the report concluded, 'the Indo-American race has extended itself in two directions:

'1 Over the whole Malay archipelago . . .

'2 Along the coast region towards the northeast . . . the race came to what is now America and extended without obstruction over the whole of that continent as America's aborigines.

'One branch of the Northwest Coast Indian fishing people seems later to have crossed to Hawaii and, still with the northeasterly trade wind behind them, to Savaii in Samoa, and the whole of the uninhabited Polynesian archipelago as well as New Zealand. Only in the islands farthest to the east—Easter Island and the Marquesas group—were they forced to conquer an earlier culture—people, probably off-shoots from the highly civilized Indo-American branch in Peru. Towards the west, this race came up against the racial barrier of the Austro-

Melanesians, and interbreeding here produced the Micronesian population.'

Thomas Olsen was immediately fascinated. What he had expected to be a short business-like meeting developed into a long exciting discussion, and to a friendship later on. The outcome of their conversation was that Thor would be allowed to travel to Vancouver with his wife and child for a purely nominal sum.

On my desk was an illuminated globe that had always attracted Thor. Now we turned the world around until an entire hemisphere was filled by the blue Pacific, and as he talked we ourselves suddenly became Stone Age people living somewhere on the coast of Asia long before pottery and the loom were known. With a small band of local coastal voyagers we were helplessly caught in the offshore current and drifted, half starved, to the Northwestern American coast. Here we struggled ashore among island-dotted fjords swarming with fish in the warm water that had carried us from the Philippine Sea. Untold generations passed before, somewhere around A.D. 1000-1100, we put to sea once more in our double canoes, driven away from the fertile Bella Coola valley by intruders, to be carried by wind and current to the hidden world of Polynesia, where we encountered the bearded people who carved stone statues and had come from Peru some centuries before.

It was evident that all Thor's energy and interests were now woven together into the line he was to follow from then on. He had found his vocation in life. He was bursting with eagerness to get to Bella Coola and start his work there. Liv was just as enthusiastic. The Fatu Hiva adventure, far from robbing her of her spirit, had kindled a fever in her blood. Travel was life, she said. There was nothing to equal getting out into the world, meeting other kinds of people, and learning to know them.

When they left, Thor promised to be back within a year. Although England, France, and Germany were at war, certainly nobody would interfere with the shipping lines between Norway and America.

'Once more', wrote Thor on November 23rd, 'we are on an island in the Pacific—Vancouver Island. We are sitting in a top floor room of an English villa on the outskirts of Victoria. There is a bright moon outside, and we can catch a glimpse of the Pacific. It is a remarkable country, this Pacific coast of Canada. It is midwinter, with glittering ranges of snow-clad mountains, but along the coast here the grass is green. There are roses and fruit. And they are even bathing on the beach! In the parks, bears, bison, and deer are strolling about, and masses of wild duck are swimming along the shore. There are even seals. Of course there are skyscrapers to spoil the whole thing. But all the same, if there must be a town, it can't be more beautiful than Victoria. . . .'

The letter went on to tell that he had begun his research at the museums in Victoria, Vancouver, and Seattle, going thoroughly through the archaeological collections there. At the same time he had tried to make contact with the local scientists, and it was not long before he and Liv had made a number of good friends. All this time Thor attempted to keep his migration theory secret, partly because he wanted the strongest possible cards in his hand before he produced them, and partly because he was afraid that someone might steal his idea before he had time to publish it.

At the University of Seattle he met Professors Erna Gunther and Verne Ray, two of America's foremost experts on Northwest Coast Indian cultures. During a luncheon with them, he merely told them he had come to study the points of similarity between the Polynesians and the Northwest Coast Indians.

'Do you too believe that the Polynesian islanders reached this coast?' asked Erna Gunther with a smile. 'You are not the first to have noticed the parallels. Our colleague, Dr Dixon, has pointed out that as early as when Captain Cook and Vancouver came on their respective voyages of discovery to the territory of the Northwest Coast Indians, they wrote down that the huge canoes, houses, fortifications, weapons, clothing, and tools all reminded them of Polynesia. But we who have ourselves studied the archaeological development of the Northwest Coast culture know that all the special features of its culture were developed locally step by step here on the coast, so they cannot have come here from Polynesia.'

Thor swallowed a retort. Professor Ray said that the Northwest Coast Indians had needed no inspiration from Polynesian sailors to build up their maritime fishing culture.

'They have managed to develop a type of canoe that is probably better fitted for deep-sea navigation than any other known primitive craft in the whole world.'

'But can you give me any reason', Thor blurted out, 'for not suspecting that the Northwest Coast Indians may have got to Polynesia?'

Professor Ray was evidently caught by surprise, and could only answer:

'Well, you may not think it is a very good reason, but we American anthropologists, and Americans in general, like to think of America as a unity; we have been brought up to look on the American Indians as a unity isolated from the rest of the world. We who belong to the school of Boas don't like to think of it in any other way.'

Thor was baffled at such an argument, but took note of the reply and made no further comment.

Soon afterwards he was invited to the home of T. P. O. Menzies, the elderly director of the Vancouver City Museum, who related how he had carried out research in Polynesia and New Zealand many years before. When he had later compared his observations with finds made in ancient Northwest Coast Indian sites, he had become convinced that there must be a connection between the two regions.

'The difficulty', he said, 'is to discover in what direction the cultural transfer had gone.'

His own opinion was that probably some Polynesians had come to this coast from Hawaii. He brought out a bundle of photographs of Kwakiutl Indians, insisting that they might just as well have been of Polynesians. Then he took Thor around the museum and pointed out similarities in utensils and weapons.

Yet another of the local authorities invited Thor to visit him. This was the old linguist, Professor Hill-Tout. He took from a bookshelf a scientific periodical of 1898 and produced his own article, 'Oceanic Origin of the Kwakiutl-Nootka and Salish Stocks of British Columbia.' In this treatise he had presented a comparative study of the languages in question, and had concluded that there was a convincing linguistic relationship between tribes of the Northwest coast of America and the natives of Indonesia and Polynesia. But he too had come to the conclusion that it was not possible to explain these 'marvellous and far-reaching similarities' without assuming that the Northwest Coast Indians had originally come from the South Sea islands.

Thor was left with the impression that nearly all these local scholars, whether they were archaeologists, ethnologists, or linguists, suspected that there must have been some former connection. They could not, however, give any satisfactory explanation, since they all based their views on the accepted dogma that the Polynesians had at one period or another come from somewhere in Asia, following the global curve of the equator rather than that of the Japan current. It would have been so simple if they had just visualized that the local American coast was the natural geographical stepping-stone from Asia to the Polynesian islands.

After these meetings, Thor was more careful than ever not to indicate to anyone his own theory of the direction of the migration.

About three hundred miles north of the Canadian–United States boundary line, a narrow valley makes its way inland between precipitous mountains till it comes to a dead end deep in the interior. This is Bella Coola, one of the largest and most fertile valleys on the whole coast. Along its floor a deep river sparkles among wooded flats. Towards the ocean it debouches into a long channel lined with perpendicular mountain walls. The wealth of the valley at the time of Thor's visit consisted primarily of fabulous runs of salmon, heavy timber, and extremely large stocks of game, both in the valley and in the mountains: bears, mountain goats, mountain lions, otters, and large game birds. The sparse population in the valley was engaged for the most part in agriculture, salmon fishing, and hunting.

'Are there many white people in Bella Coola?' inquired Thor of the captain of the passenger boat *Cardena*, which took them north.

'Only three', was the reply. 'The rest are Indians and Norwegians.'

Some distance up the valley, not far from an Indian village, they found a primitive guesthouse in western style, Mackenzie's Hotel, clumsily put together from old logs and what seemed to be the boards of packing cases. Here they managed to rent a room which served them as living room, bedroom, and workroom all through the winter. The floorboards creaked and gave way under their feet and, if there was a wind, it blew out their candle. An elderly Norwegian couple ran the place, with a half-wit as their only helper. If he was not fetching wood for the stoves, he would sit playing over and over again his one and only phonograph record. At all times of the day 'Oh, dem golden slippers' came through the thin walls.

With the guesthouse as their headquarters, Liv and Thor pursued their field work, taking little Thor everywhere with them, papoose style. If they came across interesting finds, the small boy was usually put down on a nearby tree stump, with a few pine cones to play with. Since many of the trees were about two yards in diameter, a tree stump made a pretty good play area. Nevertheless they had to keep an eye on him all the time, since there were bears and mountain lions prowling around. One day they heard the little fellow call out, 'Bow-wow! Bow-wow!' They turned around and saw a tiny bear cub standing staring at the boy, who was making straight for it. But when the child stretched out his hand to pat the 'pretty dog' it made off and the next moment was halfway up a tree. There it stopped and peeped roguishly down, a little daisy sticking out from the corner of its mouth.

Among the thick timber they discovered old, deserted burial grounds, with wooden statues of various sizes. Some were simple, representing a whale, a bear, a raven, or some other creature. Others were elaborate combinations of beasts and demon masks, hewn out of huge tree trunks into the form of totem poles. Thanks to Judge Fougner, Thor made close contact with the natives in the village. Before long he was adopted by the tribe, and with the Indians as guides he was able to penetrate further into the forest where he discovered a long series of petroglyphs, both near the bed of the river and under layers of turf in the woods.

It was remarkable and unnatural that here, in the central part of the territory of the Kwakiutl tribe, there was not a single Kwakiutl Indian to be found. The valley was completely dominated by another tribe, the Salish, whose principal district was farther south, but who had at some time forced their way into the rich and fertile Bella Coola. These people too were strongly reminiscent of Thor's Polynesian friends. However, there was nothing puzzling about this, since all the Northwest Coast Indians have many traits in common.

But what had become of the local Kwakiutl tribe? That they should have retreated across the precipitous mountains was scarcely credible. Probability suggested only two alternatives: either the invading tribe had slaughtered them to the last man, or the survivors had fled in their canoes out of the narrow river channel. The mountains on both sides were so steep all along the way that it was difficult to find a site for even a foothold. Outside lay the Pacific, with currents and a wind that led straight down towards the Hawaiian Islands. Thor had read when the first Europeans came to Hawaii, they found huge Polynesian canoes hewn from massive fir trees that had drifted there from the Northwest coast of America.

All the finds Thor made at this time confirmed his suspicion that he was now in the region where the ancestors of the Polynesians had made a halfway halt during their migration from Asia to Polynesia. Toward the end of his stay in Bella Coola, he was so sure of his case that at lunch one day in the guesthouse he yielded to the temptation of mentioning his discoveries and his theory to an interested fellow visitor, who turned out later to be a reporter.

Later Thor, the reporter, and an Indian named Moose-skin Tent went on a bear hunt in the valley of Kwatna, south of Bella Coola. In the hunt itself Thor felt little or no interest, but the possibilities of new archaeological discoveries were great. Among other things, Moose-skin Tent had told him of two dried or mummified Indians who were sitting in an ancient canoe in a burial cave high on a mountain.

They spent the night in a shanty at the lower end of the Kwatna valley. The next day they paddled inland with the tide along a calm river. Every time they landed they saw tracks of bear and other game. The Kwatna valley was a real hunter's paradise. It was not long before they sighted a great grizzly in a meadow. It lowered its head and stood watching them gliding nearer. Moose-skin Tent held his rifle ready and Thor cautiously got out his camera. Then the bear suddenly raised itself on its hind legs and stood like a great forest troll, its forepaws hanging over its belly. Moose-skin Tent stood up slowly in the unsteady canoe and fired over Thor's head. In a fraction of a second Thor was hanging over the gunwale, fumbling desperately under his collar. It felt as if the Devil had stuck his claws into his neck and as he fished out a cartridge case so hot it burned his fingers, he caught a glimpse of the Indian falling headlong into the river, while Bruin hurriedly retreated into the forest.

The following day they moved inland again up the valley. They visited the decayed remains in the burial cave, and in several places Thor saw primitive rock paintings on the cliffs: ancient drawings in red, depicting whales, otters, and other creatures. Late in the afternoon they caught sight of a dark shadow at the edge of the wood. It was a splendid specimen of a black bear.

'What a sight! What a world there still was here in Kwatna! I hated the idea of shooting, of bringing civilization into all this virgin paradise. But it was too late. The canoe moved to the edge of the reeds and, soundless as a cat, Moose-skin Tent crept ashore with his rifle. . . . By this time I also was on land. Was the bear suspicious? It kept lifting its head and peering nearsightedly in our direction, and then it began to move slowly but deliberately towards the edge of the wood. With a flash and a bang, off went the shot, and a piercing, heart-rending howl rang through the forest. Half unconsciously the great beast swung about and came towards us. I ran behind the upturned stump of a huge fir tree, the only cover in the place, with the heavy brute rushing around after me. Then, with only six yards or so between us, Moose-skin Tent fired again and the bear fell. Moose-skin Tent's Indian instincts were now aroused in earnest. While the dying bear was still gnashing its teeth, he grabbed one of its hind legs with his bare hands. It was a grotesque struggle, but the odds were all on one side, and the forest rang with howls that I shall never forget.'

They then started home with their prize. They were on the way up Bella Coola valley when they met a man on horseback who stopped for a moment and shouted:

'Norway has been invaded!'

For two or three days Liv and Thor sat with their ears glued to the headphones of an asthmatic radio in the kitchen of the guesthouse. With growing despair they listened to the news of the German entry into Oslo and other major towns in Norway. They thought of their families and friends.

The propaganda machinery was already going full blast. Rumours said that in Norway all the cattle had been slaughtered and sent to Germany, that the corn would be handled in the same way, and that the Norwegians were getting nothing but bark-bread, moss, and dried leaves! The school mistress in Bella Coola was most sympathetic and did her very best to console them. They ought to hope, she said, sincerely that their dear ones had already been killed by the invaders, and so had escaped the horrors that a Nazi occupation brought.

Something must be done, but what? Thor detested the idea of going into the regular army where he would lose his right to think and act as an independent individual. But where could he be of use? Of course— the mountains! Few, if any, knew the mountains and wilds of Norway better than he, particularly in winter. There he certainly could be useful in acts of sabotage, or guerrilla warfare from bases in forests or mountains.

They hastily packed their trunks and travelled south by the first boat.

On their arrival in Vancouver they learned that Thor had become news throughout a great part of North America. The reporter to whom he had confided his theory had sent a story on it to the *Vancouver Sun*. His story had then been picked up by other papers, including the *New York Times*, which had asked the famous Polynesian anthropologist, Margaret Mead, to express her views. Without any knowledge of the nature of his discoveries, she had dismissed Thor's theory with the remark that when Captain Cook and other early explorers had come from Hawaii to the coast of Canada, they had probably brought with them a number of Polynesian objects, which they had then left behind in the Bella Coola area.

On the basis of this hasty suggestion from a recognized authority, Thor's theory was discredited. No one would listen to his argument that Cook would hardly have gone ashore in order to make the rock carvings Thor had discovered, far inside the Bella Coola valley, nor would he have distributed thousands of Polynesian stone adzes and bark mallets among the local Indians. In fact, Cook himself had been the first to point out some of these similarities. Again, the archaeologists had found that the Polynesians could not have brought these things to Northwest America because they were locally developed. How, then, could Captain Cook have brought them?

Nobody cared about Thor's comments and arguments. His theory had been rejected; it was no longer news. All he could do was to promise himself that he would return to the fray—and with redoubled strength— when the war was over.

F

Chapter 6

THE BALL GANG

THE April sun made the European war seem distant and unreal, yet the people in the hustling streets of Vancouver, the headlines in the papers on the news-stands, and the strident voices of radio commentators sounding from the bars, all reflected the increasing gravity of the world situation.

When Thor reported at the Norwegian consulate for active service for his country, the consul, a German-American, greeted him with:

'Why in heaven's name didn't you stay up there with your Indians instead of coming here to make trouble? Norway is *not* at war. She has surrendered.'

He pointed to the door.

In search of an explanation, Thor called on his acquaintances in the town. The few who were willing to receive him were extremely reserved and did not seem in the least surprised by the consul's remarks. It was a fact, they said, that the Norwegian people had gone over to the German side. Later, it turned out that an American newspaperman had sent from Norway a sensational dispatch that had been printed in American and Canadian newspapers and reported that the Norwegians had offered no kind of resistance, but had assisted the arrival of the Germans with the greatest good will; that when the Allied forces had been routed, the principal cause was the widespread sabotage by the Norwegians. This report did immense harm and affected the attitude of the majority toward Norway and the Norwegians for a long time. Neither the press nor the authorities made any real effort at first to change this point of view. Doors that had formerly been open to Liv and Thor were now coolly shut in their faces. There were even those who suspected Thor of being an enemy agent. Things went so far that he and Liv did not dare to speak Norwegian together in public.

The future looked grim. The Nazi invasion of Norway had cut off all contact with family and friends at home. They could get no news and no help from what was now enemy-occupied territory. When Thor called at the shipping agents of the Fred Olsen Line in Vancouver, he was told that he could just tear up their return tickets, which were now valueless. He had planned to stay only for a few more weeks in Canada and had budgeted fairly accurately for this period. Now the position was quite different. To make the money last as long as possible, they left the hotel where they had been staying and moved to an attic in a cheap boarding house in the harbour quarter. Their furniture consisted of one decrepit bed, a table, and a stool. For little Thor they found an old cradle. From the window they looked down into a huge coalyard, lighted by a single bare bulb. The landlady was sulky, shrill-voiced, and full of suspicion. After she learned they were Norwegians, she trusted them even less.

When all their attempts to get in touch with Norwegian and Canadian authorities failed, there was only one course left open to Thor. He must get a job as quickly as possible. But what kind of job? And where? Having come in on a visitor's visa, he had no work permit. Besides, there was a great deal of unemployment in the town, for Canada had no conscription, and its war industry had so far made only a feeble start. Outside the labour exchanges, long queues were standing every day. Embarrassed and unsure of himself, Thor joined these queues, always with an uncomfortable feeling that he was intruding where everyone else had a better right than he. Around him stood the most varied types of humanity, but they all had one thing in common, knowledge of a trade. When Thor took his turn at the window and was asked what experience he had, he answered each time that he had studied zoology, geography, and ethnology. Sometimes the clerk would ask him good-naturedly if there was anything else he could do—bricklaying, perhaps, or a little carpentry?

'Unfortunately no', Thor would reply, 'but I'm ready to try anything.'

The interview always ended with a regretful shake of the head, and Thor was swept out of the queue.

Day after day he was to be found in one queue or another, and if he had felt a stranger on the first occasion, the feeling grew even stronger as the days went by. It was seldom that anyone spoke to him, and if he dared to ask a couple of questions, the replies he got were curt. His clothes, his face, and his hands gave him away. Otherwise there was plenty of talking and grim jokes in the queues. Most of the unemployed showed little or no sign of resentment. They were all resigned to their lot. Such was life, and such it must be for the man who, whatever the reason, had lost his footing in the community. But this did not make them any happier. Poverty and want were mustered here, and among the most unfortunate were a number of immigrants who could not even make themselves properly understood in English.

The days went into weeks, grey depressing weeks. The last traveller's cheque had been cashed when Liv found one day that she was expecting her second child. At this point the coal heap outside the window seemed to grow and grow, until it filled the whole world and not a glimmer of daylight was left. In desperation Thor tried to sell his precious collection of archaeological and ethnological objects from the Marquesas, including the complete royal robe of human hair and many other rare and valuable pieces. He did not succeed in finding a purchaser, which meant that their ration of food had to be still more drastically reduced, saving for little Thor everything they could possibly spare.

It was not the first time they had known hunger. They remembered Fatu Hiva in the rainy season. Yet when they had really searched, the jungle had always yielded something to keep them from starving—coconut, or crayfish in the stream. In Vancouver there were streets of shops full of the most delicious food, and restaurants displaying juicy steaks or long spits rotating with rows of sizzling roast chickens. But this was not the jungle: here food had to be paid for, and without money one had to go without. Liv and Thor had never seen life from this angle, hunger in the midst of plenty, but for most of those in the long lines of unemployed it had become something natural. When an ordinary citizen was dangerously ill, the ambulance arrived with its horn at full blast. If his home was threatened by fire, firemen were there in a few minutes. But who came to the help of these unfortunates, in imminent danger of perishing from starvation? In the midst of the crowds of a great city no sirens sounded for them.

Then came the darkest day of all. It was a Sunday, and the rent had to be paid the next morning. They emptied their purses and ransacked all their pockets. Their total cash came to thirty cents. Liv sank down onto the stool by the window. She sat for a long time with her chin on her hand, staring out miserably at the coal dump. Thor, in a terrible mood, started pacing up and down, while the little boy lay sobbing in his cradle. Then Liv suddenly got up, swept all the coins into her hand and went out. She came back with three large currant buns, and with little Thor between them they went out into the sunshine and found a quiet spot on the green lawn of Stanley Park. Close beside them stood a brightly coloured totem pole, wonderfully appropriate at the moment, with grotesque figures climbing up over one another as in a fight for survival against tooth and claw and the teeth of greedy beasts of prey. At the top sat a figure staring down at the young couple with eyes as big as saucers. It was like a half-contemptuous greeting from Bella Coola, reminding them of those carefree days that were now nothing but memories.

Little Thor sat on the grass happily munching his bun, while Thor and Liv discussed what would happen the next day when, if they knew their landlady, they would be turned into the street. Unless something fell from heaven, those buns might be the last food they would taste for a long time. What would happen now? What *could* happen? It seemed like the end of everything. They could do no more than leave the matter in the hands of Fate. For a quiet moment Thor prayed—as he had not prayed since he was a child.

Monday morning came. If there was a ray of sunlight, it did not shine in that harbourside alley. The world was coal—enormous heaps of coal. Soon the cradle and their pile of luggage would be out in the street, with nowhere to take them to. Even in the rainy season in Fatu Hiva things had never been so hopeless as now, in the centre of a normal, civilized city.

There was a tap on the door. The landlady came in with a curious expression on her face. She handed Thor a letter from the shipping agent, the first letter he had received in seven months. He asked Herr Heyerdahl to call upon him as soon as possible. Could it be . . .? Suppose it was a job? Thor dashed to the door and ran all the way.

The agent had had a telegram from Thomas Olsen, who had helped Thor get to Canada and was now himself in exile. After a dramatic flight from occupied territory he had arrived in England, but in the midst of all his personal difficulties he had remembered the young explorer, who was undoubtedly in a tight spot. So he had sent his agent orders to lend the Heyerdahls whatever monthly sum was needed till the immediate emergency was over.

'How much would you like?' asked the agent.

Thor mentioned the smallest amount they could possibly live on if they went on staying in their attic.

The landlady was on the lookout when he came back. She followed him up the stairs and it was with real joy that he pulled out a roll of bank notes and counted out the rent. For several days he went about in a whirl of happiness, full of gratitude to an invisible protector who must have heard his secret prayer in Stanley Park. Although the time of trial was far from over, it looked as if his luck had changed. Just before Liv was taken to the maternity clinic, a cheque for two hundred dollars arrived. An article he had sent months before to the *National Geographic Magazine* in Washington had been accepted, and the sum was sufficient to cover Liv's stay in hospital and provide a layette for her second child, a boy, who was born on September 15th. They decided to call him Bjorn and give him the Norwegian nickname for a bear cub, 'Bamse', after the one with the daisy in its mouth in Bella Coola.

Now that his family was no longer in urgent need, Thor was able to carry on a little with his studies, but he still continued his daily round of the labour exchanges, always with the same depressing result. Then he met on the grounds of the University of British Columbia, a young Norwegian student, Gunnar Lepsoe, the son of Robert Lepsoe, an outstanding chemical engineer employed by the Consolidated Mining and Smelting Company of Canada. When Lepsoe senior heard of Thor's situation, he very much wanted to help, but Thor was not an immigrant and therefore had no work permit. It was only after a lot of difficulty with the authorities that he was permitted to work as a labourer. He was more than grateful to Lepsoe for his assistance, but insisted that, since they were both Norwegians, Lepsoe should not prejudice his own position by helping him further, then or later.

The Consolidated Mining and Smelting Company was the largest of its kind in the world, extracting great quantities of such nonferrous metals as lead, zinc, and cadmium, and also producing sulphur, phosphates, and other chemical substances. It employed at that time over seven thousand people. The lowest grade, known as the 'ball gang', was made up of unskilled workers who were given all the rough jobs, often the heaviest and most dangerous. Thor, untrained as he was, became a member of this team.

The home of the gigantic plant was Trail, four thousand feet up in the Rocky Mountains. The plant was built on a lofty hillside terrace, and the town lay directly below it, on the banks of the Columbia River. Today the factory is a model one, in all respects, but at one time the dust and poisonous gases polluted the air, killing crops and other vegetation as far away as the other side of the United States border. To correct this condition, Lepsoe had been called in to evolve a system for separating solid matter from the sulphurous smoke pouring out of the skyscraper chimneys. Railway cars of pure sulphur were filled daily, yet on Thor's arrival the town of Trail was still covered with thick layers of grey dust under drifting clouds of yellow smoke. It was there that most of the workers lived, while the senior officials and engineers had their residences at Tadanac, a high area about the same level as the plant but on the windward side of the heavy pall of smoke, where the sun shone on green lawns and snug villas.

It had been arranged for Thor to live in Trail, but when he stood outside the factory and looked down at the town, it appeared to him as an anteroom to Hell. He would never live there with his wife and children, where it seemed to him that every breath would fill the lungs with poisonous air. Luckily he managed to rent a room with kitchenette in the old miners' town of Rossland, far up the mountain. A few of the workers were already living there, travelling to and from the factory in a small bus.

When the ball gang assembled in the morning in the factory yard it was like a kind of international committee of hard-bitten, tough workers from many lands. Thor later identified seventeen nationalities. Remembering how people in the queues outside the labour exchanges had regarded him as an outsider, he found a coarse pair of green working pants covered with lime and paint, a dirty cloth cap, workmen's gloves, and a battered lunch box. With a three days' growth of beard and the cap worn carelessly at the back of his head, he reported for work in the ball gang. As soon as the foreman caught sight of the newcomer, he stopped, ran his eye over him, and grinned. Thor had been found out.

The foreman sent him with two other men to the store-yard where, among piles of scrap iron, there was a mountain of used bricks, to be sorted and scraped clean of lime and mortar. The usable bricks were neatly piled up, and the rubble was shovelled into railway cars and taken away. The job seemed to have gone on for years, and the spacious yard was a maze of great stacks and heaps where Thor's fellow workmen had a knack for disappearing for a forbidden smoke or a nap. One day the foreman turned up and was clearly displeased by the general lack of progress.

'Come here, Mac!' he yelled, catching sight of Thor. 'I'll find you a better job.'

Thor answered politely that his name was Thor not Mac.

'I don't give a damn what you call yourself. To me, you're Mac. Understand?'

The 'better job' was to fill a gap in a line of labourers working hard to feed a huge cement mixer. They filled their wheelbarrows, pushed them up a narrow plank to a platform, tipped the load into the mixer, then wheeled the empty barrows down another plank. The whole thing was done at a fast pace and it was essential to keep one's place in the line. The loads were heavy, even for those with experience. Over and over again Thor had to back his barrow into a new position on the steep plank, while the man behind him cursed and yelled because the rhythmic pace was thrown off. On the way up with his seventh or eighth load, when his heart was beating wildly and he could hardly see for the sweat pouring down his face, he pushed the wheelbarrow over the edge of the plank and upset it. The men roared with laughter, but the foreman raged about 'this greenhorn who's never done a real day's work in his life' and increased the pace. One more round, and another and another, the blood pressing behind his eyes and hammering in his ears.

Every quarter of an hour there was a short rest period. Thor threw himself down flat on his back, using every second to regain his breath and relax his aching muscles, until the 'on again' came once more. The last few rounds that day did not seem to bother Thor. He just pushed on as if in a trance, and the insults of the foreman sounded as if they came from another world far away. On his arrival home he collapsed on the couch, his body so swollen that Liv could barely pull off his clothes.

Next morning he had difficulty in holding the wheelbarrow, his fingers and limbs were stiff, his back ached, and the months of undernourishment still took their toll, but by the third day he had gained strength and had acquired some tricks that made it much easier to master the heavily loaded barrow. Triumphantly he realized that from now on he would be quite on a par with his mates on the wheelbarrow circuit.

On the fourth day, however, he was called from the job by the foreman, who said that 'Mac' was now to have a less exacting task, working with a second man on some tanks in another part of the factory yard. Thor had heard that these gigantic containers were only cleaned out every fifth year and it was a truly infernal job. A narrow ladder led up to a hatch in each tank, and another ran down into the interior. Thor and his co-worker were equipped with long-handled shovels and hip length rubber boots. Not until they were on their way down the inside ladder were they warned from the hatch above to watch their footing, for the slippery stuff at the bottom was sulphuric acid.

Before Thor let go of the ladder he felt his way forward with one foot. There was a thick layer of slime, as slippery as soft soap. While they cautiously tried to move forward, the foreman hung over the edge high above them, shouting down orders. Most of them they could not understand, for his voice rolled like thunder around the tank, but they heard enough to grasp that the acid was to be shovelled out through a waste pipe. With legs apart they slid through the slush like skaters in a slow motion film, pushing their shovels carefully to avoid splashing. If they pushed too hard they slid backward, and the smallest untoward twist could cause them to fall into a devil's brew which would eat away clothing and flesh in a moment. When the task was finally completed Thor felt as if he had escaped from a cannibal's cauldron.

In the days that followed he was continually moved from job to job. Sometimes it was another turn on the wheelbarrow circuit, sometimes digging trenches, sometimes loading railway cars, always the hardest physical labour that the foreman could think of at the moment for 'this greenhorn'. But the greenhorn was now in top form. He enjoyed the manual labour as long as it went on in the open air, and he soon annoyed the foreman by proving that he could lift weights that few of the strong men in the gang could tackle. In many ways he began to feel happy in the ball gang. It felt good to do physical labour; it felt good to draw the weekly pay cheque, which was big enough to support his little family and also to pay off gradually his debt to Thomas Olsen's agent in Vancouver. And when he sat down at lunch break on a pile of bricks in the sunshine, wet with perspiration, dirty, tired, and hungry, the milk and the cheese sandwiches from his lunch box tasted better than a banquet.

Then winter came to the Rocky Mountains, and when once its claws had taken hold it did not let go. It hung lowering on the mountains on wings of frosty mist, and a piercing north wind made twenty degrees below zero a real torment for anyone who had to work out-of-doors.

The iron girders of a new factory building were now sticking out from the yellow fumes like the skeleton of a prehistoric monster, and when the roof was ready to be laid, Thor was moved out of the ball gang into a permanent asphalting team of four men. Three of these worked on the icy roof and the fourth stayed below, boiling asphalt in a pot over an open fire. The asphalt was hauled up in buckets and used to stick together the lengths of tarred paper being spread on the roof. Thor was ordered to fix the overlap of tarred paper firmly to the underside of the eaves, and also to haul up the buckets. The building was five stories high, and when he lay on his stomach with his head over the edge, exactly what he had dreaded took place—he was overcome by giddiness. It felt as if an invisible magnet was trying to drag him over the edge. Somehow he managed to control his feelings, but he was always relieved when he could take a turn with the swabber on the roof when one or the other of them became so frozen he had to go down and thaw out by the fire.

It was in this team that Thor encountered Jimmy McDonald. One bitterly cold day, Thor hauled up the rope and found tied to the end a hot brick instead of a bucket of asphalt. He peeped over the eaves and saw a little man, the new asphalt boiler, gesticulating with another brick, which he then pushed down inside his pants. Thor did the same—a blessing in the biting Rocky Mountain wind. When lunch break came he climbed down and thanked this sturdy little man with ruddy cheeks and white teeth flashing in a growth of stubbly beard. They became friends at once.

Now the other two men came shivering down to warm up by the fire. One of them grabbed an extra bundle of wood to throw on the flames, but Thor stopped him and repeated what a Bella Coola Indian had once said:

'White man him dum. Him buildum big fire. No can get close. Red man him smart. Him buildum small fire and sit on Him!'

They laughed heartily at this, then each raked out his own little heap of embers and squatted over it with loud expressions of approval.

Now Jimmy introduced himself as a professional hobo, adding, with a twinkle in his eye, that he had been in every prison in Canada except one in Winnipeg. Jimmy was a great joker, a good-hearted companion full of amazing stories about his adventurous life off the beaten track, whether it was panning for gold in the deep forest or 'riding the rods' under freight cars from coast to coast.

During one lunch break Jimmy found shelter in a big toolbox near the fire, leaving the lid propped open as a windbreak. He was in a canoe, dreaming about the heat of the tropics. Then Thor joined him and soon, shovels in hand, they were paddling up the Amazon. They had completely forgotten the time, when an inspector feared by the men, came in their direction. They scrambled out of the box, and Jimmy began stoking the fire under the asphalt kettle with his shovel. Caught eating after the siren blew might mean dismissal, and Thor was still holding a brick-hard macaroon. He crammed it into his mouth, hoping the inspector would pass him by. And so he did, but only to ask Jimmy if there was a worker named Heyerdahl in the gang. Jimmy pointed hesitantly at Thor.

'Did you write that article about the South Sea islands in the *National Geographic?*' the inspector asked him.

'Um-hm', replied Thor.

Further questions forced him to spit out the entire macaroon. But the inspector took no notice and simply asked if he would consider delivering a lecture on the South Sea islands to the local Rotary Club. Thor said yes, the date was immediately fixed, and the inspector hurried away. Jimmy was bubbling with excitement.

'Boy, your fortune's made! Only white collars get into the club!'

On the day of the lecture, Thor was asked to bring a dark suit with him when he came to work. Half an hour before lunch break he was rushed off to shower and change before appearing as guest of honour at the luncheon meeting. It was like awakening from a bad dream. Everyone smiled at him in the friendliest possible way, the food was superb, and the applause after the lecture was hearty and long. Afterwards, he was driven straight back to the factory to change into his working clothes again and resume work with the asphalt team on the roof.

His fellow workers in the factory now left him alone. It was just what they had thought from the start. He was not one of them. He was in league with the white collars. Only Jimmy was still his good friend.

Work on the asphalt team came to a sudden end when one of the men fell off the roof while hoisting up the bucket. The boiling asphalt poured down onto the head of the ground man below. Both were rushed off to the hospital, the asphalt team was temporarily disbanded, and Thor had to go back to the ball gang.

At this time there arrived a welcome and unexpected inquiry from a new magazine in New York called *International Science*. It was to be a forum for European refugee scientists who had fled to America during the war. The editors invited Thor to send them an article on his scientific work. He had already managed to save enough money to repay the whole of his debt, and could afford a 'holiday' as well. He asked for and was granted three weeks' leave to write the article, which he entitled, *Did Polynesian Culture Originate in America?*' It was published in May of the following year, 1941, and in it for the first time his theory was laid before the public, a theory which in all its main features remains unaltered today.

'After a year of research along the British Columbian coast', he wrote, 'I believe that I possess sufficient material to trace two separate migrations from the American mainland to the Polynesian island world: (a) a pre-Incan civilization, with its centre near Lake Titicaca and along the Peruvian coast below, seems to have swept the islands at a comparatively early period, via Easter Island; while (b) a later migration, the descendants of which dominate the present Polynesian race, reached the islands via Hawaii from the Bella Coola area of British Columbia about A.D. 1000.'

When the article had been mailed, Thor put on his cap and green working pants once more and went back to the ball gang. The foreman put him on loading some railway cars with logs. Thor went to join the loading gang in a contented frame of mind, but was taken aback when they all stopped work and just stood scowling at him. Then one fellow spat past him, hitched up his pants and said:

'Well, did you tell Hitler all about it?'

It came like the whiplash. Again he had to suffer for being a Norwegian. The newspapers reaching Trail had as yet made no attempt to correct the false rumours. Filled with resentment, Thor tried to clear Norway's name, but no one took any interest in his explanations. It was only with the help of Jimmy, who did all he could to defend his new friend, that gradually the general feeling improved.

Work in the ball gang continually involved new jobs. For a time Thor was a mason's assistant on the construction job of a four-storey building. The work was not only hard but dangerous, for the scaffolding was only two planks wide and had apparently been put up very hastily. The heavy buckets of mixed mortar were hooked onto the end of a rope and hauled up to the scaffolding. Thor had to carry the buckets, one in each hand, to two masons who were working on the other side of the building.

The mortar was used up so quickly, that the men were always waiting with empty buckets. They kept shouting, 'Mud, mud!' Thor had to run to keep them supplied. At one point a plank had been thrown only loosely into position. It gradually shifted, then suddenly tipped up as he set foot on it. He dropped the buckets as he fell and managed to hook his fingers firmly around a crossbar, where he hung until he could get his breath. Then he climbed up, replaced the plank and went on with the job as if nothing had happened.

The place the workers feared most was the lead smelting works, since it was said among them that all who went there were gradually stricken by lead poisoning. In his search for an 'easier job' for Thor, the foreman sent him there next. Everyone worked with a gauze pad over his nose and mouth, to filter away most of the lead dust that filled the air and lay in a thick coating on everything with which it came in contact. The stuff was constantly swept up, but the air was nonetheless a grey mist of metallic dust. The days Thor spent there remained one single, continuous horror. As an outdoor man he hardly dared draw a breath in an atmosphere like this.

Thor's job was easy enough, usually consisting of sweeping the cement floors. Nevertheless he always felt short of breath, sweaty and filthy, with a pad, stuffed with cotton, over his nose and mouth. The pad had to be constantly turned around or moved, for two thick coal black spots formed where his nostrils drew in the air.

Soon afterwards he was given a compressed air drill and a respirator. After brief instructions in their use, he was sent inside a smelting oven where, by the light of a single bulb on a length of cord, he had to break off the slag from the walls. This was the worst job he had had since he had been with the smelting company. The heat inside was intolerable; the air was soon full of metal dust which mixed with perspiration, and clung to the edges of his respirator almost like mud. But worst of all, the drill hopped and jumped as if possessed by a devil, and made such hellish noise in the narrow metal chamber that he thought he would go mad. The infernal hammering seemed to burst his eardrums. He gradually felt he was losing control of himself as he became filled with rage. He began shouting, without hearing his own voice, 'I hate! I hate! I hate!' Scared of his own behaviour he tried to work out against what or whom this hatred was directed, but the horizons of his mind were so narrow that there was room for no other thought than how to master the madly jumping drill.

He was kept on this job for days until he felt as if soul and brain had been flogged out of him. He thought of the countless factories all over the world where men led lives like this and then he thought of primitive man's simple harvesting from nature as on Fatu Hiva. Listless and defeated, he went about in a kind of daze. Then he developed a high fever, with pain in his eyes. He only just managed to get home to Rossland. A doctor was called and diagnosed measles.

After the illness was over and Thor returned to the ball gang, he asked hesitantly for a change of job, with the result that he was transferred with Jimmy and another man to a branch that produced arsenical powder. The foreman of this factory was a lean and sallow man, with boils on his throat and neck. When he saw the new hands stealing glances at his neck, he opened his shirt, showed them his horrible boils and said, with a sly grin, that they would be like that too before very long. Then he threw them each a shovel and sent them up to the loft, where there was a thick layer of arsenical powder, as fine as dust, evenly distributed over the whole floor. With masks over mouth and nose, they were to push the powder to a narrow shaft in the floor, where it poured down through a long pipe into the open cars of a miniature railway three floors below. To prevent the dust from flying in all directions below, an inverted funnel of cloth, its upper end fixed to the mouth of the pipe, was spread over the car being loaded. From his post, the foreman would signal up to the fellows in the loft, a green light instructing them to start shovelling and a red light to stop. By pressing down on the cloth covering he was able to tell when the truck was full enough. He then pushed the red button, removed the cloth, and ran the next car forward under the mouth of the pipe.

However cautiously the men in the loft used their shovels, the dust around them flew up in the air. They had heard from fellow workmen that half a teaspoonful of the stuff was enough to kill a man. During the lunch break Thor sat and reflected. What could he do to escape from this dangerous work? He could not very well refuse to do it, for he had his family to support, and yet . . . Then an idea struck him: the only way to get transferred to some safer job was to make a mess of this one. He devised a plan which the others agreed to at once. When they went up to the loft after lunch they started shovelling at such a rate that the powder filled both the car and the pipe right up to the shaft three floors above before the unsuspecting foreman pressed the red button and took the cover off the car.

A couple of nerve-racking minutes followed in the loft; then the foreman appeared in the doorway, white with arsenical powder from head to foot, and so furious that the words stuck in his throat. They assured him that they had only been working hard, but it was no use.

Thor then confessed that the whole thing had been his idea. He was sacked immediately.

At this point Robert Lepsoe considered it time to disregard Thor's wishes and intervene. He had Thor transferred to a new research department, where his job was a simple one: To keep the operator of the smelting furnace supplied with lead. The best thing about it was the abundance of daylight and fresh air, since one wall was open towards a stockyard.

During the first days Thor, who was not technically minded, was greatly impressed by the manipulations of his new superior, the trained worker who turned levers, pulled handles, and opened peepholes in the furnace to watch the boiling lead while he scribbled observations in a register. One day this man was sick, and Thor was ordered to take his place. He was panic-stricken when the superintendent explained briefly what he had to do, but he wrote down all he could remember and started on the job. Soon the pages of the register were filled with observations from the experimental furnace, the times of smelting, changes of colour, and movements and formations of crust on the surface of the molten masses.

Thor's self-confidence rose appreciably as his understanding of the knobs and needles on the control panel increased. Soon everything was running smoothly and his superiors began to realize that they had a man with abilities far above the average. Robert Lepsoe wrote of him later:

'As a worker Thor Heyerdahl was quite unusual. He displayed a concentration and interest as if the research was his own child. He would also undoubtedly have gone far in the technical field if his interest had lain in that direction.'

The foreman in the research department was a broadly built and jovial Italian, with a smile reflecting the Mediterranean sun. In the factory his only name was 'Mystery'. Nobody could say why. Mystery was highly thought of, but the gossip was that he could neither read nor write. Someone had seen him scrawling an 'X' on the paper when he signed for the roll, saying to the timekeeper with a broad grin:

'Well, you know me!'

Thor found this difficult to believe, for Mystery carried a big pencil like a torpedo behind his ear, with a whole arsenal of pencils and fountain pens stored in his breast pocket; and each morning he came to visit Thor at the experimental furnace, he opened the register on the desk, read a couple of pages, nodded approvingly, and said:

'Looks good. Looks good.'

Unable to resist the temptation Thor turned the register upside down one day. The unsuspecting foreman went through the usual procedure.

'Looks good', he said after careful study. 'Looks good.'

Thor came to value this man highly. He was far from lacking in intelligence and could find a solution to any problem, including his own. When Thor came on the job one morning, a machine part had been unloaded in front of the open wall of the research plant. On it was a label inscribed: 'Not to be removed.' Mystery arrived soon afterwards, looked at the label and scratched his head. He looked anxiously around without detecting Thor behind the furnace, then went off with rapid strides. A couple of minutes later his voice came from a distance:

'Thor! Thor!'

Thor ran outside and saw Mystery's head sticking out of a window on the very top floor.

'Is there a label on that machine part down there?'

'Yes.'

'What's on it?'

On another occasion Mystery received a written message. He folded it up and put it in his breast pocket, went away, rolled up his sleeves and thrust both arms deep into a barrel of muck. With dripping fingers he came to Thor, pointed with his thumb to his breast pocket and said:

'Will you read that scrap of paper to me?'

A new and happier life had started when Thor had been transferred from the ball gang to Mystery's department, and from the day he was promoted from 'helper' to 'full worker', he was unreservedly accepted by his fellow workers as one of them.

Another promotion soon followed. He was put at the head of a small experimental branch producing magnesium powder for incendiary bombs. This material was so important that the branch worked in shifts around the clock. The pay was extremely good, probably because it was the most dangerous work in the whole factory. The magnesium powder was highly explosive, and the least spark might be disastrous. It was put into containers as quickly as possible and shipped out.

Now the blessed mildness of spring reached the Rocky Mountains. When the snow thawed, Lepsoe asked whether Thor and his family would like to borrow his cabin by picturesque Arrow Lake for the summer. To Thor this would mean a long journey to his job, but Liv and the children would be able to live in very pleasant surroundings. Full of gratitude, he at once accepted. The life was happy for the family out there in the great forest. Although weeks might pass without sight of anyone except the farmer who sold them milk, they never lacked company, for the woods around Arrow Lake were swarming with animals that did not run away at the sight or scent of a human being, so unspoiled was this wilderness. Skunks and giant porcupines were regular visitors. Chipmunks and gophers came confidently right up to the cabin and played with the boys. By the brook lived a pair of pheasants, and small broods of ducks moved in and out among the reeds on its bank. Several times they saw bears in the meadow, not just an occasional straggler but an entire family with cubs.

Thor himself had little chance to enjoy all this. He had to get up when it was still dark, and when he got home late in the evening it was only to have a bite to eat and tumble into bed again. The bicycle ride along the narrow forest path from the cabin to the ferry took an hour and a half before sunrise; then he had to ride the ferry and travel by bus to the factory, well over twenty miles away.

One morning when he came to work, the area around the research department was fenced off. The ball gang was clearing up splinters of glass and fragments of concrete. The whole building producing magnesium powder had blown up, and his colleagues on the night shift were no more.

Thor was immediately offered the superintendency of another research department that had been planned for some time. Almost simultaneously a letter arrived from the President of the University of British Columbia, with an offer of a permanent appointment as curator of the university museum. It was clear that opinion about Norway and Norwegians was now swinging back to normal.

Both offers were tempting, but Thor was restless. The thought of his native country tormented him incessantly. A year had passed without his achieving anything more than earning a living for himself and his family. For some time he had been in touch with the Norwegian Embassy in Washington, D.C., which had by now procured him a visa to the United States, a work permit, and the offer of a job in a laboratory in Baltimore. Once there, he told himself, he could more easily contact Norwegian authorities who could tell him how he might best serve his country. To the surprise of everyone he therefore declined both the other offers, packed his suitcase and rucksack and set off for Baltimore, while Liv and the boys moved in temporarily with the Lepsoes at Tadanac.

Chapter 7

LITTLE NORWAY

A week later he was in Baltimore, once again without employment, for the offer from 'the laboratory' turned out to be a fraud. His thoughts went back to those dark days in Vancouver, but now he had self-confidence and could stand up for himself. His work permit was in order so he soon got a menial job loading and unloading railway cars in a welding-rod factory. The men he worked with were the roughest types he had ever encountered.

Liv joined him shortly with the children. Bamse had not yet been christened, although he was big enough to toddle up to the font. They arranged for the christening to take place on Sunday, December 7th, at the Norwegian Seamen's Church, and were on their way in a taxi when they heard the shouts of newsboys. The Japanese had bombed Pearl Harbour.

Thor had been in that church before to deliver a lecture to his country-men. He had become acquainted with an engineer named Aronsen, the superintendent of the engine department in the Bethlehem Fairfield Shipyard where Liberty ships were being built. Aronsen, a religious man, was deeply concerned about the environment in which Thor was now working, and he offered him the post of timekeeper in the yard.

This new post was a gift from heaven. The work was easy and he was well paid. It was a curious feeling to be seated again with pencil and paper at a desk, even though he was now working on something utterly different from manuscripts and scientific literature. After a short time he got the knack of filling in the time cards, so for much of the day he had nothing to do, but this did not suit him at all. Since his arrival in Baltimore he had been in touch with the famous geographer, Isaiah Bowman, at Johns Hopkins University, with whom he had been in correspondence since the Bella Coola days. Dr Bowman now provided him with new and valuable material which he could study during working hours without neglecting any of his official duties.

G

In these favourable circumstances he could once more return to the task he had set for himself in the log cabin at Lillehammer. He began to assemble his arguments in a large notebook, and he wrote in the preface that he did not merely hope to throw light on the unsolved problems of the Pacific, but had another and more important aim—to demonstrate certain shortcomings of conventional scientific methods.

'Science is in need of new blood, *organizers*', he wrote on January 28, 1942. 'It is like a nation without leaders, like an army without officers. We have countless men who dig, dig, dig. They dig up thousands of fragments, but where are those who ought to work across rather than down, those who know where to harvest and what to put together to get the full picture? They are nowhere. Indeed, in science today you have to conform to existing patterns, follow the beaten track, become a specialist. . . . My aim would be to shake the confidence in the existing pattern. *We need a new kind of science*, scholars able to cross the various field of investigation picking up the shreds brought forth by those who dig, specialists in piecing together. We need universities for such men, professional background and education along special lines. . . .'

In the Bethlehem Fairfield shipyard Thor made a number of good friends, with whom he and Liv spent many pleasant evenings. These days would have been happy and carefree if thoughts of his homeland had not tormented him. Here he was drawing good wages and enjoying himself while his family and friends were groaning under the Nazi yoke. It had been impossible to get information about them. Were his parents alive? Had they any food? What about his mother, who never made any secret of her true feelings and who loved England—had she been put into a concentration camp? And his father, who was an admirer of anything German—had he been able to distinguish between the Nazis and the highly cultivated Germans he had met during his apprenticeship in Worms?

The stream of news from Norway spoke of determined resistance by all sections of the population, of women and men dying in concentration camps, of young boys and old men shot down by execution squads, of innocent hostages executed for acts of sabotage carried out by others.

The American newspaperman's report was refuted at last. Every day the papers wrote of Norway's heroic fight against superior forces, until the King and government had to flee to England because they would not surrender or comply with the demands of the enemy. Now the population had built up the Home Front, an underground resistance movement so tough and unyielding that the Nazis were never able to cope with it.

Sitting at his desk busy with his papers, Thor suddenly threw down his pencil. This would not do! He shouldn't be scribbling away in Baltimore, but helping to throw out the Nazis at home. He had heard that there were Norwegian forces in England. Once again he approached the Norwegian Embassy in Washington. They advised him to go to New York where a Norwegian recruiting office had recently been opened. He immediately resigned his post in the shipyard, sent Liv and the boys back to the Lepsoes at Tadanac, packed his bags and left for New York.

At the recruiting office, Thor explained that he was an experienced skier and had a thorough knowledge of the Norwegian mountains. Although he had no military training, he could be a special courier of secret information, or could carry out sabotage behind the German lines in Norway; in fact, he could undertake any task calling for outdoor life, strong nerves, and the ability to look after himself in difficult situations. After some discussion with a couple of high-ranking officers, it was decided that he should be sent overseas on a suitable mission after a short but necessary course at recruit school. It was agreed, however, that he was to be exempt from all mechanical or technical training, for which in his own view he was entirely unfitted.

An important problem was still unsolved. Norwegian privates were paid at the usual rates calculated for unmarried soldiers in the home country and, since Thor had to start his military career as a private, his daily pay would be far too little for Liv and the children to live on, with prices as high as they were in America. No exceptions could be made, although it appeared that Thor was the only Norwegian private with dependants in the United States.

As a temporary solution he once more resolved to sell his Marquesas collection. After several vain attempts, he came into contact with Professor Ralph Linton in New York, an archaeologist of worldwide fame, and the only man who had made archaeological studies in the Marquesas. The Professor became greatly interested in the collection and put Thor in touch with a number of prominent scientists in leading museums and universities. One of these was Dr Herbert Spinden, a well-known specialist in Mexican archaeology, who at that time was president of the Explorers Club in New York. After a thorough investigation, and on the recommendation of some eminent scholars, the young Norwegian was elected a member of that very exclusive club. But the sale of the collection went off badly. There was plenty of interest, but the financial resources available were slender. Finally the whole collection was sold to Brooklyn Museum for one thousand dollars, much too small a sum even for the royal robe alone. But at least Liv could be sure of a modest monthly payment for the time being.

Being a soldier was something Thor had never envisaged, even a couple of years earlier.

'Now I've become *completely* civilized', he remarked to a friend when first he appeared in uniform.

The training camp to which he was ordered lay near the seaport of Lunenburg in Nova Scotia. Norwegians came there from both North and South America, and the first Company had already been established with a couple of hundred men already hard at work in the recruit school. To catch up with them, Thor was assigned to an extra course, along with two other men. One was an artist of about his own age and it was not long before 1132 Stenersen and 1136 Heyerdahl discovered that they had a good deal in common.

Björn Stenersen had taken part in the fighting in Norway as a civilian. When all hope of effective resistance was at an end, he felt, like so many others, that the only thing to do was to get over to England. In Tromsö lay the steamship *Heilhorn*, an old coaster of about two hundred tons, equipped with a Bofors gun, a number of machine guns and rifles, and ammunition. The Germans were approaching, and when Stenersen found out that the ship was deserted, he collected fifteen men, provisions and enough coal, and appointed himself captain. One of the 'crew' knew enough about machinery to get the engine going, Stenersen at the wheel gave the order to start, and the ship smashed into the quay and reduced it to matchwood. After this the 'captain' was sent down to the galley and degraded to cook. For the rest of the voyage he was known as 'Captain Cook'. They got across to England, and after many remarkable adventures Stenersen reached the Free Norwegian training camp in Canada to learn to become a soldier.

Stenersen was a delightful companion, a strong individualist, with a markedly artistic temperament. He was burning with pugnacity and courage when it was a matter of doing his bit for his country, but he preferred to conduct the fighting in his own way, not by marching in the ranks. The normal military methods he regarded as tomfoolery.

The first thing to be learned was to stand at attention, heels together, feet at an angle of sixty degrees, body leaning forward but straight as a gun barrel, eyes firmly directed towards an arbitrarily selected point in front, all thoughts out of the brain, ears open to receive orders. They stood like tin soldiers, turning to left or right, just as the sergeant thought fit. Only Stenersen was a constant source of disturbance. In a tunic much too long and a cap much too small, he stood staring at something or other in the distance, with a half-smile that told the sergeant clearly what he thought about the whole business. It was worse when this impossible recruit argued with the sergeant about the position of his feet, maintaining that they *were* at an angle of sixty degrees; it was merely that the boots were too big, but if the sergeant would look inside . . . Besides, 1132 Stenersen had not the slightest doubt that the Norwegians could drive out the Nazis, even if their feet were at an angle of forty degrees.

By the time the course came to an end, the men could drill, crawl through mud and brushwood, break through every kind of obstacle, and kill enemies swiftly and efficiently. Ten of them—those with sufficient mathematical knowledge, among them Thor and Stenersen—were selected, much to their disgust, for radio training in Canada; the rest were to cross to England and join the Free Norwegian Forces there.

Thor had now finally managed to find a small flat in Lunenburg for Liv and the children. On the very morning of their arrival, after a four day train ride from British Columbia, the detachment received sudden orders for their new assignments.

They paraded in the camp gymnasium, as stiff as statues and all alike, with their knapsacks, gas masks, steel helmets, and weapons, in strict conformity with regulations. The lieutenant in charge, who was to travel with the main party to England, ran his eye along the ranks. One place near 1136 Heyerdahl was vacant. Uneasy and irritated, the lieutenant looked at his watch; there was not much time to catch the train.

Suddenly the two heavy swinging doors of the gymnasium opened and in tumbled Stenersen with all his kit. On top of his military gear swayed an artist's easel and a guitar, and he was dragging a suitcase full of philosophical works and anthologies of poetry. When he took his place in the ranks the men on either side had to make so much room for him that the symmetry was ruined, which enraged the lieutenant, who shouted:

'Eleven thirty-two Stenersen! What you want is a nurse-maid!'

'Don't stand there making a fool of yourself', was Stenersen's calm response, 'just because you've got two stars.'

There was no time now for disciplinary action.

'You'll hear more about this later!' stormed the lieutenant.

But Stenersen never did. The ship carrying the main force across the Atlantic was torpedoed.

On the shore of Lake Ontario, not far from Toronto, lay 'Little Norway', a camp erected by Norwegian airmen who had escaped from their homeland. Here they had laid the foundation of a new air force under the command of Hjalmar Riiser-Larsen, famous for piloting the airplane *Norge* across the North Pole. From a small beginning the camp had grown rapidly, and after only six months the first squadron was ready for coastal service. It was soon followed by fighter squadrons. The reports of the many courageous men who came to Little Norway by the refugee routes on sea and land, and the organized drive in Canada and the United States to publicize the facts about Norwegian resistance to the German invaders, soon gave new lustre to the name of Norway.

In Little Norway the ten selected men from Lunenburg were enrolled in the radio school of the air force. Radio! Technical training! This was directly counter to the agreement and Thor was badly shaken. His only consolation was that radio was only a means to an end, sabotage behind the German lines.

The Norwegian polar explorer and author, John Giaever, who was commandant of another camp, Little Skaugum, where he and Thor met later, wrote on this 'cultured savage' in an article at the end of the war:

'Thor reported for war service, and that quiet, decent, neat man of the wilderness put on the blue uniform. Thor was asked about his training and other qualifications. But since the air force concerns itself neither with zoology nor with archaeology, he came under the category "a good basis for special training". In the air force this can lead to a number of things. In Thor's case it led to—believe it or not—the *radio school*. So that is where this quiet, hawk-faced scientist is put. He looks as if he is made for tapping a radio key. He is as game as anything, will not accept any privileges, only wants to do his duty. Says nothing. He accepts the blow with a poker face—and with stone in his wild heart. He, who burned his bridges to turn back to nature and despised any technical apparatus, answers "O.K." And on top of it all, it turns out that someone in England has given orders that a special group is to be formed which is to have a special task and a specially long and thorough training in radio. The whole thing is very secret, but it smells like guerrilla warfare in the Norwegian mountains some time in the future. Anyhow, Thor is included in that group. He draws the curtains on the wilderness and bends over books and radio keys. Orders are orders, and duty is duty. Captain Nicolaysen, who is an experienced radio instructor, says that Thor is sure to become a super radio expert.'

Eleven thirty-two Stenersen and 1136 Heyerdahl of the Norwegian Army were now 2208 and 2209 respectively of the Norwegian Air Force. They were side by side again, this time with their own desks, earphones clipped to their heads, changing rapid sequences of short and long sounds into written dots and dashes and then into letters and words. If the discipline in recruit school had been strict, it was even stricter in radio school. The head of the school was an outstanding teacher, but he was also a zealous officer who, in Stenersen's opinion, would turn them all into 'Prussian soldiers'. One morning 2208 shocked everyone by appearing in his large red painter's bow tie instead of the green regulation tie. After a term in the guardhouse his opposition to his officers increased so much that finally the air force sent him back to the army.

The day of Stenersen's departure was a dark one for Thor. In the midst of a system that was unnatural, inflexible, and mechanical, Björn Stenersen had represented something of human value. He was impossible, no one could deny that; but he was true to himself. Even in the joint struggle against the Nazis he would not and could not give up his personal freedom or submit to decisions that struck him as comic and contrary to common sense.

On church parade that next morning the men stood at ease, listening to the chaplain. They were called to attention for the 'Lord's Prayer', the officers holding the salute until the chaplain said 'Amen'. Thor wanted to shout out that a service like this was blasphemy. God himself had now been made a military leader, a commander-in-chief who was honoured by a salute and entreated to help some soldiers against other soldiers who perhaps at that same moment were standing and presenting arms during the 'Lord's Prayer' on the other side of the front line. It was against these church parades that Stenersen had reacted most violently, muttering bitter curses at Thor's side. Now he was gone and there was silence. Was it right to submit to all this? Was it not Stenersen who was right? This was indeed hypocrisy disguised as virtue. Yet how could tyranny be crushed if everyone acted like Private 2208?

There followed a period when the body marched, ate, and slept, while the mind concerned itself only with formulae for high frequency, spools, and condensers. Training reached a tempo when each hand tapping on the key of the transmitter looked as if it was trembling with fever, and the unpractised ear heard no dots and dashes but only a continuous piping vibration.

After many vain attempts, Thor finally managed to rent a cheap room for Liv and the boys in the neighbourhood of the camp; but by the time they arrived in Toronto after the wasted journey to Lunenburg, the money from the Marquesas collection had come to end. These days were really bad ones for the family, who often went to bed hungry, while Thor could eat his fill at the camp. When he left the soldiers' mess after a meal, the long tables were still loaded with food, much of which would find its way into the garbage cans. He soon yielded to temptation, stealing a sausage, half a loaf of bread, a little butter, or anything else he could take with him. He did it with bitterness, but without any feelings of guilt. Although he was now required to teach mathematics to the whole radio school in addition to his own radio studies, he still received only a private's pay. He could not expect any raise until the end of the course when, if he passed the tests, he would be promoted to sergeant. He therefore devoted all his energies to what was to him a most distasteful task.

Of the ten who came from the army to Little Norway, only eight remained. They were now without Stenersen and another man, who had resigned. Under instructions from headquarters, they were given the title of 'I-Group', but no one knew what it meant. Some thought it stood for 'Information', others 'Intelligence', but it was pure guesswork. The only thing certain was that the group was of an extremely secret character.

When the tests were passed with good results, Thor was relieved. On a sergeant's pay he would be spared the humiliation of having to steal food for his family. However, he was soon disillusioned. All the other graduates of the Air Force radio school were automatically promoted to the rank of sergeant, but instructions were received that I-Group could not be promoted because it belonged to a special branch of the army whose high command was in London. From the same source came a brief order that I-Group was to go to another special school for radio and electrical technique.

As the new course was top secret, it could not be held in the camp at Toronto. They were sent to Little Skaugum, named after the residence of the Norwegian Crown Prince, and it was not far from the town of Huntsville in Eastern Ontario. It was a group of long, low timber huts on a strip of land between two lakes, deep in the huge Muskoka forests, and was a rest camp for Norwegian Air Force personnel. Not far away was a hunter's cabin Thor was able to borrow for Liv and the children, and he himself lived partly there and partly with his comrades in camp.

Four special instructors were sent along with the eight men in I-Group with only one objective: to give them thorough training in advanced radio technique. By the end of the course, they were expected to be first-class telegraphers for the air force, the army, and the navy, and qualified for radio service in the merchant marine. In addition, they had to be able to construct receivers, transmitters, and telephone exchanges, and to have a thorough knowledge of television and other advanced branches of modern military and civil communications. To this objective their enthusiastic instructors applied themselves wholeheartedly.

The activities of I-Group in the Muskoka forests were supposed to be top secret. Supposed to be. Their exercises included the use of eight

16. Thor Heyerdahl and little Thor, at the time he worked on the 'ball gang' and when his family lived in the wilds of British Columbia.

17. (*next page*) The half-bred Indian, Moose-Tent, took Thor deep into the forests of Canada at Kwatna for bear hunting.

17

18

19

20

21

enormous loudspeakers, which were hauled around on a sled by huskies while officers shouted:

'One, two, three, four. This is a trial transmission from the radio school at Little Skaugum. One, two, three, four. We are training with a specially constructed loudspeaker. Can you hear me?'

Soon letters arrived from the people of Huntsville, who wrote:

'Yes, indeed we can hear you—and so can the folks way down in Gravenhurst.'

In spite of his antipathy to the technical training, Thor enjoyed being in the Muskoka forests, reunited with his family who could live there more comfortably and cheaply than in a big city. Besides, and this was important, they were living in a spot of rare beauty, one that almost seemed to have been carved out of a Norwegian forest. Bears, skunks, porcupines, and other wild creatures frequently came right up to the doorstep.

One great adventure for little Thor and Bamse was when they got a bear as a playmate. Word had spread that there was a thirsty fur trapper going about Huntsville with a little bear cub in a box which he was willing to exchange for a bottle of whiskey. The camp commandant, John Giaever, wanted the bear as a camp mascot. He had the advantage over Thor, who wanted it as a pet for the boys. Giaever sent out a whole body of men to scour Huntsville, find the trapper, give him the whiskey, and bring back the bear cub. Thor could do little to match this, but two of the men in I-Group volunteered to cycle into town after duty and see what they could do. While Giaever's men moved from bar to bar with their bottle of whiskey, one of Thor's friends went into the only movie house in town and arranged for a message to be flashed on the screen. The trapper just happened to be in the audience, and the deal was concluded. Thor paid for the bear with a bottle of whiskey he had to borrow from the commandant.

When the bear cub came to Little Skaugum he was no bigger than a cat, with coal black fur and a white V on his chest. They called him 'Peik', a name from old Norwegian fairy tales. At first he struck out and snapped at anything approaching his wire-netted box. But Thor knew how to handle him. He pushed a stick covered with honey through the netting. Peik buried his teeth deep into it, then stopped in surprise and licked his lips. Thor dipped his finger in the honey and pushed that

18. (*previous page*) 'Spring House', Mesa Verde, deserted centuries before Columbus. Visited by Thor during his anthropological investigations.

19. (*previous page*) The I-Group with Air Force Private 2209 Heyerdahl, first row, third from left.

20. The soldier and his mascot 'Peik', the black bear who grew up as a domestic animal.

21. A farewell to 'Bamse', his younger son, before leaving for Europe.

through the netting. Peik sniffed at it a little, then licked it clean. Before the day was over, all his wildness had gone. Thor took him out of the box and he was never again penned up.

To the delight of the children and to Liv's despair, Thor kept the cub in the cabin to make him housetrained and accustomed to people. In a short time Peik became a perfect domestic pet. In the evenings he would sit on a stool in front of the fireplace and have supper with the children. He was washed and brushed before he went to bed and his coat was as dry and fine as fox fur. At first he would lie on the foot of Thor's bed, but he soon grew so heavy that Thor could not stand it. He persuaded Peik to move up to the head of the bed and serve as a pillow.

Like most youngsters, Peik was a mischievous little rascal, and full of surprises. When the family of Crown Prince Olav of Norway came to Canada to inspect the air force, Crown Princess Märtha lived for a time in Little Skaugum with the Princesses Ragnhild and Astrid, aged twelve and eleven respectively and Prince Harald, who was six. The Crown Princess took her children with her several times to the little log cabin for a chat or perhaps especially to see Peik. On one of these visits she sat on a wooden pier below the cabin with her lacework on which she had been working for months. Peik, tethered to a nearby tree, had discovered that if he pretended that his leash was shorter than it really was, he could have the pleasure of startling people. Like a flash he lunged and stuck his claws into the royal lace. There was a furious tug-of-war between the Crown Princess and the King of the Forest before Thor came to the rescue.

That same day, Prince Harald wanted to photograph Peik. He placed himself on the edge of the pier and asked Thor to take Princess Astrid and Peik with him in the canoe and paddle around the tip of the pier. All went well until the camera began to whir. Then Peik, in the bow, rose up on his hind legs with his head on one side and listened. This alarmed the Princess. She got up too, and the next moment the canoe was floating upside down, and Thor, Peik and the Princess were splashing about in the water. Prince Harald was delighted with such a fine picture.

Early in the spring of 1943 Thor came nearer to death than he had ever been before.

Having been granted leave, he and two of his air force friends, Per and Rulle, decided to go on a canoe trip to the Algonquin National Park, a sanctuary for big game. The Muskoka region of Ontario lies in what is known as the Lakes Peninsula, with hundreds of lakes connected by as many streams, and portage paths along which campers can carry their canoes from one stretch of water to the next.

Before they left, Thor and his companions planned their route according to the existing portage paths shown on the map in red. One of these red lines led to a point on the bank of the Oxtongue River, just above High Falls. Here the line turned upstream as far as the next lake.

One day the three men stood on the cliffs overlooking the breath-taking cataract of High Falls. Enormous masses of water tumbled over the precipice with a deafening roar, and drifting trees were splintered into matchwood as they were hurled to the bottom. It was a magnificently beautiful but awe-inspiring sight.

Much to their surprise the portage trail they had followed ended on the banks of a great back-eddy of calm water about fifty yards above the falls. According to their map, they were to relaunch the canoe at this spot. They were horrified by the sight of the tossing rapids running outside the eddy and heading straight for the falls. Thor said at once that there must be a mistake on the map; it was madness to set out so near the draw of the falls. Per and Rulle had another look at the map and decided that as there was no other portage in the area, this had to be the place. Farther up, the riverbanks were sheer drops and inland were large expanses of snow. It would be impossible to continue on shore with the canoe. They must either put it into the water and try to go against the current up to the next lake, or they must abandon their trip. Thor was in favour of the second course, but Per and Rulle protested and hinted that he was not much of a sport if he didn't dare do what others obviously must have done. The map clearly showed that this was the correct route. For fear of spoiling the trip for them, Thor allowed himself to be persuaded, but only on condition that they kept close to the shore, clinging fast to roots or cracks in the bank, until they had gone far enough upstream to be out of danger from the draw of the falls.

Rulle squatted in the bow of the narrow canoe, Thor squeezed down in the stern, and Per slid his legs under the middle crossbar. Tent and rucksacks were firmly tied under the two other crossbars so men and cargo were as close to the bottom as possible to keep the slender canoe balanced, and off they started.

The thundering roar of the falls made it necessary for them to shout at the top of their voices to be heard. In the middle of the river the current was running with tremendous strength, the water greyish-white in colour with angry crests of foam from the rapids. Close to shore, however, the current seemed comparatively weak, which gave them hope. With strong strokes of the paddles Thor and Rulle kept close enough to the steep bank for Per to catch hold at a moment's notice. All went well.

They had gone a good distance away from the falls, perhaps a couple of hundred yards, when they reached a promontory where an under-current suddenly swung the canoe's bow away from the cliff. Per flung himself sideways across the gunwale, but could not reach a handhold. It was a dangerous situation and Thor and Rulle paddled frantically to turn the bow back toward the land. But the current had taken a good hold and slowly and mercilessly the canoe was forced sideways towards the middle of the river.

All three were aware of the danger at the same moment. Rulle stood up and dived in. His parting kick made the canoe heel over. Thor felt the ice cold water strike his left arm and shoulder, and then the canoe capsized. Everything was a whirl of water and foam until he got his head above the surface, and found the red canoe drifting bottom upward right beside him. He got his arms across the slippery hull and was able to look around him. Rulle was already climbing ashore. Of Per there was no sign.

Dressed as he was, in thick winter uniform and boots, Thor had little chance of getting to the bank, which was now a good way off. As the current took hold of the canoe it looked as if the trees along the other bank were rushing upstream at increasing speed, while the deep, hungry roar of the falls grew in strength. If he stayed with the canoe he would be swept along with it straight over the falls. He let go and struggled to swim across to calmer water nearer the bank, but the current was too strong and he was drawn into the middle of the river.

The falls were now less than a hundred yards away, and the whole world was nothing but roaring noise and wildly whirling masses of water. He was panic-stricken as he saw that he was making no progress, and he suddenly realized that in a moment or two he would tumble through the air down into the foaming cataract and then the question about life after death so often discussed by his parents would be decisively answered. In a fraction of a second his father's simple bedside lesson forced itself upon him. He prayed. He swam and he prayed. Something happened inside him; he became determined and confident; nothing could beat him. His strokes became calmer, longer, and more powerful. In spite of his heavy boots, in spite of the thick uniform saturated with water, in spite of the tremendous suction from the depth of the falls, he pulled himself slowly from the grip of death. He held his course obliquely in towards land, and if he did not make noticeable progress at every stroke, he still kept the falls at the same distance. Once or twice his strength began to fail and he was on the verge of giving up, but each time something filled him with fresh strength and confidence. Slowly, as if a mist was slipping from his eyes, he saw the shore growing closer; the current was gradually slackening its grip. Now he *would* manage it. And there, only a few yards away, Rulle was hanging out from the edge of a rock, his hand out-stretched towards him. Thor gripped it and was pulled ashore.

He lay gasping on the bank when suddenly a thought stabbed him. Per! He scrambled to his feet and saw Rulle running towards the falls. There, in the back-eddy, the canoe was slowly drifting around and around in the calm water, drawing nearer to the abyss with each turn. There was no sign of Per.

Just on the brink of the falls, the canoe remained hanging and swaying against some rocks. Rulle managed to catch hold of the bow and with Thor's help, succeeded in getting it ashore. Turning it over, it was with both horror and relief that they found Per's motionless body wedged with the only remaining rucksack under the crossbars. They dragged him free, lifted him under the stomach, and forced the water out of him. Then they gave him artificial respiration. To their great joy he soon began retching, and opened his eyes.

As they sat on the bank above the waterfall, three deer appeared on the other side of the river. They posed on a projecting crag above the falls, clearly outlined against a pale sheet of snow. For a time they remained motionless, staring at the three weary men, then they turned slowly around and with a couple of graceful leaps were gone in the shade between the fir trees.

Not long after their return to Little Skaugum they read in a newspaper about a father and son who had been caught by the current and killed in High Falls. The article also explained the mystery of the portage path. Due to the spring floods, the water level at this time of the year was more than three feet higher than in the tourist season. In the summer the river bank at the foot of the mountain was dry and the portage path continued for a considerable distance upstream, so that canoes could be carried well away from the falls before being put in the water.

The mystery was solved, but the miracle of their deliverance remained. Discussing it, Per said quietly:

'I take this as a sign that I shall survive the war.'

A couple of months later he was shot down in a plane over Norway.

Chapter 8

I-GROUP

THE months went by, and still no instructions regarding I-Group came from the Norwegian G.H.Q. in London, nor was there any more mention of promotion. Then, towards the end of August, a telegram suddenly arrived saying that training was to stop and the group be sent overseas immediately. The order to move was top secret.

It was a sad moment for Thor as he sat with the rest of the group on the floor of an army truck bumping through the gates of Little Skaugum and waved farewell to Liv, the boys, and Peik, who were to go on living in the log cabin.

Eighteen thousand Allied servicemen arrived from camps in Canada, Australia, and New Zealand, and were mustered in one night in Halifax, Nova Scotia, to be packed on board the Cunard liner, the *Queen Mary*. It was the greatest number of passengers she had ever carried, and I-Group completely vanished in this floating city. There were so many people on board that half of them had to spend the night on deck, where they sat propped against one another or against their baggage because there was no room to lie down. Every other night they were allowed to sleep below. As many as ten men were squeezed into one ordinary cabin, and through-out the twenty-four hours of day the corridors were packed with con-tinuous queues moving to or from the dining saloons, the lavatories, and the cabins. One single torpedo from a U-boat could have disposed of a whole army of well-trained troops.

The *Queen Mary* sailed so fast that an escort would have been of no ad-vantage. At full speed she raced forward on a zigzag course and reached England after five interminable days.

I-Group went to London by train, full of expectations. In a brief farewell speech to all the troops on the day of their departure from Little Skaugum, the commandant had said with an air of envy and admiration:

'Now at last the veil of mystery over I-Group will be lifted.'

They arrived in London on September 1, 1943, and were immediately called to army headquarters, where they anxiously waited to learn the reason for their sudden journey to Europe. They were taken straight to the office of the commander-in-chief of the Norwegian forces, who greeted them with:

'You have been long expected and greatly missed!'

When they left his office the purpose of the project was still a secret.

Four days later they were told that no one could discover who had sent the cable ordering their immediate posting to England. With instructions to await further orders, they were sent to a castle in a remote corner of Scotland, where they were attached to Haerens Skole-og Övelsesavdeling (the Army's School and Training Department). They were now given new numbers and Thor became Private 5268. To keep them occupied while they were waiting, they were sent out to work for neighbouring farmers. Thor spent one day carting manure.

After some time, one of their instructors came up from London to see them. He said there seemed to be some doubt as to who was in charge of them, and that so far no one had found out who had sent the cable. However, he had seen a letter from Norwegian G.H.Q., proposing the promotion of Heyerdahl, the spokesman for the group, to sergeant, and of the others to corporals.

Days and weeks passed, but nothing happened, except that they were detailed to wait at table in the privates' mess. When two months had elapsed they learned that the company commander had duly received the letter from G.H.Q., but had decided that he could not turn a whole group into N.C.O.'s, particularly a group who were nothing but unemployed holiday makers. By this time there was great discontent among the group. The radio school and military and physical training in Canada seemed remote and half forgotten. Thor was in constant anxiety over his family as he had not had a single word of reply to his letters. It was not until long afterwards that he learned that Liv and the children were now staying with the family of their friend Thomas Olsen, who had gone from England to direct his ships from New York. He wrote that Liv was sick in bed.

Mutiny was smouldering in I-Group. Week after week they were told to await orders inside their barracks, where they idled away their time as best they could. They were given no training or any organized form of outdoor exercise. One day they *were* ordered to rake up the leaves in the park, but as the officers found no rakes, they were ordered back to their bunks. Another day they were told to load a truck, but nobody found the truck. Thor did his best to keep physically fit by taking long walks and cross-country runs by himself in the evenings when the men were given leave.

Eventually an order came to move to Westerlea House, a stately old mansion near St Andrews, where a majority of officers were in charge of a minority of privates in the Communication and Pioneer Service. The days at the castle had been dreary enough, but at Westerlea House life was even more monotonous and humiliating. The captain in charge ordered two men each day to wash the broad stone staircase and the long wooden corridors. Sweeping was strictly forbidden: it was wash, wash, wash, scrub, scrub, scrub, until the whole building was reeking of mould and mildew because of the waterlogged floors.

I-Group had reached the point of revolt. They had not enlisted in the armed forces to do the housework in a Scottish mansion. They had forgotten most of the special instruction they had been given in Canada, and all would be wasted if they were not sent immediately on active service or, at the very least, allowed to keep their hand in through exercises and courses. Letters they had written to G.H.Q. through the normal service channels had found their way into the captain's wastepaper basket. Something had to be done.

An opportunity presented itself. They heard that one of them was about to be detailed to wait regularly in the officers' mess, and they decided that the only way to bring their grievances to the notice of G.H.Q. was to disobey the order when it came. It came the very next day, on morning parade. The man named, Private Erik Beyer, came to attention and refused. The sergeant marched him into the captain, who called in the military police. Thor, as spokesman for the group, told the captain that the rest of them would also have refused to obey if they had been given the same order. In the afternoon Beyer was taken under close arrest to St Andrews.

Soon afterwards they learned that all I-Group's official papers from Canada had disappeared and no one had any idea where they were. There was nothing to document their military training. Thor asked for leave, and went down to London. He laid the whole case before the Norwegian Minister of Defence, Oscar Torp, who was shocked and promised to take up the matter with the G.O.C. and the Judge Advocate General. When Thor returned to Westerlea House, Beyer had been released on orders from London. He was to carry out his normal duties until the case came before a court-martial.

The group was still kept unemployed. At length, one of the instructors persuaded the captain to let them put up equipment and practice sending messages in Morse code. They were horrified to discover how much their skills had deteriorated. Thor found he was quite unable to transmit properly, even at the lowest speed. He wrote in his diary:

'The continuous idleness since we left Canada has had destructive and demoralizing effects. This cannot go on.'

In the diary Thor refers over and over again to the contrast between the muddle that he himself had witnessed and the performance of other Norwegian units. His friends from the air force school at Camp Little Norway had been in action for a long time, and the Norwegian Navy was constantly involved in raids against the enemy in the North Sea. Even Foreign Minister Anthony Eden had pointed out the great value of the large Norwegian merchant fleet which had escaped the Nazi invasion and by itself carried forty per cent of all the oil consumed by the Allies. British Admiral Dickens said in a radio speech: 'Losses of ships and men have been heavy. So Norway's contribution, it would hardly be an exaggeration to say, has been indispensable.' In his diary Thor asks why I-Group could not fill in as badly needed radio operators in the merchant marine, since they seemed to be quite superfluous in the army.

But most of all he wanted the kind of job he had been picked for: a special assignment behind German lines in Norway. There his fellow countrymen were forwarding important information to the Allies by means of hidden transmitters, and were blowing up German ships and stores and carrying out other acts of sabotage. President Roosevelt had just said in a speech to the American people:

'If there is anyone who still wonders why this war is being fought, let him look at Norway. If there is anyone who has any delusions that this war could have been averted, let him look at Norway. And if there is anyone who has doubts of the democratic will to win, again I say, let him look to Norway. He will find in Norway, at once conquered and un-conquerable, an answer to his questioning.'

Look to Norway, Thor repeated. But not to I-Group. In an entry in his diary he wrote:

'6th January. I was mess-boy all day, and divided my time equally between anthropological studies and the washing up of greasy dishes and dirty floors. Private 1136 Heyerdahl, alias L.A.C. 2209, alias Private 5268 is dead and buried in a floor-mop.'

Shortly before Christmas Thor was told by the military police that I-Group as a whole would be charged with insubordination if they claimed that each of them, like Beyer, would have refused the order to wait in the officers' mess. Thor answered that the decision was unanimous, that all members of the group considered themselves to be in the same position as the soldier to whom the order had first been given.

Two months later the group was taken to Callander, and marched into a large room where a fire blazed in the hearth. In a semicircle behind a large

H

mahogany table stood a row of high-ranking officers, the G.O.C. in the centre. When the door was closed, the general began to speak in a surprisingly friendly and conciliatory tone. The men in I-Group were fine fellows, he said. The whole matter was simply a trifle, but unfortunately the case had taken a serious turn. He and the Judge Advocate General had agreed upon a solution. If the men were willing to apologize for their illegal act, they would receive a suspended sentence. There would be no question of punishment unless they showed a renewed tendency to disobedience. With the approval of the others Thor agreed to this, explaining that their object had been merely to make the situation known to the supreme command, and this had now been achieved. The general looked relieved and ended the interview by congratulating the group on the extremely exciting and interesting job they were to be given in the future.

That same afternoon I-Group was temporarily disbanded and its members distributed among the Norwegian mountain companies in Scotland. Thor was one of the two assigned to No. 1 Mountain Company, Dall Camps. This proved to be Thor's salvation. The officers were good-humoured and high-spirited, burning with zeal to make the men under them fit for top performance. Life in this company was extremely rugged, but soon Thor was in good form. Even in his spare time he went for long walks in the mountains. His diary contains a great many descriptions of the beautiful Scottish scenery. One such entry is characteristic:

'The great moment of this walk was when I stopped in one place because I suddenly scented warm-blooded animals. I looked about for a long time without seeing anything but the strange rectangular stone enclosures that are so often found on the mountainsides. Finally I spied fourteen deer gazing motionless at me from the heathery slope of a mountain, almost half a mile away.'

One morning on parade the whole company of two hundred men were called to attention while the commander read out a notice from supreme headquarters in London to the effect that Private 5268 Heyerdahl had been given suspended sentence of sixty days' detention for—here the commander paused dramatically—for having refused to wait in the officers' mess. There was a stir all down the line. Some men quietly sniggered. Thor thought he saw the corners of the commander's mouth twitch as he hurriedly gave the order to stand easy.

Shortly afterwards the group received instructions to re-assemble at Terregles House, near Dumfries. Forty-five large cases of radio equipment specially constructed for I-Group had arrived from the United

States, so it looked as if something was going to happen at last. More military instructors arrived and soon I-Group, which now consisted of only six privates, had a staff of one captain, two lieutenants, five second lieutenants, and four sergeants, besides two civilian engineers. I-Group was not going into action. There were to start a new special school. Now the specialists were really going to specialize.

There was a certain amount of friction among the twelve instructors as to what each of them was going to teach, and conditions were not made easier by the discovery that all of the equipment from America had been so badly damaged in transit that it was completely useless and had to be stored away. One of the officers told the group that the programme had to be altered as a result, and they were now to be trained for service in Norwegian broadcasting stations after the country had been finally liberated. Thor rose from his desk and said he no longer had any confidence in any arrangements for the group.

'You'd better be extra careful now', said the officer irritably, 'with that suspended sentence hanging over you.'

'Perhaps', said Thor, 'and perhaps just the opposite.'

The point was well made; it soon became apparent that the staff would go to some lengths to prevent the removal of all six of their students into a detention barracks.

The arrival of Lt Björn Rörholt at Terregles House promised some improvement. He was put in charge of the group's training and turned out to be a most competent officer, full of drive and making a strenuous effort to get them out of the doldrums and into action. Several times he travelled to London to try to speed things up, but without success. Nevertheless the good news did come through that the men in I-Group had been promoted to corporal, retroactive to May 1st. Immediately afterwards another order was received, promoting them to sergeant, retroactive to March 1st. The latter promotions were signed by the general himself, but were held up by the brigadier, who pointed out that a private cannot be promoted to corporal as of May when he has already been promoted to the higher rank of sergeant as of March. The general asked him to return the order through the usual military channels. When Lt Rörholt received a report of this he exploded. He grabbed a chair and threw it at the wall.

Then came the day for which everybody had been waiting. Thor's diary reads:

'6th June. I was busy in the radio laboratory drawing a broadcasting antenna, when it was announced on the radio in English, French, Norwegian, Dutch, Belgian and Danish: "The invasion has started". Now it had happened. This was D-Day, and here was I making a nice drawing of a broadcasting antenna!'

Three days later I-Group, now all sergeants, were transferred to a British unit to help women radio operators transmit and receive code messages between home stations in Great Britain and secret underground stations behind enemy lines. In September, 1944, after two wasted years, the group was finally dissolved. The men were given the choice between regular army signal service and a so-called 'risky job'. Thor chose the second, and was immediately sent to a new school. This time, however, there was clearly a plan in mind. The school was a special British training centre for Allied radio saboteurs. Thor made a full 100 per cent on his exams, which included a secret assignment in Scotland, a quite exceptional mark.

On his return from his secret assignment he wrote in his diary:

'29th October. Am now in Björn Rörholt's apartment in London. V-bombs have been crashing around us all night. Björn and I have decided to join forces and get into action as soon as we can. . . . Herewith I close this diary, the purpose of which has been to nail down what memory might otherwise let go as to the absurd career of I-Group.'

Chapter 9

OUT OF THE DOLDRUMS

THE war went on. After Thor's four diaries about I-Group, there was another, full of action and written in tiny script, some parts in cipher and some even in Polynesian. From this it is possible to find out what happened after I-Group was dissolved.

Once more the military authorities put Thor away in an old mansion. It was so secret that he was driven there in the dark and never did discover where it was. Referred to as '52', it was a training centre of the S.O.E. (Special Operations Executive) for young parachutists and saboteurs who would operate in occupied areas. They were men of various nationalities, burning with determination and fighting spirit.

The courses for novice saboteurs included coding and decoding, and rugged training in self-defence and assault. Thor detested having to learn how to stab a sentry from behind, how to break the arms, legs, or neck of an enemy, and how to put out his eyes with two projecting fingers. He fervently hoped he would never have to use this training, that he would be able to do his job by other and less objectionable means.

The final course was at a parachute school at an airfield in the west of England. Thor went with Erik Beyer and his new friend and former chief, Lt Rörholt, who was already an experienced parachutist. After a short theoretical introduction, they learned the right landing technique—how to fall. This was followed by practice jumps with long ropes from scaffolding and towers.

The night before his first jump from an aircraft, Thor awoke several times and felt his stomach tightening. What if the old fear of heights came back? He tried to calm himself by remembering the remark of an expert:

'There are only two sorts of parachutists: those who admit they are frightened and those who don't admit it.'

The next day he and seven other silent young men stood on the airfield, fitting their parachutes while the airplane was warming up with a nerve-racking roar. When they had climbed in and the door was closed. Thor knew there was no turning back; they were not to get out through that door again.

The plane took off. Soon came the call: 'Action stations'. They took their places in two rows, one on each side of the hatch in the floor of the plane. Thor was scheduled to jump second. Sitting close to the hatch he peered down at woods and green fields slowly slipping backwards in the gulf below.

'Ready . . . Go!'

The first man swung his legs through the hatch, loosened his hold and vanished. Thor took his place.

'Go!'

He pushed off with his hands, straightened up, and cut like an arrow through the air. As his speed increased his stomach pressed against his chest with such force that he could hardly breathe. At the same instant the static line—the cord attached at the other end to the airplane—tautened and tore off the parachute pack. A long, fluttering sausage skin expanded into an enormous umbrella, gave a violent jerk to the harness in which he was suspended, then held him at rest. He swayed slowly in the rigging lines with somewhat the same thrill he had felt as a boy on the swing in his yard. It almost seemed as if a strong invisible hand had grabbed him by the back and kept him from tumbling into the open abyss.

This pleasure was short-lived. Spinning hills and woods were on their way up to meet him, first slowly, then more and more rapidly. He managed somehow to get into his position for landing, pulling on the straps so he would strike the ground at an angle. The horizon swept upward around him on every side. In lightning succession the side of his right foot, hip, and shoulder hit the ground as he rolled over to distribute the impact of the blow. He then struck the parachute-release box to get rid of the harness before the wind swept him along.

In the next two days he made his second and third jumps, which went off without a hitch. But on the fourth jump things did not go so well. This time he had to jump carrying heavy equipment in a bag fastened to his legs. The first stage went exactly as before, but what followed was not the expected relieving jerk on the harness which always came when the parachute opened. The earth was twisting around and around beneath him. He looked up. The parachute had not opened properly and hung above him like an air-filled bag because the rigging lines had twisted. He struggled desperately to untangle them, but the earth continued to revolve and was coming closer at a frightening pace. A voice from below shouted through a megaphone:

'The bag! The bag!'

He hastily jettisoned it from his legs in accordance with advance instructions. The ground still shot up. The parachute had barely opened fully when he received a violent shock from ankle to shoulder, and for an instant all went black. He was shaken and badly bruised, but otherwise unhurt.

The last jump was to take place at night, when the main problem would be to estimate one's distance from the ground at the critical moment of preparing for a landing. The only assistance would be the light from two small sodium flares on the field. This was the jump Thor feared most of all, for his eyesight was particularly bad at night. Actually, he had not thought he would be accepted as a parachutist. He had passed the eyesight test by pressing his fingers into the corners of his eyes—the old dodge from his schooldays.

As he sat in the lightened cabin of the plane thinking how much better the other parachutists could see, he shut his eyes to get used to the darkness, and did not open them again, except momentarily as he took his place at the hatch, until the parachute had opened against the starry sky above him. It was an experience of unsurpassed delight and beauty. He thought he could see two dim lights far below, but he was not too sure. Then he caught a glimpse of trees silhouetted against the horizon. He pulled on the straps to get into landing position, and touched ground with a feathery lightness he had not achieved in broad daylight.

The others from his plane were not so fortunate that night. Jumping from light into darkness temporarily blinded them and led to broken bones and wrenched backs. Erik Beyer, who was to have accompanied Thor on a 'risky job', broke both ankles.

Before Thor was sent into action he was given a weekend pass. He took the train to Salisbury. From boyhood he had always wanted to see Stonehenge, that remarkable double circle of lintelled stone colossi dating back to sun worshippers in prehistoric times. When he arrived, however, he found the area surrounding the monument enclosed with barbed wire, because of a military camp nearby. As he sat on the edge of the road, the huge stones were outlined against the evening sky only a few hundred yards away behind the fence, looking like petrified giants guarding an old impenetrable secret. How did it all look from the inside? He caught sight of some flattened cardboard cartons discarded in the ditch, spoiling the beauty of the landscape. The Allied cause could hardly suffer from his trying out a trick he had just learned in sabotage school. When twilight came he crawled across the open ground to the fence and, protecting himself from the barbed wire with some of the cartons, pushed his way through. He drew his rucksack and sleeping bag after him in the same way, and moved like an eel into the open meadow separating him from his goal.

The evening was chilly and there was dew on the grass. A broad sickle moon hung above the weird cluster of stone giants looming high against the evening sky. The whole circle of enormous upright stones had formerly held horizontal stone lintels adjoining each other in a complete ring. Many of these giant capstones had fallen down, but some of the uprights still carried their lintels like enormous doors. What an incredible feat of engineering—primitive, simple, yet impressive and beautiful! He reached the stones, which were twelve feet or more in height. Near the centre of the enclosure lay the altar stone, a block of sandstone sixteen feet long. With its smooth surface it looked like the couch of some deity, some invisible god representing the secret guarded for thousands of years by the surrounding giants. Thor sat down on the starlit altar stone, opened his rucksack and had his supper. Then he unrolled his sleeping bag and went to bed on the stone, well aware of the stories of pagan rites it might have told if it could speak. For several hours he lay there in the dim moonlight, soaking up the strange atmosphere of a forgotten alien faith that seemed to seep out of the ground and the weathered blocks. He thought of the time when these stones stood for something important to the people who came there, people who like all other worshippers died in the firm conviction that they alone knew the truth beyond earthly life. Beset by their conviction, they had moved these enormous blocks from distant regions far beyond the horizon.

His reveries were interrupted when a shining object shot across the night sky high above him, perhaps a V-bomb, a sudden reminder of man's activities in his own time. At long last he fell asleep. When Stonehenge was beginning to glow in the rose of dawn he awoke filled with the joy of living. He rejoiced in the play of the warm sunlight falling on him and the altar stone from behind two lifeless colossi of stone. He felt like a late addition to the ageless succession of sun worshippers who had experienced here the same glorious rebirth of life.

During his parachute training Thor met a number of tough fighting men from many countries. One morning at breakfast he looked at the backs of the men sitting at a nearby table—and suddenly he was back at Fatu Hiva, among the skulls on the temple site in the Omoa valley. The men at the other table were modern men, with the same enemy and the same ideals of freedom as he, yet they had painted on the backs of their leather flight jackets rows of white skulls, one for each bombing raid over

Germany. Some had only two or three skulls, but one man had a row and a half, and was clearly the hero of the battle.

Among the natives Thor had met in the South Seas, none had bragged of headhunting. Old Tei Tetua had tasted human flesh only once, during a ceremony in his childhood; and real head-hunters who adorned themselves with trophy skulls on a cord around their necks were of the past, even in the most primitive tribes he had come across. Now this practice had reappeared among his comrades-in-arms, who had exchanged the bow and arrow for the bomb. The modern head-hunter flew so high he could not see his victims or collect their scalps, but if he could, how many men, women, and children did each painted skull represent?

During this time Thor often met young Norwegians who had been operating from secret bases in Norway. When they quietly reappeared in camp after several weeks' absence, all he knew about them was that they had been out on some dangerous mission behind the German lines. Although he made several friends, he never knew their real names.

One day a much-decorated lieutenant came up and greeted him. He was small and thin, but his clear-cut face and the firm expression of his mouth indicated a strong character and exceptional will power. This young man was later to accompany Thor on one of the strangest of post-war adventures: the Kon-Tiki expedition. His name was Knut Haugland. Knut had been the radio operator in the successful attack by Norwegian saboteurs on the heavy-water plant in the Rjukan valley in February, 1943. Mr Churchill had given top priority to this operation, which had prevented the Germans from producing the first atomic bomb. For his services Knut had already been decorated by King George VI and various Allied governments. When Thor met him he had just returned from another mission in Norway. He had set up his transmitter in the loft of a maternity clinic, in the middle of Oslo. The Germans had traced him there, and the building had been surrounded by Nazi police and the Gestapo, but Knut had shot his way out and escaped over the wall of the clinic.

Thor was pleased when this experienced saboteur wanted him as his assistant and proposed that they should parachute into the forests of Nordmarka, near Oslo. Thor's job would be to act as radio instructor for the central command of the underground forces, which by now had grown tremendously in size. The proposal met with the approval of headquarters in London, but once again things happened to upset the plan.

Chapter 10

MURMANSK CONVOY

UNEXPECTED events far up in the Arctic abruptly ended Knut's plans for Thor. On October 25, 1944, the Red Army occupied Kirkenes, the world's northernmost city. Having driven the Germans out of the Karelian isthmus, the Russians had marched through Finland into Finnmark, the most northern county of Norway. Until the time of its liberation Kirkenes had been the main U-boat base for the attacks on the Murmansk convoys, and it was completely destroyed by the Germans before they left. The further retreat of the 200,000 Germans, comprising the 20th Gebirgsarmee, went on more slowly, combined with further scorched-earth tactics and the forcible removal of the Norwegian population. Only small Russian forces followed them westward beyond Kirkenes and the last battle took place on November 6th at Leida, in the valley of the Tana.

A Norwegian mountain company, commanded by Colonel Arne Dahl, was hurriedly sent across from Great Britain to look after Norwegian interests. Headquarters were set up in Kirkenes, where the Russians had already established their own H.Q. Colonel Dahl and his limited staff worked magnificently to restore order for the civilians who had evaded evacuation and remained in the area. In the whole city only three small houses remained. No road was passable, not a single power line or telegraph pole had escaped the German explosives, and the shortage of food was acute.

Radio communication with London was through the Russian station at Kirkenes via Moscow, and it was now decided to set up a station at Norwegian H.Q., so that daily reports could be sent to London direct. To accomplish this, a radio group of three men—Lt Rörholt, Thor, and another former member of the I-Group, Rolf Stabell—received instructions to join a special cadre of thirty Norwegian officers preparing to leave Great Britain for various missions in Finnmark. As the local coast was still dominated by the German Air Force and Navy, the only access to Finnmark was by way of Murmansk in northern Russia. Immediately after joining the contingent Thor and Stabell were promoted to the rank of second lieutenant.

With thirteen large cases of radio equipment, they boarded an American aircraft carrier in Scapa Flow, Orkney, and sailed for Murmansk in a convoy of about eighty Allied ships. About half of the convoy were cargo vessels, most of them Liberty ships which Thor recalled so well from his work at the Bethlehem Fairfield shipyard. As they moved northwards, U-boats and German patrol planes followed at a distance like sharks and birds of prey, in the hope that one of the ships would be separated from the rest.

It was cold, dark, and eerie crossing the Arctic Circle. All the ships were blacked out, and sky and sea completely transmuted into pitch-dark night. Only at midday did a patch of dim light show blood red in the south, and then ships large and small became black shadows on the boundless grey ocean, all heading north. On the deck of the nearest ship huge locomotives, lend-lease from the United States to Russia, were visible for a short while. Then the arctic night fell once more over the convoy, and the whole world seemed congealed into ice and floating steel.

In this sinister world of armoured turrets and heavy guns, where patrol planes shot off, then dived back into landing nets, Thor's thoughts often went back to the peaceful hut on piles under the palms on Fatu Hiva. He wondered how old Tei Tetua would have reacted if he had seen his white friend on this floating monster bristling with super-weapons that made the club of Tei's cannibal father a mere child's toy.

At times it seemed to Thor that the situation was absurd. Here they were heading north to hunt and slay men they did not know. Hitler and his immediate staff were not up there in the arctic night, only innocent men sent up from different parts of the world to meet in combat; men who had to put on distinctive uniforms and emblems to show friend from foe. Occasionally he had to shake all thoughts out of his head. It was useless to think in the middle of a war, when friends and family were suffering from Nazi occupation. The thinking should be done in peacetime, to avoid the false steps that lead civilized men into savage wars. The world in peacetime was like a giant robot suffering from the constant fear of war. The medicine prescribed to prevent this threat had been armaments, always armaments. Whenever the dose proved insufficient to ward off another attack, the witch doctors' brew had been made stronger and more powerful, and the dose increased perhaps a hundredfold. But still the medicine remained the same. The robot, filled with guns and high explosives, was never relieved of his fear, and the attacks became more violent than ever. Was it not high time to stop prescribing this barbaric brew and try some remedy more in keeping with modern progress?

Pacing the armoured deck of the carrier, Thor never doubted that the Allies would win the war, but how long would they then live in peace? Would not some other potential enemy emerge when this war was over? Throughout his lifetime the Western world had visualized the 'Red Army' as something cruel and barbaric looming as a menace from the East, but recently, when the Germans invaded Russia, the Allied press and radio had needed less than a week to convert that very concept into one of an army of gallant and valiant men fighting the Allied cause of freedom.

Eight German destroyers were lying in wait when the convoy passed the Altafjord, but they did not attack. At the entrance to the Murmansk fjord, however, a pack of U-boats *did* attack. When the first explosion shook the carrier Thor and Rörholt were in a store-room down by the keel. They were trying to buy some of the American Navy's splendid arctic equipment to substitute for the inferior kind issued them on departure from England. As boom after boom shook the hull, Thor thought of all the watertight steel hatches through which they had climbed down. They would be hermetically sealed to keep the carrier afloat in case of a hit. There was no need to worry. The whole convoy took up the fight. Russian warships came to its assistance, the U-boats were driven off and the convoy glided into Murmansk fjord.

When the aircraft carrier had anchored in Polyarnyy harbour, Thor got permission to go ashore. He wandered around among tall, plain blocks of flats which looked abandoned and forgotten in the arctic darkness of this lifeless Russian town. Finally he met a bearded man in a sheepskin coat, and with his small homemade vocabulary tried to ask him the way to a lavatory. In spite of many attempts to vary his pronunciation, the other could not understand, not even when shown the Russian spelling. Then it turned out that he was English. He had escaped from a German prison camp and had made his way through Russia with the help of his new allies.

'Just smile at them', he told Thor. 'Then they'll do anything to help you.'

The next day, the radio group and its thirteen cases of equipment were transferred from the aircraft carrier to a Russian torpedo boat, badly scarred by German shells. It took six hours in heavy seas and a biting wind to go across to Petsamo in Finland, which had now been recaptured by the Russians. Hungry and chilled to the bone, Thor straddled the bouncing deck beside a gloomy and suspicious Russian sailor. Recalling what the

English refugee had told him, he smiled. The Russian's face lit up in a broad grin. He grabbed Thor by the arm and dragged him down below where he dug out a loaf of black bread from his bedding. They sat down side by side, grinned silently, and munched the dry bread.

They reached Petsamo at midnight. A Norwegian corvette, the *Tunsberg Castle*, lay waiting to carry the equipment to Kirkenes. Lt Stabell went with the cases, while Rörholt and Thor continued the trip across country by separate Russian transport. It was bitterly cold. In the gleam of flickering Northern Lights, Thor climbed up beside the sturdy driver of an army truck, which had its windshield riddled with bullet holes.

A few months later, on February 6, 1945, Thor described this trip in a talk on the Home Service of the BBC:

'I drove with a Russian soldier along the arctic highway to the Norwegian frontier. I tried to keep a conversation going by means of the only three Russian words I know: friend, enemy, house. I said: "Russia, Norway, England, America—friends. Germany—enemy." The fur-clad driver laughed heartily and agreed. "Germany—enemy. Norway, England, American, Russia—friends", he repeated. Then we both laughed happily together, and two minutes later we repeated the very same statements. And when we ran out of words we sang together the Volga boat song. Then suddenly we rolled across a new pontoon bridge. The driver got very excited and pointing to a small cottage he exclaimed: "Norvjeskij dom, Norvjeskij dom!"—"Norwegian house"—and pointing to me, "*your* house." I was back in Norway now, and to me it was a marvellous feeling, although I was a long way from any part of Norway that I knew well. It was like a Londoner arriving in the Shetlands.

'As we approached Kirkenes I looked for signs of human habitation, but the scenery here was strangely bare. There was nothing but wide, snow-clad fields, undulating hills covered with low birch-scrub, and then there were all the telegraph poles which had been blown up and overthrown, pointing toward the sky in all directions, with a tangled mass of wires. Ruins were seldom visible, but when I looked across the plains, I saw a curious pattern of squares and rectangles in the snow, the foundations of houses burnt down by the Germans. People build their houses of wood in Finnmark.

'If you take the road to Kirkenes expecting to see a grim devastated town in ruins, like Cassino or Caen, you will be strangely surprised. There is no town, there are almost no ruins, only the same patterns, like graves in a churchyard covered by snow. The solitary oven of a former bakery stands with its open mouth fringed with icicles, which hang down like a terrifying row of teeth. Its tall chimney towers like a monument raised by Adolf Hitler in memory of the Nazi occupation. At the time I saw it the only evidence to show that the destruction was recent were large burning dumps of coal and oats. Actually, they had been smouldering for over a month. . . .'

As soon as they reached Kirkenes, Thor reported to Colonel Dahl. Rörholt arrived shortly afterwards and they were quartered in a former German bunker. Two days later came the report that the *Tunsberg Castle* had been sunk, probably by a U-boat. Five men of the Norwegian Navy had been killed, and the thirteen cases of precious radio equipment were lying at the bottom of the sea. There was no mention of Stabell in the report. This was the end of Rörholt and Heyerdahl's mission.

Of conditions in the area, Thor said in his broadcast:

'This was a district of eight thousand people. The Germans tried to force everyone to go away with them, but six thousand escaped, some to the mountains. Up in the mountains they lived in any kind of shelter from turf huts and overturned rowboats to German pillboxes. It was like coming back to the Stone Age. We saw a little boy with nothing on but the hide of a reindeer—the skin was just as it had been taken off the animal, all bloody down the side. . . .

'The Germans certainly did their work thoroughly. Incendiary patrols went from house to house and set them on fire. If an unfortunate victim tried to move some furniture out into the street, he was forced to carry it all in again, while the men in the patrols poured petrol down the staircases and over the floors, and the flames spread from house to house.

'Young Langseth, a volunteer member of our unit, said:

' "If only I could come across the man who set fire to my father's house! I remember him so well."

'Langseth was eager to get to the front and meet the Germans again on equal terms. We were coming from the twisted remnants of factory buildings at Björnevatn, where we had been looking for any useful material. The road wound between bare foundations and fence railings. Then Langseth suddenly stopped before a flight of stone steps in the snow and said quietly:

' "This was where we lived." He stared sadly up into void. "My room was there, on the corner of the first floor."

'When the incendiaries came and the flames were licking walls and stairs, the lad had not been able to control himself any longer. Blind with despair and anger he dashed into the burning house to see if there was anything—anything whatever—he could save. In his haste he found nothing except a large Norwegian flag which he had hidden all through the years of occupation. He grabbed hold of this and rushed out onto the stone steps in front of the burning house, where he planted himself triumphantly in view of the enemy and let the flag flutter freely in the wind.

' "How did the Germans take that?" I asked.

' "Some of them stood laughing stupidly, others shook their heads and moved on to the next house. They had so little time, you see." '

Just before Christmas Stabell turned up unexpectedly in Russian clothes and without so much as a pair of pliers by way of equipment. As the alarm had sounded on board the corvette he was standing alone on the afterdeck when an order came from the bridge. Thinking it was intended for him, he hurried to the officers on the bridge and saluted. At the same moment thirty yards of the afterdeck were blown away. More explosions followed and he found himself struggling in the icy water. Fortunately it was not long before he was picked up by one of the rescue boats. He was taken back to Petsamo, where he learned that the large convoy they had been on had been attacked by fifty Junker 88's and a whole pack of U-boats after leaving Murmansk fjord. The Allies reported twelve U-boats sunk or badly damaged, while admitting the loss of several cargo vessels and heavy damage to one of the destroyers.

Stabell's miraculous escape was suitably celebrated on Christmas Eve. They had procured a joint of reindeer from a mountain Lapp. As the little group of Norwegian officers sat around the table in the bunker there was a knock on the door and in came the Russian commandant and a couple of officers with a keg of vodka and a bag of Russian rice. The commandant had heard about Norwegian Christmas parties and very much wanted to join them. It was a Christmas Eve without parallel. Toasts of friendship were drunk to victory and eternal peace and the Russians assured them that they would withdraw from Norway as soon as the German resistance was crushed. Norwegian carols and Russian folk songs were sung, while a green aurora borealis flickered across the winter sky, and vodka helped them to forget for a while the follies of the world.

On December 26th, an order arrived from the Russian supreme command that Heyerdahl must return immediately to England. The reason given was that his name did not appear on the list of personnel that had been cleared through the Russian embassy in London. Colonel Dahl sent a message back saying that Heyerdahl's name would be found on the supplementary list from London, and owing to the shortage of officers he could not be spared. To this the Russians replied that in the supplementary list a Sergeant Heyerdahl was included, but no officer of that name. Colonel Dahl then explained that Heyerdahl had been promoted after the list had been dispatched, and that the sergeant and the lieutenant were one and the same man. Hoping that the Russians would accept this explanation, and to avoid further pointless discussion, the colonel sent Thor into the field as second-in-command of a small Norwegian commando group, seven carefully selected men. The order was:

'Attack on your own initiative.'

They decided first to make contact with the mountain company of seventy men who were holding the most advanced outpost in the desolate and war-devastated district near the Smal fjord, far from all Russian and Norwegian forces. The German rear guard still held positions besides this fjord.

The commando group crossed the Varanger fjord from Kirkenes to Vadsö, where they commandeered a civilian lorry to take them westward across the land-mined Finnmark plateau. The bridges over the Tana and the Guljok had been blown up by the Germans, but the driver took the lorry across the ice. On the last day of the year they reached the frozen trenches left by the Germans and now occupied by the most advanced unit of the mountain company. Lying huddled in one of the snow-covered foxholes, they celebrated New Year's Eve with their scanty field rations and listened to the news from the BBC. They were astonished when it was announced that 'the Norwegians are advancing on a wide front while the German divisions are retreating'. If these seventy-seven had advanced on a wide front, they would have had to look through telescopes to see from one man to the next.

Just as the commandos were about to start on their first raid against a lighthouse and three German destroyers on the coast of the Porsanger peninsula, an order came over the field radio from Colonel Dahl. He had received an ultimatum from Russian headquarters that all Norwegian advance units were to be split up into patrols to search for Heyerdahl. They all looked at each other. Here seventy-seven men were sitting in their foxholes waging war on a wide front, and now they were to split up into patrols!

There was no choice. They radioed back that Heyerdahl would return at once. Luckily the lorry driver had not yet left. At one o'clock on New Year's night he and Thor set off. It was a brutally arduous trip. The engine stalled many times because of water in the petrol. New-fallen snow lay deep on the old crust, and over and over again the heavy vehicle got stuck in snowdrifts. They were always able to dig their way out until the time they got stuck trying to get up on the bank from the ice on the Tana River. Thor went ashore to look for help and found a snowplough, only just visible under the drift. He tried to move it, but it was frozen fast. He tramped on through the deep snow until he came to a Lapp hut where he was able to borrow a horse. As he was digging the snow away from the plough to fasten the tow rope, he discovered a land mine fixed in such a clever way that he and the horse would have been blown to pieces the moment the plough moved.

Eventually, with the help of the horse, the lorry was pulled ashore. The next day it fell through a gap in the ice on the fjord outside Nesseby. Thor had to continue on foot. The time limit he had been given had almost run out. The last day and night he staggered doggedly through the deep snow. Later the next morning he reached Vadsö, wet to the skin and frost-bitten, and sank unconscious on the floor of the first house he came to.

While still at Vadsö, he met an enigmatic person known as Lt Pettersen, with whom he had often made radio contact since his arrival in Finnmark. Pettersen did not seem to be attached to any particular unit; he moved from place to place with a small radio receiver. It was later revealed that 'Pettersen' was a well-known parachutist, Torstein Raaby, who, after training in England, had been smuggled into the Tromsö district of Norway. For ten months, he had hidden and observed all activity around the battleship *Tirpitz* and dispatched daily reports to England with the help of a German officer's radio aerial, to which he connected his transmitter. It was on the basis of Raaby's reports that the battleship was sunk in Tromsö fjord by R.A.F. Lancasters. Raaby and Thor were to meet many times in the snow-covered wilderness in the far north, but neither of them dreamed that two years later they were to spend a hundred and one days on a raft together beneath the southern skies.

Colonel Dahl was greatly relieved when Thor finally arrived, but he was angry at the idea of losing one of his few officers, merely because of a trifling difference in two documents. Another Allied convoy was now on its way to Murmansk, and the Russians had ordered Thor and two lieutenants of the Norwegian Navy to return with it and report to the Russian Embassy in London, where they must procure new papers before being allowed back to Finnmark.

Shortly after Thor's return from the front, the tragic news reached H.Q. that the commando group he had had to abandon so suddenly had been discovered by the Germans while attempting to cross the Porsanger fjord in a small open boat. One of the men had been killed, the others wounded and taken prisoner.

Early in the morning on January 11th, a Russian military car arrived at Norwegian H.Q. to take the three lieutenants to Murmansk, where the Allied convoy was getting ready for its return to Great Britain. A Russian major and three Norwegian 'blue majors' (uniformed but civilian members

I

of the Norwegian administration in London), were also passengers. They had been sent to Finnmark with the mountain company to look into the condition of the populace and were now returning to England to give their report.

The car jolted in the darkness along across endless stretches of snow from Norway, through Finland and across the frontier to Russia. They met long processions of military lorries and fur-clad Russian troops. Occasionally the passengers were given a rest in some snow-covered dugout where they drank tea with Russian soldiers.

'As my listeners will know', Thor said later in his broadcast over the BBC, 'it is our own forces who have taken the initiative in Finnmark. Behind us lie the Russians—stout, fur-clad men, who look more like peaceful trappers than formidable warriors. Their exploits, however, will soon be appreciated by anyone who lives for a time among them. It would be hard to find warriors more unassuming and efficient. Their equipment is perfect. A Russian soldier in Finnmark is dressed in a long sheepskin coat, boots, padded trousers, and a fur cap. He carries no unnecessary loads. He has his weapon and a sack of black bread, fat, and onions. He is nimble and light-footed, and able to push ahead for days until the field kitchen catches up with meat and cabbage soup. In contrast with the Germans, who forced their way into every house, the Russians camp in the open. You may wake up at night to the most fantastic displays of the Northern Lights, and strange, stirring choruses ringing through the winter valleys. Here and there is a small campfire, where the Russian soldiers have thrown themselves down in the snow, without tents or sleeping-bags. If they wake at night because of the arctic cold, they dance and sing for a short time around the fire, then settle down quietly to sleep again.'

There was little to distinguish day from night as the passengers for Murmansk slept and shivered their way through the darkness, until finally one day they saw rows of twinkling lights ahead. A faint green streak along the horizon to the southeast told them that midday was approaching. Soon afterwards they swung down to the Murmansk quay. A Russian naval officer pulled open the door of the car, saluted, and said in staccato English:

'I have good news for you. We have received permission for the three majors to return to Kirkenes.'

One of the three majors smiled patronizingly and said there must be some misunderstanding; it was the three *lieutenants* who had asked to be allowed to stay.

The Russian shook his head.

'There can be no misunderstanding. It is an order from Moscow.'

So saying, he produced a crumpled telegram which he translated into English. The majors were to stay, the lieutenants to go to England. There were emphastic but still polite protests from the three 'blue majors'. A decisive refusal came from the Russian with equal politeness. He added nervously that the convoy had already left, and the three lieutenants must immediately go on board a Russian submarine chaser waiting for them by the quay. While the majors grew more and more hysterical, the lieutenants were hurriedly helped into the submarine chaser. The last thing they saw were the three majors, now literally blue from rage and cold, being pushed back into the icy car to make the long journey back to Finnmark. In the confusion, some of their reports and equipment had already been thrown on board the submarine chaser, and Thor had to take these back with him to England.

The Russian submarine chaser went at full speed north through the Murmansk fjord. In less than an hour she caught up with two British destroyers at the rear of the convoy. One of the Norwegian naval lieutenants was hoisted on board the *Zebra*, while Thor and the other one were helped aboard the *Zambesi*.

After a couple of hours' sleep on a couch in the wardroom, Thor was awakened by the dull sound of depth charges. The *Zebra* had made contact with a U-boat. Soon afterwards another U-boat appeared fifteen miles astern of the *Zambesi*, shadowing the convoy. It sent out messages in code, doubtless about the position and course of the convoy, for it was not long before an increasing number of escort ships reported contact with U-boats. One of the officers showed Thor the line-up of the whole convoy. The escort ships included an aircraft carrier, a cruiser, eight destroyers, nine corvettes, and some smaller craft. Later, Thor was given a hammock slung in a narrow open passage on the upper deck and told to sleep with his life jacket on.

Before lunch the next day there was a thumping noise along the side of the ship that came from depth charges dropped by a destroyer in front of them. As the officers started their meal, there was another thunderous boom, this time so violent that the whole ship shook.

'That was us,' said someone.

Quite calmly everyone rose from the table one by one and left the mess. Thor stuffed the last morsel of apple pie into his mouth and accompanied them up to the bridge. The destroyer turned on a new course and depth charges were thrown in a high parabola out into the tossing grey waves.

In order to throw the U-boats lying in wait outside the fjord off the scent, the convoy altered course and headed east in the direction of Siberia, and then a hundred miles due north. It ran into the towering seas of an arctic storm, and the next night the *Zambesi* was labouring heavily and at times listing at an angle of thirty-five degrees.

It was now almost impossible to keep the convoy together. It changed course again and for two days travelled southwest, but the storm increased instead of abating. On the third day there was a sudden cry of 'Man overboard!' Three of the crew had been caught by a heavy sea, but were swept back on board by the next wave and managed to cling to the lifelines.

That day the rolling of the destroyer increased until once she heeled over at an angle of forty degrees on each side. An attempt to lay the breakfast table in the messroom for the only three who put in an appearance—Thor, the ship's doctor, and a midshipman—failed completely. One huge wave sent the ship reeling. Thor managed to twine his legs around the table, which was bolted to the deck, but everything on it, as well as chairs, carpet, and the doctor, was swept across the messroom. The doctor ended up sitting sideways against the bulkhead with the carpet over him like a blanket. Simultaneously, the midshipman pitched forward, a knife covered with jam held at arm's length. The knife stabbed into the bulkhead, missing the doctor's nose by an inch. Just at that moment the door flew open and in staggered the messboy with nothing on but a short fluttering shirt. He performed a wild dance barefooted among broken glass, shattered plates, and pats of butter. The doctor blinked his eyes over the carpet and remarked dryly:

'Say, is this a striptease, or what?'

Then another wave sent the messboy back through the doorway and slammed the door behind him.

The next day the weather eased somewhat. There was suddenly a terrific bang with a curiously metallic ring. The hull shook and heeled over violently. Thor's first thought was that a torpedo had hit the ship, but a series of explosions followed: the *Zambesi* herself was dropping depth charges.

On deck the crew was reloading the depth-charge throwers. Once more a series of barrel-shaped objects were thrown out in a high parabola. Shortly after each explosion a quivering marked the surface where the depth charge had fallen, but nothing else was to be seen. Then a report came from the 'asdic' room:

'Echo bearing 207, seven hundred yards. Probably U-boat.'

The *Zambesi* altered course, ran on until the submarine lay straight beneath her, and dropped more depth charges. Then the radar broke down and before it could be repaired the destroyer had lost touch with the convoy. Without waiting to see the effects of the depth charges, the captain gave orders to increase speed to twenty knots until they overtook the other vessels.

That day the convoy crossed the Arctic Circle on its way south. The wind rose to another terrific gale. The waves swelled into mountains of hissing dark grey water, which crashed against the bobbing destroyer. For the men in the convoy the world suddenly dwindled from shadows of many ships on a dark ocean to one lonely vessel combating the next wave—and the next—and the next.

Towards evening the aircraft carrier signalled that she could no longer make it and would have to heave-to. Soon came the order that ships unable to keep in the convoy were to alter their course to northward, head to wind. At ten o'clock the *Zambesi* and most of the other escort vessels had to give up, which led to complete chaos for a while. The *Zambesi's* radar broke down again so she could not maintain her correct station on the wing; with all the ships around her observing strict blackout, she suddenly found herself in the middle of the convoy. Cargo ships appeared on all sides out of the troughs of the waves, and she had the greatest difficulty in avoiding collisions. The heavy seas had now become a greater danger than the U-boats, so ships were instructed to show navigation lights.

In the midst of all this chaos an enormous wave struck the ship. The only motor boat on board was completely wrecked. A fixture on the deck broke loose tearing a hole in it, and the water now poured down below decks every time the waves broke over the ship. But worse still, the depth charges broke from their lashings and rolled wildly about the deck, tearing through the railing and going overboard right against the hull. With the ship unable to make more than three knots against the storm, it was fortunate the charges sank fairly deep before being exploded by the pressure of the water. But each time the armoured hull of the destroyer shook so violently that disaster seemed imminent.

While the crew were making heroic efforts to secure the charges still rolling dangerously about the deck, one of the men was swept overboard. For awhile he bobbed up and down in his yellow life-jacket, at times only a few arms' lengths from the ship's side. The desperate shouts of 'Man overboard!' were barely heard in the tumult of the storm.

It was impossible, without risking more lives, to rescue him. In a few moments he was frozen to death, covered by a sheet of ice.

'What a pity', said one of the officers quietly when he heard who the man was. 'He was so good at the accordion.'

He was not being callous. He just could find no better way of expressing his feelings.

All attempts to secure the remaining depth charges failed. The seas were striking the destroyer with such force that the men could no longer remain on deck, even on a line. One by one all twelve charges rolled overboard and exploded in the sea.

The weather improved a little the next day. Towards afternoon a ship was seen on the radar. The *Zambesi* began flashing signals and in a short time four ships were assembled. A cruiser, which was fifteen miles away, issued orders to alter course southward once more. Soon signals were flashing on all sides. One ship had a hole in her side and water in the oil. Another could not get up speed. Something was wrong with most of the ships, but it was not possible to estimate the full extent of the damage as many of them were still missing.

New orders now came from the cruiser that assembled ships were to proceed in independent groups to the Faroe Islands, north of Scotland. Next day the *Zambesi* caught up with many more ships, including the *Zebra,* and towards evening the black cliffs and snow-covered mountain ranges of the Faroes loomed up in the dusk. As the ships were about to enter Thorshavn harbour they were once more attacked by U-boats. The *Zebra* dropped depth charges while the other ships reached safety; the *Zambesi* received orders to patrol the entrance. In the early dawn as the *Zambesi* herself entered the harbour and anchored among the other ships in the convoy, a gleam of sun shone through a gap in the clouds for the first time in six weeks.

When Thor finally arrived in London he called at the Russian embassy. He was immediately issued papers authorizing his return to Finnmark.

Chapter 11

BACK TO THE FINNMARK FRONT

On Tuesday, February 6, 1945, Fru Alison, now seventy-two years of age, was hiding in the loft of her villa near Lillehammer, secretly listening to the BBC in London. Beside her sat a young man who called himself 'Per', which was all she knew about him. Both kept glancing impatiently at their watches, which were infuriatingly slow moving that afternoon. Time was precious for at any moment the Germans might search the house. If they found Per there he was done for. A group of the Norwegian underground had been broken up after the torture of a prisoner by the Gestapo, and Fru Alison's villa, which had long been a refuge for saboteurs and parachutists was now no longer safe. Per was supposed to have gone to Sweden the day before, but he had heard the announcer say from London:

'At half past five tomorrow evening Lieutenant Thor Heyerdahl will be giving a report on Finnmark.'

Per decided to take the risk of staying in the loft for another day with his radio. It was the only way Fru Alison would have a chance to hear her son's voice, as all Norwegian radios had been confiscated and listening to news from England was strictly forbidden.

Now they were both waiting. At last, at 5.30 p.m., they heard Thor say:

'I am just back from the arctic front and I still have clearly before me the picture of a place which—incredible as it may seem—is our own Norway. There is permanent semi-darkness, a constant dawn, and it is bitterly cold. As my listeners will know, it is our own forces who have taken the initiative in Finnmark. Behind us lie the Russians. . . .'

The broadcast, from which excerpts have already been quoted, lasted only a few minutes, but they were minutes Fru Alison would never forget. After nearly five years she knew that her son was alive and doing what he could, just as she was. And *her* contribution was not a small one for her age. After the war the leaders of the Home Front presented her with a citation for bravery; and from London she was sent a signed photograph of

Winston Churchill and a letter from General R. A. Allen that ended:

'Mr Churchill desires me to express his gratitude for your great help and begs you to accept the enclosed photograph as a small token of his recognition of what you have done.'

Great was Thor's surprise when, shortly after his arrival in London, he ran across Björn Rörholt, now a captain. He had managed to get back from Finnmark through neutral Sweden, leaving Rolf Stabell in Kirkenes. Rörholt was in London to try to interest the Norwegian high command in a new plan to improve communications between the military detachments and the civilian population, both in Finnmark and with the outside world. The last attempt had failed because of the loss of all the equipment on the *Tunsberg Castle*. The new plan was to set up a radio school in Sweden, then parachute men equipped with long-range instruments into Finnmark.

Ten thousand Norwegian servicemen were being trained in Sweden. Because of its neutral status, these men were disguised in police uniforms and were officially referred to as 'policemen'. Many of them were training in a camp at Axvall, outside the garrison town of Skövde, about a hundred and fifty miles southwest of Stockholm. If some of these young men could be formed into a radio unit many problems in northern Norway would be solved.

After a series of meetings in London with the G.O.C., the Norwegian Foreign Minister, Special Operations Executive, and officers of the American Air Force, Rörholt finally got permission to proceed. Thor was appointed his assistant, responsible for personnel and instruction, while Rörholt undertook the difficult task of procuring the necessary radio equipment. Stabell was to join forces with Thor when he arrived in Finnmark.

On the completion of the preliminary arrangements, Thor left Rörholt in London and flew in a small British military plane across occupied Norway to Stockholm, and from there to Axvall. He was allowed to select sixteen of the best 'policemen', all high school graduates who had recently finished a five-months' course in radio. Later he was given eleven others trained in cipher work. He set up a course for these men in radio transmission and reception, Norwegian and British procedure, codes, security, and weather reporting, as well as hard physical training. More men joined the group until he alone was responsible for the administration, instruction, and discipline of thirty-five privates.

22-3. In England, training as a parachutist.
24. (*next page*) Liaison officers Rörholt, Heyerdahl and Stabell in Finnmark.
25. (*next page*) Capt Rörholt and Lt Heyerdahl planning radio links and the dropping of supplies.

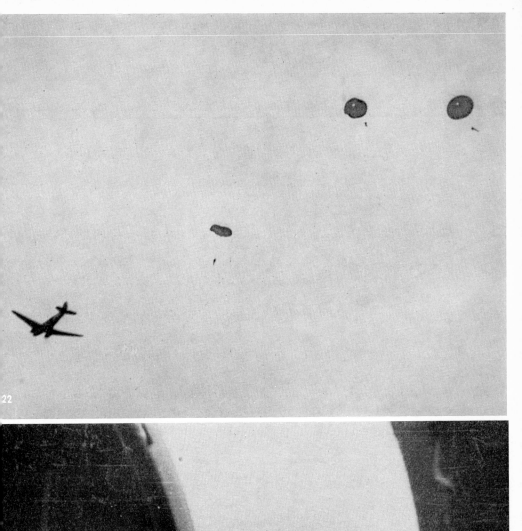

22

23

24

25

28

After three weeks Rörholt phoned from Stockholm to say that the group was to leave at six o'clock the next morning and report to the main Stockholm railway station for a secret destination. He had organized the technical details, established contact with Lt 'Pettersen', and enlisted the co-operation of the famous Norwegian pilot, Bernt Balchen. At that time Balchen was a colonel in the American Air Force, with ten planes at his disposal, now operating undercover from a remote air base of the Swedish Air Force in the extreme north of Sweden near the borders of Finnmark.

The sudden order created an unforeseen problem for Thor. He had arrived at the Axvall camp in clothes borrowed from Rörholt, but thirty-five men in police uniforms could not be marched through the streets of the Swedish capital by a man in civilian dress. Inside the camp he had worn his British army uniform; so, counting on the likelihood that the neutral Swedes had scant knowledge of various types of uniforms, he decided to set out with his body of 'policemen' on the long journey through Sweden in full Allied attire.

After a train ride from Stockholm to the remote northern city of Luleå, the small Norwegian unit was installed with the greatest secrecy at the Swedish Air Force camp at Kallax, from which Colonel Balchen's Dakotas were operating. It was here that the main station of the new radio section was to be set up as soon as Rörholt arrived with the equipment. When the members of the group had been trained in parachuting, other stations would be established in Finnmark.

Being completely cut off from contact with G.H.Q. in London, Thor, although a mere lieutenant, promoted on his own initiative his most able man to sergeant and a few others to corporal. With no confidence in the Army's winter equipment which he had already tested in Finnmark, he began teaching his group primitive man's means of survival in arctic conditions. The Swedish Air Force personnel were surprised one morning when they arrived at the airstrip and found a long row of Eskimo igloos along the side of the runway. He also started a ground course in parachute jumping, and when Rörholt arrived the men were ready to make their first trial jumps from Balchen's planes. Soon afterwards certain members of the group were dropped with their transmitters on both sides of the German lines in northern Norway. While Rörholt remained behind, Balchen flew Thor with the rest of his men across Finland to the airfield in Kirkenes. Immediately after landing, Thor was embraced by the same Russian officer who had sent him back to London four months earlier. He was visibly glad to see him back safe and sound with all his papers in order.

26. (*previous page*) Lt Heyerdahl in the field.
27. (*previous page*) The enemy had done a thorough job on the Finnmark front.
28. On board an Allied man-of-war in the convoy to Murmansk.

'We soldiers would have liked to keep you here', he smiled, 'but the order came from Moscow.'

It was a small but efficient unit that now pitched its camp in the area of Kirkenes. Thor gave a quick course of training to about twenty volunteers from Finnmark who joined his group, while he prepared for an all-out expedition to the south. On radio instructions from Rörholt at Kallax, Thor was to set up radio stations at strategic points in the vast sort of no-man's-land between the Russian and German lines, into which only a handful of Norwegian soldiers had infiltrated. From one of the under-cover stations behind the German front, they received a report that some armed Norwegian Nazi spies were heading north by small boat from the city of Narvik. Under the pretence of working for the Home Front, their object was to find out the strength and position of the advanced Allied forces. If the Germans discovered that the Russian Army had stopped its advance in the vicinity of Kirkenes, and that only a few insignificant Norwegian contingents occupied the wide area in between, it could be disastrous. Thor's party was first to establish a small radio station at an advance point along the coast where the northward movement of any sus-picious-looking boats could be reported to the Norwegian H.Q. The remainder of the party were to continue with Thor to the front line.

Thor, with a force of about twenty men, commandeered a fishing smack at Kirkenes for the trip along the precipitous coast of Finnmark. He was joined by Lt 'Pettersen', who had suddenly turned up again like a jack-in-the-box. The skipper of the smack raised strong objections, saying he was short of both fuel and provisions. Thor procured a barrel of fuel and sufficient rations for the boat's crew, but it was still necessary to brandish a revolver and gently remind him there was a war on.

Lt Stabell with another group took over a second fishing smack and followed close behind. In Baatsfjord they passed the place where the *Tunsberg Castle* had been sunk, and nearer the shore, another ship was lying with a yawning hole in her side. It was here that the first radio patrol was put ashore to keep watch for the Norwegian Nazi spies.

Allied warships had not gone along the coast beyond Baatsfjord during the war, so at this point the two smacks entered water mined and patrolled by U-boats. Stabell and Thor had agreed on radio contact every hour, on the hour, day and night, and the next part of their plan called for putting into the harbour at Hopseidet on the Nordkinn peninsula.

Just before they arrived there late in the evening, Thor began to feel uneasy. Instinctively he felt that something was wrong. He remembered Hopseidet as the first port of call of the unlucky commando patrol he had been forced to leave before they were ambushed by the Germans. Perhaps

Hopseidet involved danger. He sent a message in code to Stabell, who was following, suggesting they avoid Hopseidet and try to sneak past the advance German positions. The chances were that the Germans had already observed the two smacks heading for Hopseidet, but they probably never expected them to go beyond the Nordkinn peninsula and the mouth of Laksefjord. Stabell agreed to the plan and they decided to chance it.

German observation posts must have seen the two smacks before they changed course. That night three U-boats came into Hopseidet and put ashore a squad of marines, who took six Norwegian civilians prisoner, tortured them to obtain information, and afterwards shot them. Eye-witnesses said later that the marines were drunk.

If winter in Finnmark had been one long black and gloomy night, now in May the nights were so bright that one could see for miles. Putting out all lights on the smacks was no help as they crept into the seemingly endless Porsanger fjord where German land forces still held positions along the western shore.

At nine o'clock the next morning they reached Hestnes, far up on the eastern shore of the fjord. The whole area was covered with barbed wire defences and land mines. Only the previous day two men had been killed by one of these mines. From his base at Kallax, Colonel Balchen had attempted to drop radio equipment near Hestnes. Thor found two of the parachutes but neither had opened, and valuable equipment, including a generator, had been completely smashed.

After protesting anew, the skipper finally agreed to take them all the way to Hamnbukt, at the southernmost end of the fjord, since all the roads in this section of the front were rigged with German mines and booby traps. They reached Hamnbukt at 11.00 p.m., where they landed and camped among a group of Lapps who were celebrating the surrender that day of the German troops in Denmark.

A horse was needed to help transport the equipment inland to Skogan-varre, in the central section of the front, where they were to establish the main radio station. The next day, Thor and 'Pettersen' found a Lapp who did indeed have horses, but wanted first to have a nice long chat, for he enjoyed hearing Norwegian again. He talked and talked and almost choked to death on the tobacco they gave him. Finally Thor grew impatient. He looked at his watch and said:

'Now you must get your horse before it gets dark.'

This child of the midnight sun calmly took the pipe out of his mouth, smiled, and replied reassuringly:

'It won't be dark till autumn.'

The Germans had laid large quantities of mines and traps in this area as well, and both civilians and soldiers were killed or wounded every day. The next morning, the two patrols proceeded inland, following a partially snow-covered valley. It had been a beautiful place and reminded Thor of Bella Coola. However, the woods had been devastated by the retreating enemy and only a few scattered firs and birches were left standing.

The enemy must have had a strong force in this area, for the patrols were always coming across deserted camps, surrounded by minefields and littered with abandoned tanks and cars, broken glass, enormous heaps of empty bottles, and refuse of all kinds. They pitched camp that night at Skoganvarre with the forward unit of the Norwegian mountain company. 'Pettersen' left for Sweden the next morning, while Thor gave his unit new instructions in the various types of land mines and booby traps, a constant danger for all of them.

Coincidentally, at the same time, another Norwegian officer was similarly instructing his men at Karasjok, nearer to the Swedish border. He had placed a Teller anti-tank mine on the ground and explained that it would explode under the weight of a tank or a heavy vehicle, but not under the weight of a man. To demonstrate this he stepped square on the mine. It exploded, killing him and twenty-one others and wounding nine. One of Thor's former trainees happened to be present with his transmitter. He at once got in touch with Rörholt at Kallax. With amazing speed Rörholt and Balchen dispatched two doctors and a nurse, who all had to go in by parachute after only brief verbal instructions, and luckily landed safely in the deep snow. When the doctors could do no more, one of them skied across to Skoganvarre, where he reported that before the mass burial could take place, even the churchyard at Karasjok had to be cleared of mines.

On May 7th, they picked up on the radio vague rumours that the Germans in Norway had surrendered. Only the bugler reacted. He ran excitedly into the camp and blew the cease-fire, but it turned out to be premature.

On May 8th, it looked as if victory for the Allies was imminent, but no orders arrived for a cease-fire. German outposts were known to be stationed just behind the nearest hills to the west, and it was possible that they might make a last ditch attack if cease-fire orders did not reach them.

On May 9th the soldiers at Skoganvarre, surrounded by mines and booby traps, lay in their tents listening to Oslo radio broadcasting the news of Allied victory, and describing the capital's joyous welcome of Norwegian troops from England. Rejoicing with their liberated countrymen in the far south, they suddenly heard the announcer exult:

'At this very moment the first Norwegian troops are back on Norwegian soil!'

The men smiled wryly at this comment, and one of them thumped his fist hard on the ground.

'Isn't *this* Norwegian soil?' he demanded. 'And haven't we been here the whole darned winter?'

It was not until 9.37 p.m. on May 13th that the cease-fire order came over the radio from London, but surprisingly, it applied only to units of a full division. Since there was not even one regular division on the Finnmark front, the cease-fire did not apply to Thor's unit! Thus a state of war continued in the wilderness—not with military operations, but with daily accidents caused by the mine fields. Seventy mines surrounding one single bomb crater in the road were discovered.

The entry in Thor's diary on May 16th is typical:

'Stabell was standing in the sun shaving when he remarked to me: "Feel this spring air. Doesn't it have a faint scent of honey?" I had hardly time to answer when there was a loud explosion from the plain outside. An unnatural silence followed, until the noise was echoed from the distant hills. When I came out, Lieutenant Asbjörnsen and two stretcher-bearers were on their way right out to the minefield, where more fiendish devices might explode anywhere—below the sand or among the rubbish on the ground.

'I followed them in the direction of the explosion. We had run a couple of hundred yards when a bloodstained soldier came staggering towards us from some twisted scraps of rusty iron that had once been a hangar. "Rolf is hurt", he gasped. He himself had splinters in his eyes, and his nose was badly cut. He turned around and ran ahead of us to show the way. We came to a sandpile, and there was a man lying on his back about eight yards from a hole in the ground. The white birch stems around him were spattered with mud and blood. The poor fellow's face was just one mass of wet pulp. He was fully conscious and complained of pains in his legs. Blood was flowing through his ripped pants. We took a knife and cut away his pants, shorts and socks. There were great gaping wounds full of mud. It was no use cleaning him up here. We bandaged his head and thighs temporarily to check the worst of the bleeding. Then the stretcher-bearers carried him back in our own tracks.'

On May 22nd, he wrote: 'Moved to a new camp. The engineers have pitched their camp in our old place. They had a practice today with mine detectors and were a little startled to find a large Teller mine in the sand below our tent.'

On July 13th, Thor applied for his discharge, having seen a circular from

G.H.Q. saying that university graduates could now be demobilized. His application was rejected on the grounds that his services were still needed, so he remained in Finnmark during the summer. He managed to help a number of his N.C.O.'s and privates become discharged before he was informed that his radio unit would, from then on, be subordinate to the regular signal corps of the North Norway Command. The head of the signal corps proved to be an old acquaintance who had just come from Scotland: the captain who had driven I-Group crazy with his non-stop washing and scrubbing orders. Visualizing a new service with scrub brushes and pails among the rubbish and refuse of the Finnmark ruins, Thor decided to take direct action.

In August he got the news that Liv and the children were on their way from America by ship. He applied for leave to meet them in Oslo and was granted fourteen days. Balchen flew him to Kallax, and from there he went by train to southern Norway. On his arrival in Oslo he wrote an order on official army paper saying Lieutenant Thor Heyerdahl was to be discharged from military service, to take effect immediately.

He took this document to an administrative office in G.H.Q., where he, a first lieutenant, deliberately handed it to a second lieutenant with a brief order to have it passed through the proper channels. Having duly stamped the order, the unsuspicious administrative officer went into the next room and left the document on an empty desk. A few days later, before his leave had expired, the same order came back to Thor by mail, approved and signed by two officers of high rank.

He was a civilian again.

PART III

THROUGH THE STORM

Chapter 12

BURNING ALL BRIDGES

A telegram in my roadside mailbox on a sunny August day in 1947: 'From Norwegian Relay League, main station LAIO, *Kon-Tiki*. We enclose herewith a radio message picked up last night through the U.S.A. Yours respectfully, Egil Berg: To Arnold Jacoby, Larvik, Norway. Our raft is approaching its goal. All well. Greetings to our old friend from Thor and Erik.'

When I read this note my thoughts flew halfway around the world to six young daredevils sailing across the vast Pacific on a primitive raft. I could picture them, tanned and weather-beaten, half naked and bearded, looking like real savages. What were they doing just at that moment? Perhaps the raft was bobbing gently on the waves. Perhaps the men were fighting for their lives against the wind or monsters of the sea. Perhaps— but I could only speculate. I knew so little; not much more than that this voyage, one of the strangest the world had ever seen, had been undertaken in spite of the fact that experts on sea and land had scoffed at it or doomed it to failure.

I myself had had doubts. In March of the previous year I had stayed for a week with Liv and Thor in their cottage near Lillehammer. Thor was working every day on the manuscript of *Polynesia and America, A Study of Prehistoric Relations*, but in the evenings we revived memories from childhood and from the senseless period of darkness that had kept us apart. It was grand to renew our old association, yet in our hearts we knew that nothing would ever be the same again. The war had left its mark on all three of us, Liv perhaps the least. Those trying years had dampened her ebullient spirit but had given her in its place maturity and, above all, self-reliance. Thor was still the cultured savage with boyish charm, but the last remnants of uncertainty had been swept away. Something strangely dynamic, which up to then had appeared in him only occasionally, had become a fundamental characteristic. I remember how I sat trying to find the right word for this, some expression to describe this new quality.

K

He was a 'man of iron' I told myself without quite knowing what I meant; a 'man of iron' with a great sense of humour and with spirit and warmth behind his armour.

When we spoke of the future, Thor expressed his firm determination to establish his theory of the two migrations to Polynesia. During our conversations he would state the problem in a few words, presenting his ideas in the form of questions, then give the answers himself, coming up with a solution so simple and clear that no alternative seemed probable. He expected, he said, strong opposition from the experts, who maintained that primitive navigation from South America to Polynesia had been impossible. They were in unanimous agreement that the South Sea islands lay far beyond the range of the ancient civilizations in South America. The whole American continent was looked upon as a watertight bag from which nothing could escape until Columbus opened it. Thor's task was to show that there was a leak in the bag long before that.

When the Europeans came to the Pacific islands they were astonished to find that many of the natives had almost white skins and were bearded, unlike the American Indians and the peoples of Southeast Asia. On many of the islands, in the midst of the normal Polynesian types, there were whole families conspicuous for their remarkably pale skins, hair varying from reddish to blond, blue-grey eyes, and almost Semitic, hook-nosed faces. The genuine Polynesians had golden-brown skins, raven hair, and flat pulpy noses. The redheads said they were directly descended from the first chiefs of the islands, such as Tangaroa, Kane, and Tiki, who were white gods. On Fatu Hiva old Tei Tetua had spoken of Tiki, the god and chief who had brought his ancestors to the Marquesas from 'a great land far beyond the sea'.

'As I pursued my research', said Thor, 'I was impelled to go on digging deeper and deeper, trying to identify the place of origin of the all-Polynesian tribal god Tiki.'

He had finally found traces of the legend of Tiki and the bearded white men, not only in Polynesia but also in ancient America.

When the Spaniards, led by Francisco Pizarro, appeared in Peru in 1527, they noticed that the mass of Andean Indians were small and dark, while the members of the ruling Inca family were tall, with fairer skin and beards. Pedro Pizarro, Francisco's young cousin, mentioned in particular that some of the whitest inhabitants had naturally red hair. Modern research has confirmed this. On the Pacific coast of Peru, in the desert sand, there are large man-made burial caves in which numerous mummies have been found perfectly preserved. Some have the thick, stiff black hair of the present-day Indians, while others have red, often chestnut-coloured hair, silky and wavy, as found among Europeans. They also have longer skulls and remarkably tall bodies and are very different from the Peruvian Indians of today. Experts have shown by microscopic analysis that the red hair has all the characteristics that ordinarily distinguish Nordic hair from that of Mongols or American Indians. Other features, and the entire culture of these redheaded Indians, clearly show that they were not Nordic, but merely a variety of early American aborigines, of which there were a great number of different types in the New World.

Pedro Pizarro asked the Inca Indians who the white-skinned redheads were. They replied that they were the descendants of the *viracochas*, a divine race of white men with beards, who had lived there before the Incas became rulers. They were wise, peaceful instructors who had come from the north long ago and had taught the Incas' primitive forefathers architecture and agriculture, as well as manners and customs. They had finally been attacked by a chief named Cari, who came from the Coquimbo valley in central Chile. In a battle on the island in Lake Titicaca, now known as the Island of the Sun, the fair race had been massacred, but their leader Contici had escaped with his closest companions, first northwards to Cuzco, the subsequent Inca capital, and then down to Puerto Viejo, on the Pacific coast of Ecuador, where the local craft were balsa rafts. Because they were white-skinned and vanished like foam into the sea, they were given the Inca name of *viracocha* (Sea Foam) and their leader became known as Kon-Tici Viracocha. In pre-Inca times he had been called Kon-Tici (Sun-Tici) or Illa-Tici (Fire-Tici). He was high priest and sun-king, said the legend.

It is historical fact that when Pizarro and his Spaniards landed at Tumbes on the north coast of Peru, they were thought to be *viracochas* who had returned from the Pacific. For this reason alone the handful of Spaniards were able to march straight into the heart of the fortified Inca empire and capture the sovereign Atahualpa, without the vast and valiant Inca armies touching a hair of their heads. To this very day white men are called *viracochas* in Peru.

When the Spaniards came to Lake Titicaca, high up in the Andes, they found the mightiest ruins in South America—Tiahuanaco. They saw a hill reshaped by man into a stepped pyramid, classical masonry of enormous blocks beautifully dressed and fitted together, and numerous large stone statues in human form. The noted Spanish chronicler, Cieza de León, who visited the ruins in 1549, asked the local Indians about these impressive structures and was told that they had been made by the *viracochas* long before the Incas came to power.

The same strange types of stepped pyramids, colossal stone masonry, and giant stone men were later found by early European explorers on Easter Island and other Polynesian islands nearest to South America, and here, too, the natives considered them remains from the earliest race of god-men.

'I am no longer in doubt', said Thor, 'that the white chief-god Sun-Tici who left Peru was identical with the white chief-god Tiki, son of the sun, who reached Polynesia and became the legendary founder of the earliest island culture. And the details of Sun-Tici's life in Peru and the ancient names of places around Lake Titicaca, crop up again in historical legends about the ancestral homeland still current among the natives of the Pacific islands.'

But how did the sun-king and his *viracochas* reach Polynesia?

On balsa rafts with sails. Many old Spanish documents have left descriptions of their construction and efficiency. The first Inca Indians seen by the Spanish explorers on their way to Peru were a score of men and women on a thirty-ton raft, with masts and yards and excellent cotton sails. The large raft was heavily loaded with trade goods. When the explorers reached Peru they met a whole flotilla of such rafts putting to sea at full sail towards Puná island off Ecuador and loaded with Inca troops. For more than three hundred years after the Spanish conquest the coastal Indians continued to use these characteristic rafts for fishing and transporting cargo, sailing among the unpredictable currents sweeping along their unsheltered shores. At the end of the nineteenth century this seagoing type of raft disappeared, and when modern scholars took an interest in the voyages of the Incas, the balsa raft had been forgotten in Peru. It could be studied only in the ancient writings and drawings.

In 1932 the eminent American archaeologist, Dr Samuel K. Lothrop of Harvard University, published a treatise entitled, 'Aboriginal Navigation off the West Coast of South America.' After giving a detailed description of the balsa raft, its mast, rigging, sail, and curious steering gear, he stated that the raft had a dangerous weakness: the balsa logs absorbed water so quickly that they sank in a short time. The raft had to be beached at certain intervals to be dried out, so it could not have carried people on the lengthy voyage out to the islands of the Pacific.

Dr Lothrop's brilliant treatise was generally accepted, together with his conclusion that the balsa raft had to hug the coast as it was seaworthy only for one short trip at a time. Ten years later the Inca historian P. A. Means, in *Pre-Spanish Navigation off the Andean Coast*, described the balsa raft as 'a type of boat that would awake nothing but scorn in the breasts of shipbuilders of almost any other maritime people in the world'. Pacific island specialists now introduced this same opinion into the literature of Polynesia. The ethnologist J. E. Weckler thus maintained that 'no American

Indians had sea-going ships that were capable of such passages as the voyage to Polynesia'. In his widely read book, *An Introduction to Polynesian Anthropology*, published in 1945, the leading Polynesian authority, Sir Peter Buck, wrote about the bringing of aboriginal culture elements, such as the sweet potato, to the South Sea islands: 'Since the South American Indians had neither the vessels nor the navigating ability to cross the ocean space between their shores and the nearest Polynesian islands, they may be disregarded as the agents of supply.' Other leading authorities such as Dr Roland Dixon and Dr Kenneth Emory, who had both previously suspected that Peruvian civilizations took their own plants and masonry technique to Polynesia, now abandoned their own theories because they had become persuaded that balsa logs absorbed water so quickly they sank after a short time. Everyone was now agreed on this point.

With no more than his biological training and independent anthropological studies behind him, Thor felt that he was standing at the foot of an enormous mountain of traditional thinking and prejudice. He had to convince people who were all experts, each within some distinct and narrowly limited field of study. He had to expect—and he took this for granted—that the ethnologists would dismiss his arguments as dilettantish, because he had no degree. The archaeologists, sociologists, and linguists would likewise regard him as an outsider, a disrespectful buccaneer sailing in forbidden waters. Such scepticism was natural, he had to admit. He conceded that his work might have some weak points of detail when seen through the eyes of specialists in the many different fields of science he was combining into one amalgamated study. This ought to be of secondary importance, however, compared to the fact that by thus approaching the problem from all angles he had managed to pick to pieces all the old theories of migrations in the Pacific, none of which proved tenable when confronted with known facts from more than one field of science. His own theory, even if a few details should prove wrong, stood up to these many-sided tests. He was not afraid of taking up the battle, for he had himself, in a sense, become a specialist, not a specialist in a restricted field or one who had himself brought to light hitherto unknown evidence, but one who had thoroughly studied and combined all available data pertaining to the problem of human migrations in the Pacific. He was convinced that he had found the true answer to the old riddle of Polynesia.

How was he going to convince the others?

He would go to America with the manuscript of *Polynesia and America*, and if the experts were not prepared to listen to him, he might have to cross the Pacific on a balsa raft in order to convince them that the Polynesian islands were within reach of primitive seafarers from Peru.

Liv thought the plan was madness, and so did I. Couldn't the same point be proved by setting a bottle adrift? Certainly not. The point to be established was that *men on a balsa raft* could have surmounted all the obstacles and dangers that a voyage across this precise stretch of sea involved. I was uneasy when I left them at the end of the week. Apart from the possibly disastrous consequences of such a voyage, the crazy plan seemed likely to bring about a strain in relations between Liv and Thor. Nevertheless, I suspected that this man would not hesitate, if it was necessary, to stake his life in support of his theory. And so it proved.

In his book on the Kon-Tiki expedition, Thor passes lightly over what was perhaps its most remarkable feature—his lonely struggle beforehand against contempt, mistrust, and intrigue—which he thought was not relevant to the narrative of the voyage. In fact, for months before the raft left Lima harbour he was engaged in what he has referred to as the hardest and most desperate battle for his whole life.

On arrival in New York with three copies of the manuscript of *Polynesia and America* in his suitcase and only a modest sum of money in his pocket, he circulated the copies among a number of well-known scholars in several of the American universities. From some he received polite though discouraging replies. Others merely returned the manuscript without comment. Most of them had probably not even read it. It was like a fight with an invisible monster of conventional thinking and unlimited trust in the opinions of experts.

Among those to whom he sent the manuscript was the noted archaeologist Dr Herbert Spinden, president of the Explorers Club and Director of the Brooklyn Museum. Receiving no acknowledgement, Thor plucked up courage and called upon him at the museum. On Dr Spinden's desk lay the manuscript—unopened.

The old scientist shrugged his shoulders when Thor briefly outlined his theory.

'You're wrong, absolutely wrong', he said, and shook his head indignantly to drive out the idea.

'But you haven't read my arguments yet', Thor urged, nodding hopefully toward the manuscript.

'Arguments! You can't treat ethnographic problems as a sort of detective mystery!'

'Why not? I've based all the conclusions on my own observations and the facts that science has recorded.'

'The task of science is investigation pure and simple. Not to try to prove this or that. It's quite true that South America was the home of some of the most curious civilizations of antiquity, and we know neither who they were nor where they vanished to when the Incas came into power. But one thing we do know for certain—that none of the peoples of South America got over to the islands in the Pacific. Do you know why? They had no boats!'

Once again it was the same old negative attitude.

'They had rafts', Thor objected hesitatingly. 'You know, balsa-wood rafts.'

The old man smiled and said calmly:

'Well, you can try a trip from Peru to the Pacific islands on a balsa-wood raft.'

Thor could find nothing to say. He put the manuscript under his arm and found his way out of the museum and into the crowded streets of Brooklyn.

The challenge had to be met. In October of that year, 1946, he wrote to his friend Erling Schjerven in Oslo:

'One of the main arguments of my opponents is that the coastal inhabitants of Peru used a kind of log raft before the time of Columbus, and that these could not manage the voyage from Peru to Easter Island, which is 2,000 miles. . . . If I cannot gain a hearing in any other way, my plan is to build a faithful copy of the log rafts of which we have detailed descriptions dating from the time of the discovery. It is my intention, perhaps with a crew of twelve paddlers, to prove that the voyage is feasible, since I shall have the ocean current and the trade wind behind all the way. In other words I intend to re-enact a voyage from South America to the South Sea islands on a primitive Inca raft. . . .'

Within a month of writing this letter he discovered that he had underestimated the difficulties in realizing his plans. First of all he was facing serious financial problems. His father would have helped him, but the Bank of Norway said he could exchange no more dollars because of international currency restrictions after the war. The first thing he had to do was find cheaper lodgings, so he moved from his small Manhattan apartment to the Norwegian Sailors' Home in Brooklyn, where the food was good and the price moderate.

The Sailors' Home offered another advantage: the majority of the lodgers were seamen. When they spoke of the sea, they knew what they were talking about. They told him that waves and rough sea did not increase with the depth of the water or the distance from land. On the contrary, squalls were often more treacherous along the coast, and a vessel that could hold her own along the open coast could do so farther out as well. They also told of people whose lives had been saved in small boats, dancing over the waves like a gull, after the seas made their large ships founder. But they knew little about rafts.

'Rafts are not for navigation', they said. 'They go sideways and backwards and round as the wind takes them.'

Thor's thorough research had already provided him with a sound knowledge of how to reconstruct an Inca balsa raft. He knew precisely how they were built; that they carried a straddle-legged mast, a square cotton sail, and several wooden *guaras* which seemed to have served as a kind of centreboard. He could count on being able to steer the raft, but to what extent he didn't know.

In the Sailors' Home he met a young Norwegian engineer. His name was Herman Watzinger and he was an expert in thermodynamics. They got into conversation, and Thor felt such rapport with him that he disclosed his plan. A few days later Watzinger asked to be allowed to come with him if the voyage ever materialized.

During the same week Thor bought a pilot chart of the Pacific and went to visit his friend Wilhelm Eitrem, a former sea captain who was now office manager for the Fred Olsen Line in New York. It would be hard to find anyone who knew more about currents and seamanship than he. He listened in surprise to Thor's ideas, answered most of his questions in the affirmative, but told him straight out that his plan was mad.

'But you said just now that you thought it was possible!'

'Quite right. But the chances of its going wrong are just as great. The old Indians in Peru had generations of experience to build upon. Perhaps ten rafts went to the bottom for every one that got across—or perhaps hundreds in the course of centuries. As you say, the Incas navigated in the open sea with whole flotillas of these balsa rafts. Then, if anything went wrong, they could be picked up by the nearest raft. But who's going to pick you up, out in mid-ocean? Even if you take a radio for use in an emergency, don't think it's going to be easy for a little raft to be located down among the waves thousands of miles from land. In a storm you can get washed off the raft and drowned many times over before anyone gets to you. You'd better wait quietly here till someone has had time to read your manuscript. Write again and stir them up; it's no good if you don't.'

Thor couldn't wait; soon he would not have a cent left, and he had lost all hope of getting a favourable reply from any expert. When Wilhelm realized that he could not make his determined visitor drop his wild idea, he did everything to help him. They sat together with the map in front of them trying to work out the probable duration of such a crossing by raft.

'Ninety-seven days', said Wilhelm, 'but remember that's only in theoretically ideal conditions, with a fair wind all the time and assuming that the raft can really sail as you think it can. You must definitely allow at least four months for the trip, and be prepared for a good deal more.'

A few evenings later Thor dropped in at the Explorers Club. He happened to arrive in the middle of a lecture by an American colonel, who was speaking about new kinds of rescue equipment of the Air Force—rubber rafts, safety jackets, and other devices. He demonstrated some of these to the audience, and after the lecture there was an animated discussion. Several speakers, among them the polar explorer, Peter Freuchen from Denmark, had little faith in these new-fangled contrivances, so finally the colonel offered the equipment *gratis* to anyone who would test it.

A few days later Thor took Herman Watzinger as his guest to the Explorers Club, where they met Freuchen. Thor mentioned their plan to him, and to his surprise he was optimistic.

'Damn it, boys! I should like to go with you!'

As Freuchen's words had the weight of a life-long experience under primitive conditions, this was just the kind of encouragement Thor needed.

Through friends he came into contact at this time with a Norwegian multimillionaire in New York who offered him a private loan for the project if no other solution could be found. Other wealthy Norwegians with business interests in the United States also promised to lend him dollars. The outlook began to brighten. Just the same, he would have preferred to manage without private loans.

Then came a surprise. In his zeal to support Thor, Freuchen disclosed the raft plan to a Scandinavian paper, which at once released the news in large headlines. The very next morning Thor was phoned by a Norwegian journalist, who invited him and Watzinger to a conference in an apartment in a fashionable quarter of New York, where he introduced them to an American colleague and their host, a smart young gentleman in patent-leather slippers and a silk dressing gown.

The trio scented business. They had wasted no time in preparing a detailed plan for the financing of the expedition, on the condition that Thor gave them the 'exclusive rights' to newspaper articles, books, and motion pictures about the voyage. They had already had a good offer from the president of the North American Newspaper Alliance. To Thor it was as if with a stroke of a magic wand all his economic problems seemed to have vanished.

At the same time he received word from the chief editor of the *National Geographic*, who remembered his article, 'Turning Back Time in the South Seas', six years previously. The editor told him to apply to the directors of the Geographic Society for support for his voyage, as it would no doubt result in an interesting article.

Convinced that the economic obstacles were now surmounted, Thor burnt all his bridges and started his preparations. He even spent the money set aside for his own return ticket to Europe. With the same youthful optimism, Herman resigned his job as a thermoelectrical engineer and threw himself wholeheartedly into helping with the preparations.

First of all they had to look for a crew. Thor had reduced his original estimate of twelve paddlers by half, since he was now convinced that the steady trade wind would give sufficient propulsion to the raft. He and Herman were both landlubbers, so they had to find someone experienced in navigation who could plot the daily drift on a map. The crew had to be well qualified and have strong nerves, first and foremost. Thor could think of three such men. He recalled his boyhood friend, Erik Hesselberg, who had been his companion on strenuous mountain trips. Erik, who had later graduated from navigation school, was now an artist. He had a sailor's experience, played a guitar, and was full of fun. Thor also remembered those daring wartime radio operators, Knut Haugland and Torstein Raaby, alias Lieutenant 'Pettersen'. He wrote to them all. Torstein replied by telegram in one word: 'Coming.' Knut and Erik, too, accepted. They all bought tickets to America with money borrowed from Thor's father, who also undertook to support the families of Erik, Herman, and Thor for the duration of the expedition.

Finding the sixth member of the crew was a problem. One man after another was considered and tested, but something was always wrong.

While Thor and Herman were busy with their preparations, a new assistant to the Norwegian military attaché arrived in Washington. He turned out to be Thor's wartime superior, Captain Björn Rörholt. Thor informed him of the plan, and asked him to find out whether the American Army had any field rations or other gear they wanted tested. Rörholt mentioned the matter to the Norwegian military attaché, Colonel Otto Munthe-Kaas, who got in touch with the foreign liaison section of the American War Department. Arrangements were made for Thor and Herman to go to Washington for a meeting in the Pentagon on December 26th.

So far they both had striven to avoid public attention, but when they arrived at the Pentagon with its thirty thousand clerks and sixteen miles of corridors, the public relations officer had invited a large number of reporters to create maximum publicity. The meeting with Colonel Lewis and other members of the quartermaster general's staff was most re-warding, until the colonel said they must have a talk with the 'boss' before they could be issued with the equipment and field rations they required.

The boss was a serious little officer with keen blue eyes.

'Well, what do these gentlemen want?' he asked the colonel, without taking his eyes off Thor.

'Oh, a few little things', answered the colonel, and stated the case briefly and clearly.

'And what can they give us in return?'

'Well', said the colonel in a conciliatory tone, 'we hoped that the expedition would be able to write reports on the new provisions and some of the equipment, based on the severe conditions in which they will be using it.'

The intensely earnest officer behind the desk leaned back in his chair with unaffected slowness, with his eyes still fixed on Thor's, and said coolly:

'I don't see at all how they can give us anything in return.'

There was dead silence in the room. Colonel Lewis fingered his collar.

'But', the chief suddenly broke out, 'courage and enterprise count too. Colonel Lewis, let them have the things!'

This was fantastic and Thor heard it all as in a dream. He was hardly aware of what went on at the unexpected press conference that followed, and he still felt he was dreaming as he and Herman rode back to their hotel in a cab. But by now it had become an evil dream for he knew that at this very moment the news about the raft expedition was being sent to all main American newspapers, and would spread from them all over the world. Yet, just before the meeting at the Pentagon, something had happened that had made the whole plan collapse like a house of cards. What actually happened was a mystery, and has never been properly explained. Only one thing was certain: all those who had promised financial help suddenly got cold feet.

The trio who had offered to provide the backing for exclusive rights to the story withdrew with the empty excuse that the young man whose flat they had visited was ill in bed. The president of the North American Newspaper Alliance was still willing to contribute £700 for newspaper rights, but the money would be paid in two instalments, the first when the raft was halfway across, the second when the voyage was completed. What, asked Thor, could the expedition do with a cheque in the middle of the Pacific? It was *now* that the money was needed—immediately. Simultaneously a letter came from the chief editor of the *National Geographic* stating that the technical consultants of the board had advised against any support, because the planned expedition was sheer suicide. The Norwegian multimillionaire who had guaranteed a loan if everything else failed, suddenly refused to assist, and an urgent appeal to the other persons who had promised support resulted in the advice that Thor ought to approach 'American business'. The final showdown with his financial backers had come earlier that morning, but now that the news was released Thor neither could nor would give up. It was too late to postpone the project.

That same evening Thor scribbled some lines on a sheet of notepaper headed Wardman Park Hotel, Washington, put the sheet in an envelope which he sealed, then wrote on it: '26/12/1946. To be opened in due course of time. T.H.'

The envelope was opened by the author of this book on November 19, 1962. The note read:

'Let this be just a page of a diary. Let the day be December 26, 1946, for never in my life have such great contrasts been set side by side on one and the same day. Success and humiliation have followed one another step by step for many years, and in turn. Today they have both risen side by side to dangerous heights, so dangerous that one of them must collapse in the next few days. For long months I have been moving alone in a metropolis with a manuscript which no one would read. Day by day my money grew less. Before it was too late, I decided on the raft trip and staked my whole life on the plan, leaving no way of retreat open, in order to be able to concentrate on the way forward. I've gone straight ahead as never before in my life, I have *believed* and *willed* and the obstacles have collapsed, one after another, until today. Many are still willing to contribute their name, some are willing to contribute from the government's abundance. But no one is willing to give anything of his own. We have arrived at a point where we have attracted abundant interest, have obtained most of the important equipment, but have not a penny with which to start the expedition. The snowball has rolled too quickly; we could not stop it, for then the whole expedition would crumble to nothing. What has been done hitherto has been necessary to get money and to make the machinery work. Today that side of the proceedings culminated in an official "release" from the War Department and with a press conference at which all American news agencies were represented.

'After the meeting we all separated: the Americans, the Norwegian military attaché, Rörholt, and Watzinger. Back in the hotel I made the following calculation: my cash in hand amounts to $35.35, all that remains of $200 which I borrowed from Rörholt when I ran short of money on my arrival in Washington. I am to return to New York tomorrow evening. My $35.35 is not even sufficient to pay the hotel bill here. Watzinger has twenty dollars left. That is not enough for his hotel and his food. . . .

At the moment I can see no possibility of getting any money at all. . . . This is the day after Christmas, 1946, and I am alone. There is one way forward and none back. I *believe* it will work out; and I am determined that it *shall* work out. But I should like to remember this day, this struggle and this experience for the rest of my life till the day I shall be forced to give up my very breath.'

Colonel Munthe-Kaas, the military attaché, evidently guessed that something was wrong. He turned up unexpectedly the next morning and straightforwardly asked if the boys were in trouble. When he heard of their plight he quietly pulled out a cheque book and a pen, and offered Thor a loan of £350, an amount sufficient to help them over the first obstacle.

Once the colonel had identified himself with the cause, others gained faith in the enterprise too, and Thor was given more loans. He now also received a letter from Gyldendal Norsk Forlag, the publishers of his book on Fatu Hiva, who said they were prepared to invest four thousand Norwegian kroner in a future book on the expedition.

The days that followed became a period of triumph mixed with despair. Very slowly the money from loans increased, which carried the preparations forward step by step. Yet Thor knew that some day these loans had to be repaid with interest, and sometimes he felt he was tottering on the brink of financial disaster. Still, he pressed on with faith and confidence. It *must* work out. It *had* to work out. And it *did* work out. Gradually the private loans were big enough to permit Thor and Herman to book their passage to South America, where they were to start building the raft.

Before they left, the backing in equipment by the United States War Department aroused interest in official British quarters too, and they were called to a conference at the British Military Mission in Washington. Here they were given plenty of good advice, and a selection of British equipment which had been flown over from England to be tested on the raft expedition. A British medical officer was especially anxious for them to try out a mysterious shark powder. They were merely to sprinkle a few pinches of the powder on the water if a shark became too impudent, and the shark would vanish immediately.

All told, the situation now seemed brighter than it had for a long time. In South America, however, they met new and unexpected obstacles. The greatest problem was the scarcity of whole balsa logs necessary for building the raft. They flew first to the tropical city of Guayaquil on the Pacific coast of Ecuador, which was known as the main centre of balsa exportation. The balsa tree still grows along the northwestern coast of South America, but during the war they had been felled by the thousand for use in the aircraft and deep-freeze industries, as balsa is the lightest wood in existence. Large trees could now be found only in the interior jungle. Since none could be purchased in the saw mills, Thor and Herman decided to go inland and fell the balsa trees themselves.

'Impossible', said the authorities. 'The rains have just begun, and all roads into the jungle are impassable because of floodwater and deep mud. If you want balsa wood you must come back to Ecuador in six months.'

Six months! In half a year little or no money would be left. They had to get their balsa *now*. If they could not get in through the flooded lowland jungle, they could try to get to the trees from the inland side. In a little cargo plane they flew over the jungle to Quito, the capital of Ecuador high up on the Andes plateau, 9,300 feet above sea level. Here they managed to borrow an American jeep and make their way down into the jungle. They cut twelve large, sap-filled balsa logs near the banks of the Palenque river, lashed them together with lianas into a sort of raft, and floated them down through the marshy jungle lowlands and out to the Pacific coast near Guayaquil.

Leaving Herman to organize the transport of the logs down the coast on a cargo steamer, Thor continued southwards by plane to Lima, the inland capital of Peru. The authorities there displayed great interest in the plan. On instructions from his Excellency Don José Bustamante y Rivero, President of the Republic, the Minister of Marine gave permission for the raft to be built within the area of the naval harbour at Callao.

On the same day the Lima newspapers wrote about the Norwegian raft expedition that was to set out from Peru. A few hours later Thor was visited by a red-bearded Swede who introduced himself as Bengt Danielsson and said he was a sociologist who had come up the coast to Peru by canoe after an expedition among the jungle Indians of the Amazon regions. He had read about the raft project and would like to join it. Thor knew nothing about the man except that he was a graduate of Uppsala University, but he needed a sixth man, and 'if a solitary Swede had the pluck to go out on a raft with five Norwegians, he could not be squeamish'. And not even that imposing beard could hide his placid nature and gay humour. Also, he was then the only one of the six who could speak Spanish.

By this time Knut Haugland and Torstein Raaby had arrived in Washington. Björn Rörholt had interested the Radio Amateur League of America to listen in for weather and other reports from the raft, and Knut and Torstein were now busy assembling the transmission equipment. Leaving Bengt to purchase hemp ropes and other necessities in Lima, Thor flew back to join the others in Washington, where there were a thousand things to be done. In a room set aside for them in the Norwegian embassy the piles of papers in the files grew. 'Military and civilian documents—white, yellow, and blue—in English, Spanish, French and Norwegian. Even a raft trip had to cost the paper industry half a fir tree in our practical age! Laws and regulations tied our hands everywhere, and knot after knot had to be loosened in turn.' In the paper work they had the assistance of Gerd Vold, the popular London secretary of the Norwegian parachute saboteurs during the war. She was now secretary for the expedition and would be the contact on the mainland after the raft put to sea.

At length all preparations in Washington were complete, and they flew to Lima, where Erik Hesselberg had arrived with his guitar from Oslo via Panama. Herman had now reached Callao with the logs, and for the first time the six members of the expedition were all assembled. Although Thor knew them all, none of the others had met before, and all were entirely different types. Each had an exciting life behind him, so weeks would pass before they tired of each other's stories. It was the danger of mental friction Thor feared most, the nervous strain on six men forced to share cramped quarters day and night for an undetermined period.

The men wasted no time in moving into the Callao naval yard. To assist in the raft construction, they hired some Peruvian seamen with Inca blood in their veins. Never had modern man seen such a strange craft as the one now being built. An exact copy of the old rafts of Peru and Ecuador began to take shape among the destroyers and submarines in the naval base. Nine balsa logs, two feet in diameter, were lashed together with lengths of rope and, across these, thinner logs were placed at intervals of about three feet. Deep grooves were cut in the circumference of the logs to prevent the ropes from slipping. The longest log, running from bow to stern, was forty-five feet in length. Shorter and shorter logs were laid symmetrically on both sides of it, so that the bow stuck out like a blunt plough. Astern, the raft was cut off straight across, except for the three middle logs which projected and supported a thick block of balsa wood that held the tholepins for the long steering oar.

A cabin was erected amidships to shelter the crew, their personal possessions, the radio equipment, and the meteorological and hydrographic instruments. It measured eight by fourteen feet, and to diminish the pressure of wind and sea it was built so low that a man could not stand upright under the ridge of the roof. Walls and roof were made of strong bamboo canes lashed together and guyed. The walls were covered by a tough wickerwork of plaited bamboo reeds, and the roof was of bamboo slats with leathery banana leaves overlapping one another like tiles. The floor, of split bamboo, was also covered with wickerwork in the form of loose mats. The open doorway was in the centre of the starboard side.

Only a part of the raft was decked with split bamboo and wickerwork; on the port side, in the bow, and in the stern, the logs were not decked in at all.

A large bipod mast of heavy mangrove wood, on which the square sail was to be hoisted on a bamboo boom, was raised forward of the cabin.

Five solid fir planks one inch thick and two feet wide were pushed down at various places where there were large chinks between the logs so that they stood on their edges in the water under the raft. This form of keel, or *guara*, was used by the Incas on all of their rafts for navigational purposes.

In the whole construction of the raft not a single spike, nail, or wire rope was used. It was laboriously fastened together with about three hundred different lengths of one-inch and quarter-inch hemp rope, each firmly knotted.

The Peruvian Minister of Marine was horrified when he saw the craft for the first time. He summoned Thor to his office and requested him to sign a paper freeing the navy from all responsibility for the construction of the raft.

The projected voyage produced a variety of reactions from specialists and the general public alike. Many thought it was simply the product of a boyish thirst for adventure. Others thought it a mere advertising stunt. Most people laughed at the whole business, and continued to laugh even when the raft was a good way out at sea.

But a large group of professional sailors and scientists were not amused; they regarded the experiment with fear and foreboding. Ahead lay a whole complexity of known and unknown perils. The heavy and violent storms in southern latitudes could tear both sail and rigging from the raft. Waves as high as battleships could reduce the logs to matchwood. The raft could be driven off course and lie adrift long after the provisions had been exhausted. Hurricanes could wash the crew overboard, or they might be sucked down into the depths by giant octopuses that climbed on board at night. Even in an ordinary sea the crew would be wet continually, the skin would be worn off their feet, and everything on board would be ruined.

An admiral who inspected the raft thought they would never come out alive. The measurements were completely wrong! She was so small that the waves would capsize her, and so long that she would ride on the crests of two waves at the same time and then the brittle logs would break under the strain. One of Peru's leading exporters of balsa shared Dr Lothrop's view that the porous logs would become so waterlogged in a short time that they would sink. The skipper and two experienced old salts on a Norwegian ship in the harbour looked as glum as undertakers when they set eyes on the raft. It couldn't even be steered! It would take a year or more to drift across with the Humboldt current—if indeed she kept afloat so long. The boatswain took one glance at the lashings joining the logs together and shook his head. They would be worn through in less than a fortnight by the continuous up and down movement of the logs.

An ambassador of one of the Great Powers made a last earnest effort to dissuade Thor. He appealed to his sense of responsibility, spoke of his wife and children, and finally said desperately:

'Your mother and father will be very grieved when they hear of your death.'

In the midst of all these warnings of impending disaster came these encouraging lines:

'I only wish I knew you were all six safe on board the raft.'

The writer was Fru Alison.

Chapter 13

THE *KON-TIKI* ODYSSEY

ON April 27, 1947, all flags were hoisted on the raft. The Norwegian flag fluttered on a bamboo pole astern and the banner of the Explorers Club waved at the masthead, surrounded by the colourful flags of the nations which had in some way supported the project.

The expedition was again running short of money. Some ropes and provisions had been stolen and had to be replaced at considerable expense. For this reason work had been accelerated and the day of departure moved forward to avoid further living expenses ashore. Nevertheless, the quay was black with spectators the day the raft was to be christened. In the front line were representatives of the Peruvian government and navy, the Ambassadors of the United States, Great Britain, France, China, Argentina, and Cuba, the ex-Governor of the British colonies in the Pacific, the Swedish and Belgian ministers, and friends from the little Norwegian colony in Lima with the consul general at their head. Autograph hunters flocked around to get signatures of the crew, perhaps because they felt this was their last and only chance! 'There were swarms of journalists and clicking of movie cameras; indeed, the only things that were lacking were a brass band and a big drum. One thing was quite clear to all of us—that if the raft went to pieces outside the bay we would paddle to Polynesia, each of us on a log, rather than dare come back there again.'

The raft was christened with coconut milk *Kon-Tiki* after the legendary sun-king who had led his fair-skinned people westward to Polynesia more than 1,500 years ago. Milk and bits of kernel filled the hair of all those who stood reverently around.

The next day, April 28th, the *Kon-Tiki* was towed out to sea by the tug *Guardian Rios*. Immediately outside the harbour mole, high seas were encountered, and all the small boats which had accompanied the raft, turned back one by one. The *Kon-Tiki* followed the tug 'like an angry billy goat on a rope'. Finally the tow rope broke, and while the men were trying to splice it, the raft ran in under the stern of the tug and had her bow knocked askew by the propeller.

On the following day they entered the Humboldt Current which comes up from the Antarctic, sweeps its cold waters along the coast of Chile and Peru, and swings west just below the equator. The tug heaved to, cast off the tow rope, and the *Kon-Tiki* was left alone. The sail was hoisted, but hung slack, showing Kon-Tiki's bearded head painted in red by Erik, a copy of an ancient stone statue of the god at Tiahuanaco. When the *Guardian Rios* disappeared over the horizon, the raft still lay dipping up and down on the same spot. But the breeze came, blowing up from the southeast, and by late afternoon the trade wind was blowing at full strength. Thor wrote in *Kon-Tiki*:

'As the troughs of the sea gradually grew deeper, it became clear that we had moved into the swiftest part of the Humboldt Current. This sea was obviously caused by a current and not simply raised by the wind. The water was green and cold and everywhere about us; the jagged mountains of Peru had vanished into the dense cloud banks astern.

'When darkness crept over the waters, our first duel with the elements began. We were still not sure of the sea; we were still uncertain whether it would show itself a friend or an enemy in the intimate proximity we ourselves had sought. When, swallowed up by the darkness, we heard the general noise from the sea around us suddenly deafened by the hiss of a roller close by and saw a white crest come groping towards us on a level with the cabin roof, we held on tight and waited uneasily to feel the masses of water smash down over us and the raft.

'But every time there was the same surprise and relief. The *Kon-Tiki* calmly swung up her stern and rose skyward unperturbed, while the masses of water rolled along her sides. Then we sank down again into the trough of the waves and waited for the next big sea. The biggest seas often came two or three in succession, with a long series of smaller seas in between. It was when two big seas followed each other too closely that the second broke on board aft, because the first was still holding our bow in the air. It became, therefore, an unbreakable law that the steering watch must have ropes round their waists, the other ends of which were made fast to the raft, for there were no bulwarks. Their task was to keep the sail filled by holding stern to sea and wind.

'We had made an old boat's compass fast to a box aft so that Erik could check our course and calculate our position and speed. For the time being it was uncertain where we were, for the sky was overclouded and the horizon one single chaos of rollers. Two men at a time took turns as steering watch and, side by side, they had to put all their strength into the fight with the leaping oar, while the rest of us tried to snatch a little sleep inside the open bamboo cabin.

'When a really big sea came, the men at the helm left the steering to the ropes and, jumping up, hung on to a bamboo pole from the cabin roof, while the masses of water thundered in over them from astern and disappeared between the logs or over the side of the raft. Then they had to fling themselves at the oar again before the raft could turn around and the sail thrash about. For, if the raft took the seas at an angle, the waves could easily pour right into the bamboo cabin. When they came from astern, they disappeared between the projecting logs at once and seldom came so far forward as the cabin wall. The round logs astern let the water pass as if through the prongs of a fork. The advantage of a raft was obviously this: the more leaks the better. Through the gaps in our floor the water ran out but never in.'

As the days and nights passed, the six men steadily gained confidence in their raft. What did it matter if a mountain of water rose high around them, so long as they now knew the raft stayed on top? However, the next question was—how long could they count on it staying on top?

As the raft approached the Galápagos islands, six hundred miles off Ecuador, it was clear that the balsa logs absorbed water. The aft crossbeam was worse than the others; one's whole finger tip could be pressed into the soaked wood till the water squelched. Without saying anything Thor broke off a piece of the sodden wood and threw it overboard. It sank quietly beneath the surface and slowly vanished down into the depths. Later he saw the other fellows do exactly the same thing when they thought no one was looking. They stood looking reverently at the waterlogged piece of wood sinking quietly into the green water. They had noted the water line on the raft when they started, but in the rough sea it was impossible to see how deep the craft lay, for one moment the logs were lifted out of the water and the next they went deep down into it. But when a knife was driven into the timber, the wood was found to be dry an inch or so below the surface. All they could hope for was that the sap further in would act as an impregnation and check the absorption.

There was another question that troubled their minds at first—whether the ropes holding the logs together would bear the strain. All night they heard them creaking and groaning, chafing and squeaking. It was like one single complaining chorus round them in the dark, each tone having its own note according to its thickness and tautness. Every morning they made a thorough inspection. But the ropes held. The balsa wood was so soft that the ropes wore their way slowly into the wood and were protected, instead of the logs wearing the ropes.

After a week or so the sea grew calmer, and they noticed that it became blue instead of green. They began to go west-northwest instead of north-west, and took this as the first faint sign that they had got out of the coastal current and had some hope of being carried out to sea. For hours at a time it was just fair weather sailing across a sea teeming with fish. Tunnies, bonitos, dolphins, and unknown kinds of fish gambolled round the raft in shoals, and flying fish shot through the air and landed with a thud on the deck.

Hardly a day passed without the raft receiving visits from astonishing or alarming creatures from the deep. The book on the *Kon-Tiki* voyage, in spite of all its graphic descriptions, is actually no more than a modest extract from the logbook, which is now displayed in the Kon-Tiki Museum in Oslo. Almost every day something unexpected showed up from the depths. The logbook relates:

'6/5 10.45. Thor was working with fishing tackle on the port side, when he heard a snorting as from a horse beside him. Turning around he saw a great whale right beside the raft. It dived and shortly thereafter three porpoises surfaced. Then whales and porpoises appeared everywhere. Shoals of three or four of the big whales at a time came right up to the side of the raft, so close that only part of the whale was visible in the view-finder of the camera. . . . The greatest whales were longer than our raft, and one huge one approached us from the port bow breathing and snorting each time it came up. Six feet from where we were standing, it dived and the huge shining black body went down under us. There it stopped, and standing on the edge of the raft the whale was just under our feet. Then it sank deeper and disappeared.'

The quantity of fish was astounding. In five minutes they caught more than they could eat in two days.

Sharks, too, paid them many visits. One day Herman was standing at the helm, barefooted as usual, water constantly pouring over the steering platform, when an eight-foot blue shark bobbed up just beside him. The mysterious 'shark powder' would have been useful at that point, but shortly before they left Lima, it had been stolen by Peruvian *mestizos*, who no doubt thought it was some kind of flour or soup powder.

Here is an entry in the logbook about an encounter with a brown shark:

'Erik yelled, "Shark!" Herman and Knut grabbed one hand harpoon and Thor another. A ten-foot brown shark with a great head was following us at a distance of about fifteen feet. Erik tied a rope around the tail of a dolphin and threw it out. Quietly the shark approached the bait, which Erik pulled in towards the raft. The shark continued to follow slowly, and the third time Erik pulled the bait in, the shark was only three feet from Thor's toes as he stood on the edge of the stern logs. Thor struck and felt his harpoon slide into the neck of the shark. The shaft was wrested out of his hands, but he managed to hold the line tight only four feet from the shark's broad head. Knut threw his harpoon at the head which was so hard that it bent the quarter-inch galvanized iron shank and made it useless. Thor held the shark for a minute or two until it became furious and tried to dive. He slackened the line, then twisted it around one of the logs astern so the others could strike with another harpoon. But the shark turned, bit through the line and disappeared.'

The marine creature against which the experts had warned them the most was the giant octopus, which could get onto the raft. The National Geographic Society in Washington had produced reports and a magnesium photograph from an area in the Humboldt Current where great numbers were to be found. For protection each of the crew armed himself with a long machete knife which he took with him into his sleeping bag at night. Yet they were to see few of these monsters, and then mostly just the shine of phosphorescent eyes staring at them from the water after dark. But their offspring, the small jet-propelled squids, often came aboard, gliding through the air like flying fish, escaping from pursuing shoals of dolphins, and landing on deck or on the roof of the cabin.

On a couple of occasions the raft sailed over a great dark mass like a reef under the surface of the ocean. Presumably, this was the dreaded giant ray, but they never got close enough to make out its shape clearly.

About four o'clock one morning Torstein, who slept with his head in the doorway of the cabin, was awakened by something long and wet wriggling on his pillow. Herman woke at the same moment and caught hold of it— a snake-like fish nearly three feet long, with dull black eyes, a long snout and a jaw full of needle-sharp teeth. Bengt was the last to be awakened. The others held the paraffin lamp and the long fish under his nose. He sat up drowsily in his sleeping bag and said solemnly:

'No, fish like that don't exist.'

With which he went off to sleep again.

It turned out later that this fish was extremely rare, because it lived at a great depth. The crew of the *Kon-Tiki* were the first to see a living specimen. The fish was known to science only because two or three skeletons had been found on the coast of South America and the Galapágos islands. Ichthyologists called it *Gempylus* or snake mackerel. This one ended its days in a jar of formalin.

The days and weeks went by. How did these six men sailing in the sun-god's wake pass the time? Certainly not idly. There was always some job to be done. Each had a regular two-hour watch at the helm. In fair weather the steersman might doze for the greater part of the watch, but in heavy seas the work was hard and dangerous; then he had to get help to keep a steady course.

Thor was constantly busy with observations and experiments. He studied the effect of the *guaras* and other aspects of the balsa raft, he recorded the expedition's daily life on 16 mm. film, wrote a detailed log-book, experimented with fishing methods and the extraction of thirst-quenching fluids from raw fish, and collected and prepared samples of plankton and other marine life. He never tired of studying this miniature world with its countless variety of incredible shapes and colours when viewed under his magnifying glass.

Herman was in charge of the technical side of the expedition. He might be engaged in observations at any time of day or night—at the masthead with meteorological instruments, by the side of the raft with wave metre and with deep water thermometers, under the raft with diving goggles on to check the lashings and the *guaras*, or in the rubber dinghy with balloons and other strange measuring apparatus.

Bengt was appointed steward, and was responsible for the daily rations of water and food. Cooking duty was divided equally, in accordance with a daily rota.

Knut and Torstein were fully occupied with their little radio station, tinkering with soldering irons and circuits, and using every device they knew to keep the transmitter going. In spite of many difficulties, they sent out the promised weather observations nearly every day, which were picked up by 'hams' and passed on to the Meteorological Institute in Washington and other destinations.

Erik, the only trained seaman on board, took daily readings of the raft's position, course, and speed. At other times he was usually patching sails and splicing ropes, or carving in wood and drawing sketches of bearded men and odd fish. In the evenings he brought out his guitar and entertained the others with sea shanties and hula tunes.

It was most remarkable what a psychological effect the shaky bamboo cabin, built so low that they could not stand upright under the ridge of the roof, had on their minds. Even though the doorway was only five feet from the unprotected edge of the raft and only a foot and a half above the water line, they felt as if they had travelled many miles away from the sea and occupied a jungle dwelling, once they had crawled inside the door. They could lie and look up at the roof, enjoying the jungle smell of raw wood, bamboo, and withered palm leaves.

For their leisure hours, friends had given them a bundle of detective stories, but Erik, who suffered a little from rheumatism, used them to plug the largest cracks in the bamboo walls of the cabin. On the other hand, Bengt's textbooks on sociology and Herman's on thermodynamics were industriously studied. Most of the time, though, was spent in discussing philosophical subjects and, like so many before them, they tried to solve problems of international policy. They came to the conclusion that in times of crisis statesmen should take a raft trip together.

Thus the days went by, and most of the time this remarkable company of bearded white men felt happy and comfortable on their prehistoric vessel.

But what Thor had always feared most of all—the psychological strain of being cooped up, day in and day out, in a world made up of nine balsa logs and nothing else but water, water everywhere—was smouldering in the minds of some of them and, at times, threatened to become dangerous. Thor had announced at the start that he expected that every one of them would go through a period of crisis. When it came they must keep to themselves as much as was possible and make the best of the situation until their good spirits returned. Such times of depression did occur. For two or three days, one or other of them would go about silent and glum. But they fought through it, and if harsh words were spoken Thor was there at once to smooth things out. He had gone through it all time after time in his imagination, just as he had lived through every aspect of the journey. The surprising qualities of the balsa raft, its daily progress towards their objective, and the variety of new, exciting experience, broke the monotony and bound the six ever more closely together.

As Knut was washing clothes one day, he was confronted by the sight of the biggest and ugliest face he had ever seen:

'It was the head of a veritable sea monster, so huge and so hideous that, if the Old Man of the Sea himself had come up, he could not have made such an impression on us. The head was broad and flat like a frog's, with two small eyes right at the sides, and a toadlike jaw which was four or five feet wide and had long fringes hanging drooping from the corners of the mouth. Behind the head was an enormous body ending in a long thin tail with a pointed tail fin which stood straight up and showed that this sea monster was not any kind of whale. The body looked brownish under the water, but both head and body were thickly covered with small white

29. Drawings of balsa rafts which sailed along the coasts of the Inca Empire.
Top: A drawing by Juan and Ulloa, 1748.
Bottom: A drawing by Alexander von Humboldt, 1810.
30. (*next page*) Balsa logs for the raft had to be cut deep in the primaeval forest.
31. (*next page*) Herman and a native preparing food on the logs drifting down the Palanque River to the coast.

30

31

spots. The monster came quietly, lazily swimming after us from astern. It grinned like a bulldog and lashed gently with its tail.'

It was a whale shark, the largest fish known in the world today. Only a few specimens have been seen in the tropical oceans, and this monster was probably one of the largest. When it swam under the raft, its head was visible on one side, while its tail was still sticking out on the other.

The giant shark again and again described narrower and narrower circles just under the raft for what seemed like an eternity, often lifting the steering oar clear out of the water; and the men realized that it had enough strength in its tail to smash the raft to pieces if it attacked.

At last it became too exciting for Erik, who was standing at a corner of the raft with an eight-foot hand harpoon. He raised the harpoon above his head and thrust it with all his giant strength deep into the broad and grisly head below him. In a flash the placid monster was transformed into a mountain of steel muscles. The harpoon line rushed over the edge of the raft, flung three of the crew head over heels, and flayed and burned two of them as it rushed through the air. Then the thick line, strong enough to hold a boat, was caught up in the side of the raft but snapped at once like a piece of twine, and a few seconds later a broken-off harpoon shaft came up to the surface two hundred yards away. They never saw the whale shark again.

On July 4th the *Kon-Tiki* sailed into her first storm. It began with a black bank of clouds to the south and treacherous squalls from all directions. Then the gale fell upon them in full force. In an incredibly short time the seas round them were flung up to a height of fifteen feet, while single crests were hissing twenty and twenty-five feet above the trough of the sea. The men watched these towering waves with anxiety. Their foaming crests were the level of the masthead when they themselves were down in the trough. The silence of the crew struggling with ropes and sail reflected for a while their feeling of insecurity, but as the astonishing raft took everything with ease, the combat with the storm became an exciting form of sport.

'The sea had much in common with the mountains in such weather. It was like being out in the real highlands in a storm, up on the highest mountain crests, naked and grey. Even though we were right in the heart of the tropics, when the raft climbed to glide down from a high crest in the smoking waste of the sea, we always thought of racing downhill among the snowdrifts and rock faces.'

32. (*previous page*) The raft was made of nine balsa logs lashed together with rope.
33. Each shark killed was another enemy less in case someone fell overboard.
34. The bamboo cabin protected the men against the wind and the tropical sun. From left: Watzinger, Haugland, Raaby, Danielsson and Heyerdahl.

After twenty-four hours the storm dropped to just a stiff breeze, and when the weather moderated the sea was teeming with fish.

The sharks in particular approached the raft in great numbers, chasing the dolphins and bonitos that swam close to the raft. In one day they dragged, hooked, and hauled nine large sharks up on the slippery logs. For each shark disposed of there was one less waiting in case a man fell overboard. There was blood everywhere—on the logs and in the water, and live and dead fish everywhere, sharks, dolphins, tunnies, bonitos, flying fish, and squids, all wriggling about under the logs or on top of the bamboo deck. The next day, only the sharks were still numerous. When the men got into their sleeping bags on those nights and closed their eyes, they still saw ferocious shark jaws and water tinged with blood. Someone made the remark that it would soon be good to stretch out comfortably on the green grass of a palm island and to see something other than cold fish and rough sea.

The squally weather continued. A few days later Torstein's sleeping bag was caught by a gust of wind and went over the side. Herman tried to grab it but missed his footing and fell overboard. Although he was an excellent swimmer, the heavy seas gave him no chance to keep up with the raft, and before the rubber dinghy could be launched, he was already on a level with the steering oar, which he reached for but could not hold onto. Knut and Erik threw out the life belt on its long rope, but the wind was so strong that it was simply blown back to the raft every time. By now Herman was far astern, swimming desperately to keep up, while the distance increased with each gust of wind.

Then suddenly Knut plunged into the sea with the life belt in one hand. He and Herman swam towards each other until they were both clinging to the life belt at the end of the line. Knut waved his arm and all four on board took hold of the line and hauled for dear life, their eyes fixed on a dark object just visible behind the two men. A greenish-black triangle was being pushed above the wave crests.

It was not until the two were safely back on board that they learned from Herman that the triangle did not belong to a shark or any other sea monster. It was an inflated corner of Torstein's watertight sleeping bag. But the sleeping bag did not remain floating for long. Whatever dragged it down into the depths had just missed a better prey.

They did not have much time to discuss the incident; for before evening they ran into another storm. For five whole days the weather alternated between full storm and light gale; the sea was dug up into wide valleys filled with smoke from foaming grey-blue seas. On the fifth day the sky cleared and the storm passed on. The steering oar had been smashed and the sail torn, and the *guaras* hung loose and banged about among the logs. But the men themselves were unhurt, and the balsa raft still floated like a cork. After this second storm, however, the *Kon-Tiki* had become weaker in the joints. In fact, the strain had stretched all the ropes, which in turn had dug themselves deeper into the balsa wood. Thor recorded:

'We thanked Providence that we had followed the Incas' custom and had not used wire ropes, which would simply have sawed the whole raft into matchwood in the gale. And, if we had used bone-dry, high-floating balsa at the start, the raft would long ago have sunk into the sea under us, saturated with sea water. It was the sap in the fresh logs which served as an impregnation and prevented the water from filtering in through the porous balsa wood.'

Towards the end of the third month they got the first signs that there was land ahead somewhere out in this boundless ocean ahead of them. First they spotted some frigate birds; then in the stomach of a shark they found an undigested starfish, a certain sign of coastal waters ahead. Finally, two large boobies were sighted to the west who had come straight from the Polynesian islands. From then on they observed an increasing number of sea birds every day.

On July 30th Herman took over the watch from the masthead just at sunrise. A few moments later he was down the rope ladder again, waking the others; the first island was visible as a short blue pencil line against the red morning sky behind them. This had to be the atoll of Puka Puka, the first outpost of the Tuamotu group, and they had passed it in the night. The trade wind and the current carried the raft farther on into Polynesia, although they tried to change course to get back to Puka Puka. A column of smoke began to rise from the atoll, and soon the men were able to catch a faint scent of burned wood and of leaves and greenery as Puka Puka sank into the sea behind them.

On August 3rd another coral island, identified as Angatau, was sighted, and they set their course for it. However, as they got closer, they realized there was a dangerous coral reef a hundred yards from land. They circled the atoll, hoping to find an opening through which they could reach the palm-fringed shore. All day they zigzagged along Angatau; it was beautiful at close quarters, but inaccessible. Towards evening they saw a canoe being launched on the other side of the reef. It shot through a passage and headed straight for them, paddled by two natives. They came on board the *Kon-Tiki* and tried to help paddle it towards the opening in the reef, but a wind blew up and they could make little headway even when more natives appeared and tried towing the *Kon-Tiki* from their out-rigger canoes.

Knut decided to go in the dinghy to fetch more help from land. He was taken to a native village where the islanders did all they could to tempt him with fruit and girls, hoping that all the white men would decide to spend some time on the island. Knut's sign language did not suffice to make them realize that the strange craft now drifting further and further out to sea had no propeller and was unable to return to their island. It was completely dark before he managed to persuade three canoe-loads of natives to guide him back through the reef and only through signals flashed from the mast were they able to find and catch up with the drifting raft. Knut was therefore the only one who had landed in Polynesia after exactly ninety-seven days on the raft, the period calculated by Captain Eitrem and Thor in New York.

Three days later the raft was drifting towards the dangerous Takume and Raroia reefs. Although the crew made great effort to steer clear, and for awhile it looked as if they would succeed, as the dawn rose on their hundred and first day at sea the watch hurried into the cabin and roused all hands: Land ahead!

The wind had changed and they were drifting straight towards the Raroia coral reef, lying partly above and partly under water, like a mole where the sea was white with foam and leaped high into the sky. Behind the reef idyllic islets lay in a string around the still lagoon inside. It was obvious that they had now only a few hours more on board the *Kon-Tiki*. Everything was prepared for the push through the thundering inferno ahead. Each man was told precisely what he was to do. Life itself was at stake, and there was not a minute to waste. Torstein was trying desperately to get in touch with a radio 'ham' on Rarotonga in the Cook Islands, with whom he'd made contact the day before, while the others made an improvised anchor of scrap and tied it to their longest rope.

Thor's last entry in the log ran:

'9.50. Very close now. Drifting along the reef. Only a hundred yards or so away. Torstein is talking to the man on Rarotonga. All clear. Must pack up log now. All in good spirits; it looks bad, *but we shall make it!*'

The dramatic moments that followed are narrated by Thor himself.

'A few minutes later the anchor rushed overboard and caught hold of the bottom, so that the *Kon-Tiki* swung around and turned her stern inwards toward the breakers. It held us for a few valuable minutes, while Torstein sat hammering like mad on the key. He had got Rarotonga now. The breakers thundered in the air and the sea rose and fell furiously. All hands were at work on deck, and now Torstein got his message through. He said we were drifting towards the Raroia reef. He asked Rarotonga to listen in on the same wave length every hour. If we were silent for more than thirty-six hours, Rarotonga must let the Norwegian Embassy in Washington know. Torstein's last words were:

' "O.K. Fifty yards left. Here we go. Good-bye."

'Then he closed down the station. Knut sealed up the papers, and both crawled out on deck as fast as they could to join the rest of us, for it was clear now that the anchor was giving way.

'The swell grew heavier and heavier, with deep troughs between the waves, and we felt the raft being swung up and down, up and down, higher and higher.

'Again the order was shouted: "Hold on! Never mind about the cargo. Hold on!"

'We were now so near the waterfall inside that we no longer heard the steady continuous roar from all along the reef. We now heard only a separate boom each time the nearest breaker crashed down on the rocks.

'All hands stood in readiness, each clinging fast to the rope he thought most secure. . . .

'When we realized that the seas had got hold of us, the anchor rope was cut, and we were off. A sea rose straight up under us, and we felt the *Kon-Tiki* being lifted up in the air. The great moment had come; we were riding on the waveback at breathless speed, our ramshackle craft creaking and groaning as she quivered under us. The excitement made one's blood boil. I remember that, having no other inspiration, I waved my arm and bellowed "Hurrah!" at the top of my lungs: it afforded a certain relief and could do no harm anyway. The others certainly thought I had gone mad, but they all beamed and grinned enthusiastically. On we ran with the next enormous sea rushing in behind us; this was the *Kon-Tiki's* baptism of fire: all must and would go well.

'But our elation was soon dampened. A new sea rose high up astern of us like a glittering green glass wall. As we sank down it came tumbling after us, and in the same second in which I saw it high above me, I felt a violent blow and was submerged under floods of water. I felt the suction through my whole body, with such great power that I had to strain every single muscle in my frame and think of one thing only—hold on, hold on! . . . Then I felt that the mountain of water was passing on and relaxing its devilish grip on my body. When the whole mountain had rushed on, with an ear-splitting roaring and crashing, I saw Knut again hanging on beside me, doubled up into a ball. Seen from behind, the great sea was almost flat and grey. As it rushed on, it swept over the ridge of the cabin roof which projected from the water, and there hung the three others, pressed against the cabin roof as the water passed over them.

'We were still afloat.

'In an instant I renewed my hold, with arms and legs bent round the strong rope . . . but at the same time I saw a new green wall rise up and come towering towards us. I shouted a warning and made myself as small and hard as I could where I hung. And in an instant hell was over us again, and the *Kon-Tiki* disappeared completely under the masses of water. The sea tugged and pulled with all the force it could bring to bear at the poor little bundles of human bodies. The second sea rushed over us, to be followed by a third like it. . . .

'Then I saw the next sea come towering up, higher than all the rest, and again I bellowed a warning aft to the others as I climbed up the stay as high as I could get in a hurry and hung on fast. Then I myself disappeared sideways into the midst of the green wall which towered high over us. The others, who were farther aft and saw me disappear first, estimated the height of the wall of water at twenty-five feet, while the foaming crest passed fifteen feet above the part of the glassy wall into which I had vanished. Then the great wave reached them, and we had all one single thought—hold on, hold on, hold, hold, hold!

'We must have hit the reef that time. I myself felt only the strain on the stay, which seemed to bend and slacken jerkily. But whether the bumps came from above or below I could not tell, hanging there. The whole submersion lasted only seconds, but it demanded more endurance than we usually have in our bodies. There is greater strength in the human mechanism than that of the muscles alone. I determined, that if I was to die, I would die in this position, like a knot on the stay. The sea thundered on, over and past, and as it roared by it revealed a hideous sight. The *Kon-Tiki* was wholly changed, as by the stroke of a magic wand. The vessel we knew from weeks and months at sea was no more; in a few seconds our pleasant world had become a shattered wreck.

'I saw only one man on board besides myself. He lay pressed flat across the ridge of the cabin roof, face downward with his arms stretched out on both sides, while the cabin itself was crushed in, like a house of cards, towards the stern and towards the starboard side. The motionless figure was Herman. There was no other sign of life, while the hill of water thundered by, in across the reef. . . .

'I felt cold fear run through my whole body. What was the good of my holding on? If I lost one single man here, in the run in, the whole thing would be ruined, and for the moment there was only one human figure to be seen after the last buffet. In that second Torstein's hunched-up form appeared outside the raft. He was hanging like a monkey in the ropes of the masthead, and managed to get onto the logs again, where he crawled up onto the debris forward of the cabin. Herman, too, now turned his head and gave me a forced grin of encouragement, but did not move. I bellowed in the faint hope of locating the others and heard Bengt's calm voice call out that all hands were aboard. They were lying holding onto the ropes behind the tangled barricade which the tough plaiting from the bamboo deck had built up.

'All this happened in the course of a few seconds, while the *Kon-Tiki* was being drawn out of the witches' cauldron by the backwash, and a fresh sea came rolling over her. For the last time I bellowed "Hang on!" at the top of my lungs amid the uproar, and that was all I myself did; I hung on and disappeared in the masses of water which rushed over and past me in those endless two or three seconds. That was enough for me. I saw the ends of the logs knocking and bumping against a sharp step in the coral reef without going over it. Then we were sucked out again. I also saw the two men who lay stretched out across the ridge of the cabin roof, but none of us smiled any longer. Behind the chaos of bamboo I heard a calm voice call out:

' "This won't do."

'I myself felt equally discouraged. As the masthead sank further and further out over the starboard side, I found myself hanging on to a slack line outside the raft. The next sea came. When it had gone by I was dead tired, and my only thought was to get up onto the logs and lie behind the barricade. When the backwash retreated, I saw for the first time the rugged red reef naked beneath us, and perceived Torstein standing, bent double, on gleaming red corals, holding on to a bunch of rope ends from the mast. Knut, standing aft, was about to jump. I shouted that we must all keep on the logs, and Torstein, who had been washed overboard by the pressure of the water, sprang up again like a cat.

'Two or three more seas rolled over us with diminishing force, and what happened then I do not remember, except that water foamed in and out, and I myself sank lower and lower towards the red reef over which we were being lifted in. Then only crests of foam full of salt spray came whirling in, and I was able to work my way in onto the raft, where we all made for the after end of the logs which was highest up on the reef.

'At the same moment Knut crouched down and sprang up on to the reef with the line which lay clear astern. While the backwash was running out, he waded through the whirling water some thirty yards in and stood safely at the end of the line when the next sea foamed in towards him, died down, and sank back from the flat reef like a broad stream. . . .

'Bengt had had a slight concussion when the mast fell but had managed to crawl under the wrecked cabin alongside Erik. We should all of us have been lying there if we had realized in advance how firmly the countless lashings and plaited bamboo sheets would hang on to the main logs under the pressure of water.

'Erik was now standing ready on the logs aft, and when the sea retired he, too, jumped up onto the reef. It was Herman's turn next, and then Bengt's. Each time the raft was pushed a bit further in, and, when Torstein's turn and my own came, the raft already lay so far in on the reef that there was no longer any ground for abandoning her. All hands began the work of salvage. . . .

'I shall never forget that wade across the reef towards the heavenly palm island that grew larger as it came to meet us. When I reached the sunny sand beach, I slipped off my shoes and thrust my bare toes down into the warm, bone-dry sand. It was as though I enjoyed the sight of every footprint which dug itself into the virgin sand beach that led up to the palm trunks. Soon the palm tops closed over my head, and I went on, right in towards the centre of the tiny island. Green coconuts hung under the palm tufts, and some luxuriant bushes were thickly covered with snow-white blossoms, which smelled so sweet and seductive that I felt quite faint. In the interior of the island two quite tame terns flew about my shoulders. They were as white and light as wisps of cloud. . . .

'I was completely overwhelmed. I sank down on my knees and thrust my fingers deep down into the dry warm sand.'

The strange journey was over, and all hands were alive! Once again in his life Thor was filled with a gratitude that had no boundaries. *He* had been responsible. His relief was not for his own life alone. The unshakable faith in Providence that had welled up in him in those moments of supreme peril had been the very same that had saved his life during his desperate fight for survival in the rapids above High Falls. As he lay in the warm sand watching the white clouds in the blue sky above him, he recalled one by one the times he had been saved from danger or from the depth of despair. He would never again forget that with unqualified faith nothing was impossible.

Their tiny island was barely two hundred yards across, and uninhabited. However, the palms were full of coconuts, and hermit crabs crawled everywhere. Food was no problem. It was now important to get in touch with the radio 'ham' at Rarotonga before the thirty-six hours had elapsed, to stop him from sending out appeals for rescue operations. Knut and Torstein had salvaged the soaked equipment, but to get it going was far from easy. All the components had to be detached and dried in the sun. Since all the batteries had been completely ruined, they got power from a tiny hand generator. Throughout the next day Torstein and Knut worked on the radio parts, while the others took turns at cranking the generator. It was not until after the time limit at ten o'clock in the evening had expired that they managed to make contact with Rarotonga and stop all attempts at rescue.

Some days later natives arrived in outrigger canoes from the main island of Raroia, on the other side of the big lagoon. When they returned, they took the six white men with them where they were greeted by chief Teka and his people singing, not a Polynesian song of welcome, but the Marseillaise! Their stay on Raroia was one long period of feasting and rejoicing. The six mariners in their long beards, with wreaths of flowers adorning their necks and heads, were plied with food, songs, and hula dances. This went on almost continuously until the French schooner *Tamara* arrived to take them to Tahiti where they would take the regular boat home. The *Tamara* also rescued the raft from the inside of the reef and took it in tow.

At Papeete, the capital of Tahiti, their reception was tremendous. Led by the Mayor, the whole population turned out to welcome them. One burly old Tahitian pushed through the crowd calling:

'Terai Mateata! Blue Sky!'

This was Thor's Polynesian name given him on his first visit to Tahiti ten years earlier, and the old man calling him was the one who had given him that name, his adoptive father, chief Teriieroo. No other welcome, not even the most glamorous Tahitian hula parties, could match the party given by the old chief for Thor and his friends in Teriieroo's bungalow in the Papenoo valley, which had once been Thor's first home in Polynesia.

The expedition sent a telegram to its Washington headquarters, asking whether any Norwegian ship was likely to call at Papeete in the near future. In answer a message came from Norway saying that the ship owner Lars Christensen had ordered the 4,000-tonner *Thor I* to proceed from Samoa to Tahiti to pick up the expedition and take it to America, including the raft.

'If you wish to come back to Tahiti', cried Teriieroo as the ship's whistle sounded over the island on the day of their departure, 'you must throw a wreath out into the lagoon when the boat goes!'

As the ship left, six white wreaths were floating in the blue lagoon.

Chapter 14

KON-TIKI FEVER

ON September 20, 1947, M/s *Thor I* glided under the Golden Gate bridge into San Francisco harbour. On her deck lay the *Kon-Tiki*, fringed with dried seaweed, her bow and crossbeams broken, but otherwise in surprisingly good condition. The hardwood mast had been put into splints, and the pliable wickerwork walls of the bamboo cabin pulled up again. Along the rail of the cargo steamer stood the crew of the raft, six tanned men who gazed eagerly towards the long dock where only three people were waiting. After they docked they found them to be the expedition's secretary, Gerd Vold, the Norwegian Consul General, Jörgen Galbe, and an unknown gentleman who handed Thor a bill for £3,500 for the expense of the ship's making the trip from Samoa to Tahiti for the sole purpose of fetching the raft expedition. This was a blow that came like a bolt from heaven. Thor had never asked anyone to send a ship off its course. He had cabled his Washington headquarters to check the schedule of Norwegian ships out of Papeete, but questions asked by the Washington office had been misinterpreted by the shipping company and the result was that M/s *Thor I* was ordered to make the special detour by way of Tahiti to pick up the raft and crew at the expedition's expense. Where would he get the money? The thought of his debts had hung over Thor on board the raft. Now another £3,500 was piled on top and, in addition, he was responsible for getting his entire group across America and then across the ocean to their homes. He thought wistfully of the time of their arrival in lonely Raroia, where no problems had loomed.

Moreover he was suddenly faced with a new problem. He had arrived in San Francisco with a white elephant: the *Kon-Tiki*. What was to be done with the raft? The harbour authorities would not allow it to be launched and left in the water without a continuous harbour fee; at the dock there was no empty space, and permission to tow it out to sea and set it adrift was refused because of the danger to shipping. After many headaches the problem was finally solved thanks to a Norwegian ship owner, who carried the raft on one of his ships to Antwerp and from there another Norwegian ship freighted it on to Norway.

Though safe and sound back in America, and finally relieved of their white elephant, Thor and his daredevil companions faced another problem: they had no more money. Through the generosity of Consul General Galbe, he was granted another loan to fly his team across the country to the expedition's headquarters in Washington. Here the Norwegian Embassy gave a welcome party, and a cable from the Norwegian government congratulated them for 'their brilliant achievement'. But although the *New York Times* and other leading American papers had published their brief radio reports from the raft, the general public had no clear conception of the purpose of the expedition. It did not help that the Norwegian Cultural Attaché in Washington had told the American press that the voyage had certainly been a sporting triumph, but there were strong reasons to doubt its scientific value.

Among those who showed a real interest in the enterprise from the very beginning was President Truman. He had followed the voyage through a special clipping service, and he now invited the six participants to the White House to hear a detailed account from their own lips.

The President's enthusiasm was echoed in the American press, and created an interest among a number of the larger movie companies and magazines in search of good pictorial material. Besides ordinary photographs, eight thousand feet of 16 mm. film had been taken during the expedition. Very hurriedly the film was developed, and representatives from Paramount, R.K.O., and other leading companies were present when the material was run off for the first time, without having been examined or edited. The showing was a nightmare to Thor. For hour after hour they sat looking at a chaos of glimmers and flashes, interspersed with a confusion of waves, clouds, bearded faces, and wriggling fish. Only now and then were there short connected scenes where something happened. Half of the film had been totally ruined, partly by dampness and partly by rust causing shutter troubles in one of the cameras.

At the end of the showing all the movie men declared that the film was completely useless. One of the companies, however, was willing to give two hundred dollars for all the raw material, but Thor refused this. In spite of his disappointment, he noticed here and there scenes that could be used as a lecture film if cut and spliced. He decided to go to New York with Knut Haugland and begin the editing of the film with the help of a friend who did the splicing.

In New York he had two pleasant surprises. Lars Christensen, the owner of M/s *Thor I*, invited him to lunch at the fashionable '21-Club' to give him a first hand account of the expedition. When they reached the dessert Christensen leaned towards Thor and murmured in his ear:

'I hear there's been some correspondence between you and my shipping company about a bill. Just forget it.'

Never had a dessert tasted better!

At the same time *Life* had asked for an option on the still photographs taken during the voyage, and for several days Knut had helped their technical staff identify the remarkable pictures that were developed. Then Thor was summoned by the editor who asked him how much he wanted for first publication rights.

'Two thousand dollars', answered Thor, thinking he was putting it pretty high.

'Then you'll probably be satisfied with this', said the editor, and handed him a cheque for five thousand dollars.

As soon as he got over his surprise, Thor went off to his creditors, in particular to Colonel Munthe-Kaas, the Military Attaché, and paid initial instalments, with interest, off the various sums due.

From the Explorers Club, which had played an important part in the planning of the expedition, he now received an invitation to lecture on November 25th. This gave him very little time, for his work on the film was far from finished. He and his two friends worked night and day to cut down the eight thousand feet to a usable length. As late as half an hour before the lecture they were still sitting gluing ends together. Without really knowing what he had on film, Thor had jumped into a taxi and arrived at the Explorers Club the very moment he was due on the platform. All the time he was speaking, improvising his commentary as he went along, he had the feeling that both the lecture and the film were complete failures. The audience was ominously silent. When he stopped speaking some painful seconds passed, then the most tremendous applause he had ever heard burst out. The Kon-Tiki film, which gave only a faint image of the great adventure, had had a triumphant first showing.

A few days later, Thor went by plane to Oslo to start a lecture tour that would give him the means to pay off more of his debts. It seemed to have every prospect of success. In Norway he had made a name for himself with *In Search of Paradise* and his numerous articles and lectures before the war ought to insure a number of full houses. But a prophet is not without honour.

The scant and often distorted Norwegian press releases must take their share of the blame for the fact that only a few Norwegians took the expedition seriously. Most of them regarded it as a stunt, like rolling over Niagara in a barrel, or pole-sitting for sixty days. On their arrival home both Thor and the other men heard that their families and friends had had to endure many unpleasant remarks about 'boyish pranks' and 'publicity seeking'. Typical of the general opinion were these words by an Oslo journalist who interviewed Thor soon after his return:

'Why this Heyerdahl again? And why more about Kon-Tiki? We would have dropped the whole affair but for one special point we found so interesting that we had to drive the Kon-Tiki leader into a corner to get a full explanation of the first strange reports we received from out at sea. They did not in the least suggest that they had to do with a serious scientific expedition, but more with six Boy Scouts who were sending their greetings to Dad and Mom and uncles and aunts. . . .'

So the lecture tour also went rather badly. After two lectures in the capital, a few followed in smaller Norwegian towns, but then the interest waned, in spite of a very favourable press and enthusiasm among the audiences. This was another great disappointment, for it was precisely in these lectures that Thor had put his greatest trust as a source of income to pay back his debts.

The only way out that he could see was to go back to the United States and try a tour there. He signed a contract with an American agent for a hundred lectures, one per evening, at two hundred dollars each. Thor himself would pay all travel and hotel expenses. This sounded marvellous—a gross profit of twenty thousand dollars. All his remaining debts could be paid off. But this was to prove a beautiful illusion. Apart from the fact that lecturing every night for weeks on end was a tremendous strain, his profit was by no means as much as he had calculated.

Inexperienced as he was, he had signed the contract without noticing that it gave the agent the right to arrange the bookings, which he did without any consideration for distances and the cost of travel. Thor found himself incessantly on the move. One evening he might have to speak in Minneapolis, the next in San Francisco. Then Seattle, down to Los Angeles, and the next day back to Spokane. Day and night for more than three months he was moving across the country, and for a period of fourteen days he slept only on planes and trains. One day he went by plane from Chattanooga, Tennessee to the American Museum of Natural History in New York, only to be told that though he had come to the right place at the right time and on the right day of the month, this was 1948, not 1949. His agent had 'forgotten' to make a note of the year!

Inevitably his share of the profits was far short of his expectations, for often they barely covered his expenses. One trip to the Deep South cost him £64 for the plane and the hotel, leaving a balance of seven dollars. Nevertheless he did manage to make some inroads on his debts, which were still alarmingly high.

There are times when a shadow comes over one's mind; a sense of uneasiness, an intuition that something has gone wrong. As I write this my thoughts go back to an evening in the autumn of 1948. I was sitting at my desk, working on a manuscript, when the telephone rang. When I took up the receiver I heard Thor's voice, low but insistent. Could I meet him the next morning in his old home at Stengaten? There would be time for only a short talk, since he was in Larvik on a flying visit, but the matter was important.

Next day in Number 7, where his father was again living, Thor told me that he and Liv were separating. They had come to the conclusion that this was the best course to take, and they were parting as good friends. Everything they had endured together—the solitude of Fatu Hiva, the hunger in Vancouver, the dark days in Trail—should have bound them closer to one another—but this had not happened. They were too unlike in temperament. The war years forced them to grow to maturity miles apart from one another, to develop into independent personalities with widely different views of life; so that it had been almost as strangers that they met when the war ended.

He told me that in many ways life would be more difficult in the future. The financial prospects were anything but bright. The only hope was that the book he had been writing that summer would have a good reception when it came out later in the year. It was to be published by Gyldendal Norsk Forlag of Oslo and would be called *The Kon-Tiki Expedition (Kon-Tiki Ekspedisjonen)*.

It was obvious as he sat there talking about the book in his unpretentious and straightforward manner that he did not nourish any very great hopes for its success. Its publication on November 1st, 1948 did little to change this opinion. Its reception in Norway was moderate, and although it received favourable reviews in the newspapers, one could trace here and there a certain caution, based upon the mistrust that many felt about the motive of the voyage itself.

Thor went on with his lecturing, going on tour in Sweden. This was a resounding success from the very start. The enthusiasm was so overwhelming that it fully compensated for his earlier disappointments. At Stockholm he could have had full houses for as long as he stayed there, but his contract called for him to lecture in a number of other Swedish towns. One by one the *Kon-Tiki* men took his place in Stockholm while Thor completed these other engagements. From Sweden Thor went to

London to address the Royal Geographical Society on December 6th, and then he toured six other European countries.

After Christmas, the sales of the *Kon-Tiki* book in Norway dropped near to zero. While Thor continued his international lecture tour the book was translated into Swedish and was published the following year. The enthusiastic reception of his lectures was quite overshadowed by the success of the book. Adam Helms, of the publishing firm of Bokförlaget Forum in Stockholm, hit on the original promotion scheme of sending strips of balsa wood as postcards to every bookseller in the country. The reviewers vied with one another in searching for superlatives to describe this literary achievement. In its first year the book had a sale of 100,000 copies, a publishing record in Sweden.

Its success in Sweden was duplicated in other countries, and all this was reflected in Norway. Norwegian papers began to write about the book's success abroad, the sales began to pick up, and at last the Kon-Tiki expedition became a topic of conversation in the author's native country.

In 1950 the book was published in London and Chicago. As the result of a visit made by Philip Unwin to Harald Grieg of Gyldendal Norsk Forlag in 1948, when the book was virtually unknown outside Norway, Allen & Unwin had secured the British rights. As soon as their English translation had been completed they realized they had a best seller on their hands. This became abundantly evident as soon as the book was published, so much so that Sir Stanley Unwin, the head of the firm, decided that if it were humanly possible *The Kon-Tiki Expedition* should not be out of stock for a single day. In spite of the rush of orders, which continued for nearly two years, there was not a single day when the publishers were unable to supply it. It was never reprinted in quantities less than 20,000 at a time, and the British sales, including paperbacks, are now over 2,000,000 copies.

Curiously enough, Thor had great difficulty in finding a publisher in the United States. Three leading New York firms had returned the manuscript, saying that it did not suit their publishing programmes, and others had not even been interested enough to read it. One day, however, while he was in the States on a lecture tour, he spoke at the Chicago University Club. After the lecture he was approached by two enthusiastic gentlemen, one of whom was Bennet B. Harvey, of the Chicago publishing firm of Rand McNally and Company. They had both been fascinated by the story as it had been unfolded in Thor's lecture, and Bennet Harvey now asked for an option on the book. So it came about that this firm, which hitherto had specialized in atlases and children's books, captured one of the greatest publishing triumphs on record in America.

The *Chicago Tribune* called the book 'a superb record of the triumph of the human spirit', while the *New York Herald Tribune* wrote: 'It is the deep connection with nature and a tremendous simplicity that make this book great as few books in our time are great'. Reviewers in Great Britain were unanimous in their homage to the six men who had jeopardized their lives to prove a theory. Somerset Maugham wrote that it would be a very dull reader indeed who would not be full of admiration and envy at their boldness. The *Sunday Times* asserted that the narrative was 'certain to be one of the classics of the sea', and the *Daily Mail* described it as 'a book to restore one's faith in twentieth-century mankind'.

In Great Britain the author was placed beside such great names as Jules Verne, Conan Doyle, and 'Conrad at his best'. In America, *Kon-Tiki* surpassed even *Moby Dick* in excitement, had an atmosphere older than the voyages of the Odyssey, was as good as *Robinson Crusoe*—and was, moreover, true. President Truman wrote upon reading the book:

'It certainly is a wonderful thing to have people in the world who can still take hardship and do an exploration job just as the one you young men did on that raft. One of the difficulties of civilization is that people became fat and easy-going and can't accept hardships as a part of life. I am hoping that situation will not develop to too great an extent in this Republic of ours.'

As a result, the English language editions in the United States and Great Britain rose to record-breaking figures. For months it retained its place at the head of the list of best-sellers. At this very time it is being reprinted all over the world in more than sixty different languages, among them Hebrew, Eskimo, Esperanto, Telugi, Singalese, Gujarati, Marathi, Malayalam, Tamil, Indonesian, Mongolian, as well as in Braille in a number of countries. In some of the Communist countries the book was banned up to the time when Stalinism became discredited. Then within a short time it was published in the Soviet Union in seven languages, and also in all the other countries in the Eastern block, with the exception of the Chinese People's Republic, and the sale was enormous. Despite its hard birth the *Kon-Tiki* book was to sweep like a fresh breeze through the postwar world and be one of the greatest sensations in literary history.

No sooner had Thor's book become an international success than a surprisingly large number of people became more interested in its financial than in its literary achievements. While Thor was still struggling with his debts, they guessed and calculated how much money he had made. One foreign paper reached the conclusion that he must have received about five pounds for every mile of the voyage. This appeared in a little Norwegian paper as fifty pounds, and then grew to five hundred in other Norwegian newspapers. One agile brain worked out that the *Kon-Tiki* had earned more currency than the total Norwegian export of cod-roe!

To Thor, the tremendous popularity of the book was something incomprehensible. He had never dreamed of any such success, and he suddenly found himself in a whirl of events and work that quite took his breath away. Not only were there negotiations and contracts with publishing firms, but there was also fan mail in such quantities that he did not know how to deal with it. Still he found time to work at odd hours on a revised version of his old scientific manuscript *Polynesia and America* . . . which he now called *American Indians in the Pacific*.

At the same time, the *Kon-Tiki* raft caused him further headaches. Since its arrival from San Francisco in the autumn of 1947 the raft had been moored in the shoal water of a beach near Oslo, which had caused more damage to it than all the storms of the Pacific plus the final wreck on the Raroia reef. The ropes were rotting, the logs covered with oil slick, and the whole thing stank like a sewer. Souvenir hunters came with axes and knives and cut pieces from the logs, and at night lovers or tramps sought shelter in the remains of the bamboo cabin. Nothing had been done to protect it.

At first, Thor had wanted to present the *Kon-Tiki* to the Norwegian Maritime Museum, but the offer had been regretfully declined on the grounds that the expedition might prove to be of only passing interest, and the Board could not assume the financial responsibility for housing it. However, the museum did put at its disposal a free site where the raft could be kept, which was a great help. The authorities showed no interest in the matter, so in the spring of 1949 three energetic businessmen of Oslo set up a committee whose object was to provide a temporary shelter for the raft and its accessories until a permanent home could be provided. This plan of building a museum for what many still considered a mere stunt encountered opposition, and many bitter attacks appeared in the newspapers. However, the raft—every single bit of which had to be cleaned and reassembled—was installed in the shelter by the end of the year. Knut Haugland, who had continued as an officer in the Norwegian Army after the war, gave all his free time to the new venture.

Success was assured from the first day that it was opened in the latter part of 1949. The number of visitors rose from week to week, from month to month, from year to year. It was as if the little building had a power of attraction that reached out across national frontiers. From every corner of the world people came to see the raft, and many visitors to Norway had as the first item on their programme, a visit to the Kon-Tiki Museum. It was obvious, however, that this wooden shack was no real solution, since dogs, cats, and hedgehogs crawled under the walls, and souvenir hunters were still able to reach across and cut slivers off the balsa logs. In the end Thor and Knut made a final effort to save the raft. A concrete building with air-conditioning was needed, but there was no money for the project. Knut, who directed the work of this new building, later wrote:

'At first Heyerdahl raised a big personal loan to have the museum fitted and equipped for public service. Next he decided in a memorandum that an eventual profit was to go to a fund for students of anthropology and maritime history. Thus, while he was still in debt, he was able to disregard his own financial problems and instead stretch out a helping hand to needy scholars.' Years were to pass, however, before this new museum became a reality.

One morning in the early summer of 1949 I received a letter postmarked New Mexico. The envelope contained a short greeting from Thor and a clipping from an American paper with a picture of him and an attractive young woman. The caption said that Miss Yvonne Dedekam-Simonsen had become Mrs Thor Heyerdahl in Santa Fé.

The first time I met Yvonne was about half a year later, or more exactly on February 14th, 1950, when she arrived with Thor in Larvik on a visit to Heyerdahl senior. I remember the exact date, because it coincided with an event that made front-page headlines in our little hometown. They had come from abroad to attend the Norwegian première of a commercial movie version of his Kon-Tiki film, which had been just completed for world distribution. Yvonne was as charming and natural a person as I had expected her to be.

I learned that they had spent their honeymoon in a remote stone cabin high up in the southern Rocky Mountains where they had hidden away so that Thor could resume work on his scientific manuscript. An ancient Ford car was their only means of communication with the outside world. Thor had never cared for cars. He could not drive and still cannot. So it was Yvonne who had to take the car on the slippery and dangerous cattle tracks to the nearest village for provisions. And often she had to drive the long way to the state museum in Santa Fé or the University of New Mexico in Albuquerque to get reference books for Thor's work. One day she returned on foot; a wheel had come off and rolled down a precipice.

In the important American research centres in Santa Fé, Yvonne and Thor met various experts on the North American Indians. Among those who became their friends were two archaeologists, Erik Reed and Edwin Ferdon, who were later to join Thor on new expeditions in the Pacific.

The summer in the Rocky Mountains was unforgettable. Yvonne had spent her early years in Oslo. Her father was a noted businessman, and she herself had made a special study of penicillin in London, where she had worked in a laboratory. The sudden change from urban life to the silence and grandeur of wild nature was a tremendous experience for her. There was high adventure in every puff of wind and every forest sound when she and Thor, after a long day's work, took their sleeping bags and spent the night among the animal tracks in the hills. They would lie under the starry sky and talk about prehistoric peoples and ancient civilizations. As Yvonne began making an entry into Thor's world, she was completely fascinated by it. The tangled problems of Pacific migrations became of essential interest to her and made her his loyal collaborator to the present day.

The happy days in the Rocky Mountains soon came to an end as Thor's still insecure financial situation forced him to sign on for more lectures in Europe. As he and Yvonne travelled round with his lecture film, Thor did not dream that there was any great future for the material as a cinema film. It had been condemned as useless, not only by the leading American film companies, but also by the Director of State Cinemas in Norway.

One evening in a hotel in Copenhagen he received a telephone call from Stockholm. The producers of Artfilm, Olle Nordemar and ex-Prince Lennart Bernadotte, were anxious to purchase the rights to enlarge the 16 mm. film to the standard size used in cinemas. Thor replied that the film was not good enough to enlarge, and he was going to Vienna the next morning to deliver a lecture. For the moment, therefore, he did not think there was an opportunity to discuss the matter. But the gentlemen of Artfilm were so keen that they flew to Copenhagen that same evening. They hurriedly scribbled a contract, partly in Swedish and partly in Norwegian. Legally it was unsatisfactory, but it represented a gentleman's agreement which later formed the basis for contracts with film distributors that earned millions of dollars for theatre owners all over the world.

How could a little Swedish film company undertake a task which the major companies had considered impossible? The answer was that Artfilm had invested a large sum in an optical printing machine, the only one in

Europe at the time, which could make a 35 mm. copy of a 16 mm. film, improving it by cutting, changing lighting effects, and removing defects due to the movement of the camera. The machine was a technical whizz, and even now only a few exist in the world.

After his lecture tour, Thor returned to Stockholm and handled the story and text, while Nordemar did the editing and his technical staff patched bits together and stabilized scenes that danced too wildly over the screen. The result was an outstanding achievement in more ways than one. The film had been shot at a speed of sixteen frames a second instead of twenty-four, as used in all cinemas, so it became necessary to rephotograph every third frame of the entire film, and then splice in these duplicate frames to obtain the twenty-four frames per second required for standard film performances.

At length the film was ready for showing, with a commentary spoken in several languages by Thor himself. On January 13, 1950, a month before the Norwegian first performance, the world première took place in the Grand Cinema, Stockholm. Those present were the Swedish Royal Family and a long list of prominent persons, including the world-famous explorer, Sven Hedin. The film was an odd piece of work, a documentary with the glow of high adventure. The actors were the six bearded fellows on the raft, the fish, and the monsters from the depths of the sea. The scene was the raft, the sky, and the Pacific in storm and calm. There was such an impression of actuality that the spectators felt as if they were participating in the voyage. They could feel the raft rising and falling with the waves, hear the wind whistling in the rigging, and sense the smell of salt seas washing over the balsa logs. It was so realistic that several members of the audience felt the symptoms of seasickness coming on and had to leave the auditorium. One lady sitting next to Queen Ingrid at the Danish première in Copenhagen was unable to retire in time.

The very first performance of the film clearly indicated that it would be a major success. The *Stockholms-Tidningen* wrote of 'a uniquely fantastic adventure, a film achievement which is going to re-echo over the whole world'. There were many other such notices. The one criticism concerned the technical defects and the amateurishness of the photography. But, it was said, these were not disadvantages: they gave the film a stamp of genuineness that would have been lost had it had the perfection of a studio production.

All these favourable forecasts were fulfilled. Artfilm transferred its world rights to the American producer Sol Lesser, who in turn disposed of them to R.K.O. Thus the film came through these middlemen back into the hands of one of the companies who had originally rejected Thor's material as being completely useless.

To escape all the stir that inevitably accompanies public success, Thor retreated with Yvonne to Owl's Creek, his father's remote property in the great woods on the Swedish frontier, where he hoped to be able to continue in peace his work on the scientific manuscript. Here he was far from crowds and telephones. But not even Owl's Creek was sufficiently isolated.

One day a peasant arrived on a bicycle with the news that Heyerdahl was wanted at the country store for an urgent telephone call from Hollywood. Amid the chatting of local farmers he heard Sol Lesser's indistinct voice from America stating that Thor was being sued for £50,000. A Tahitian beauty, Purea Reasin, had denounced Thor for illegally filming a hula dance she and a girl friend had performed during a dinner party for the Kon-Tiki expedition in her home outside Papeete. She had learned that the film was now being exhibited in American cinemas without her consent, and was claiming that the film should be stopped and confiscated, in addition to the payment of damages. If the film was stopped, Sol Lesser and R.K.O. could expect lawsuits from more than a hundred cinemas exhibiting the film in the United States at that time, which would be a much more serious matter than any sum claimed by Purea. The financial responsibility for the whole thing was Thor's; he was the defendant and answerable to Artfilm, Sol Lesser, and R.K.O.

The film companies recommended that Thor settle with Purea out of court if she would abandon her claim that the film should be stopped. Purea, they declared, could not help winning her case in the United States, since it was an American law that no one's picture could appear on a cinema screen unless the party concerned had given permission in writing. If there was no written consent the defendant had to pay whatever compensation was demanded. No defendant had ever won a case of this kind in the American courts.

There had not been, of course, any written agreement at the party, yet the hula performance had been given in the full knowledge that it would be used as one of the scenes of welcome on Tahiti. Thor had used only twenty seconds of the dance, and the original lecture film, showing Purea dancing, had been run in Tahiti without any protest from her. But when later on it became a world success, Purea and her American husband traded on the claim that she was of royal descent and therefore unwilling to dance the hula-hula in public. In fact, it was a lawyer friend in California who had recommended a lawsuit.

Fifty thousand pounds for twenty seconds of dancing! Thor could not possibly raise such a sum. He determined to fight the case, and when he advised the film companies accordingly, Sol Lesser provided legal aid, while Thor collected written evidence from people who had been at the party. He intended at first to leave the case entirely to his American lawyers, but he suddenly decided it would be better to go to Hollywood and defend himself.

Purea grew flushed and uneasy when he unexpectedly turned up in court, but she stuck to her indictment. The judge, a puritanical gentleman who had once been a clergyman, examined Thor sternly and searchingly, and the situation looked sticky, despite the fact that Lesser had engaged three clever lawyers for the defence. Purea, her husband, and the counsel for the plaintiff all stressed the point that in modern eyes the hula-hula is an indecent dance. She had danced it at the party because of its historical interest, and if she had dreamed of the presence of a film camera she would never have allowed herself to do it. For two days the case seemed hopeless to Thor. Each time the defence sought to read a written deposition by one of the witnesses at the party, the plaintiff's lawyer jumped up and objected. Written evidence was either contrary to law or irrelevant. Every single time the objection was sustained.

On the third day a Hollywood witness suddenly and unexpectedly disclosed that Purea had taken the part of a hula-hula girl in an earlier film as a stand-in for Dorothy Lamour. Immediately afterwards the defence started its well-planned and well-executed cross-examination of the Tahitian beauty, who had to answer without having much time to think. Only a witness who is telling the truth can successfully get through this sort of interrogation. In the midst of his fire of questions, Thor's counsel asked innocently:

'But surely you must have known that the film could be enlarged to the size of a professional movie film, even if it had been taken with a 16 mm. camera?'

'No, I didn't know that.'

'But how could you know that he had a 16 mm. camera and not a 35 mm. one?'

'Because it was the same sort as my husband's.'

'Now, stop a moment. You have been insisting all the time that you had no idea there was a camera in the place.'

'I—I saw that he was fiddling around with one.'

And thereupon the young lady broke down, entangling herself in a web of contradiction while her husband and the lawyer tried furiously to stop her.

After a short pause, the judge said:

'I want to see the film.'

Purea's lawyer objected. He thought it was quite unnecessary, and moreover, difficult to arrange. While the defence insisted on having the film produced, Sol Lesser ran to the nearest telephone and returned with the news that the local cinema was ready and that a copy of the film was on its way. The court and all the spectators rose and left for the cinema. The judge took a seat by himself in the front row. He sat for an hour and a half, until he had seen the part at the end where Purea appeared, danced for twenty seconds, and finally sat down and smiled straight into the camera. When the film had finished, the judge said brusquely:

'Run it through once more.'

And so the audience had to sit through another hour and a half before it could return to the courtroom. When silence had been restored there, the judge turned to Purea and asked:

'How much have you paid Heyerdahl to take part in this film?'

'Nothing.'

'Then the film is his and you cannot have it confiscated. Besides, you ought to be proud to have danced so pretty a dance in such a good film.'

With that, the case was concluded. To Thor, Sol Lesser, and R.K.O. the decision was as pleasing as it was surprising to the film world of Hollywood. The judgment was to prove of importance for all future documentaries. Indeed, it created a precedent in Hollywood for later actions of the same kind.

After this the film was shown without interruption in all countries. More than thirty million people have seen it in cinemas, and through television it has reached almost five hundred million viewers. It also achieved the honour of being the first Norwegian film to receive an Oscar for the best documentary in 1951. Thor did not want to go to Hollywood for the award, but during a special ceremony in the Kon-Tiki Museum, he and Olle Nordemar each received their gold statuette from Sol Lesser. By 1955 the film had been awarded nearly fifty prizes in all parts of the world.

After the expedition had become famous through Thor's book and the film, a real Kon-Tiki fever broke out in the greater part of the civilized world. There seemed to be something magic about the title itself, for rarely has a name become a catchword so quickly and completely. In the course of time the name of the expedition has almost replaced the name of the man who led it. 'Heyerdahl' is difficult to remember, but 'Kon-Tiki' sounds good in all languages. Actually, Thor has become known to most people as Mr Kon-Tiki, or even more commonly, Señor Kon-Tiki.

As usual, the businessmen had the sharpest eye for the possibilities in the Kon-Tiki adventure. As soon as Thor became famous, he was tempted with a multitude of golden offers if he would endorse commercial products. He consistently refused all these, but it was impossible to prevent the name 'Kon-Tiki' from appearing on products all over the world without his consent. They might be drinks, chocolate, candy, perfume, dress materials, paints, cookies, butter, sardines, leather goods, porcelain, silverware, building sets, souvenirs, matches, and insecticides; and the rich pictorial material in the book gave ideas for calendars, ornaments, strip cartoons, jokes, games, and advertisements.

Kon-Tiki hotels and exotic Kon-Tiki restaurants, some with the most fancy special dishes and cocktails, appeared in most countries. In an international cooking competition in Berne, Norway's entry was a *Kon-Tiki* raft made of salmon mousse. The names *Kon-Tiki I*, *Kon-Tiki II*, and *Kon-Tiki III* soon appeared painted on boats of all kinds from Lake Geneva to the coast of Japan. Two new varieties of grape in Russia were named 'Kon-Tiki' and 'Thor Heyerdahl'; and when Russia sent up the world's first manned satellite, the provisions included 'Kon-Tiki' chocolate with a picture of the raft on its wrapper.

The idea was also applied in different forms to fashion. At the time when the film made its first appearance in London, the Kon-Tiki scarf was the *dernier cri*, and soon there were Kon-Tiki ties, bathing suits, shorts, dresses, and decorative materials. In Pittsburgh, Pennsylvania, a woman fashion consultant wore as a hat a Kon-Tiki raft with a sail and caused a traffic jam. At fêtes and floral processions, from the Riviera to California, pretty girls could be seen on board Kon-Tiki rafts made of roses and other flowers. In the botanic gardens of Durban, a striking increase in visitors was shown when it became known that a balsa tree was growing there.

Authors and composers vied with one another in writing verses and popular music inspired by *Kon-Tiki*. In every part of the world extracts from the book were included in school readers. In the United States alone more than thirty such textbooks have been published, and in the Soviet Union a bilingual edition of the book has been issued as an English reader for Russians.

There were other forms of Kon-Tiki fever, too. Boys in many countries built rafts and sailed them across lakes and ponds. Adults started off on pointless voyages on rafts made of ping-pong balls or empty gasoline cans, while others tried to reconstruct the exact voyage. One attempt to cross the Pacific in the opposite direction ended in an S.O.S. after six months' drifting in the stormy antarctic current. It soon became evident that the only successful voyages were those that sailed in the wake of the *Kon-Tiki* from South America to the South Sea islands. Since 1947, when *Kon-Tiki* showed the way, six more manned rafts have been set adrift off the coast of Peru. One of them reached the Galápagos, the five others landed in various parts of Polynesia. Of the latter, one continued through the island area and reached Australia on the opposite side of the Pacific.

There has been much speculation as to why the *Kon-Tiki* book and film reached such a high degree of international popularity. The book was well written, but books just as good have appeared in world literature and not left a trace worth mentioning behind them. The film was a fantastic record, but technically it had many shortcomings. The reason—or reasons—must lie elsewhere, and it was to this point that reviewers and writers in various parts of the world devoted their attention. Many suggested that it was something peculiar to the age that made a success of these dimensions possible. People were living in a postwar period of lost ideals and broken illusions, struggling to satisfy material demands, and uncertain of what the future might have in store. If they took refuge in the world of books for an hour or two, there was little comfort to be found in the mass of war literature and profound psychological novels; in books with such titles as *For Fear of Weeping*, *A Kiss for the Leper*, and *Dynasty of Death*. It was far more pleasant to sail with these six daredevils away from the troubles and anxieties of everyday life.

The noted writer and philosopher, Dr Robert Jungk of Vienna, said: 'Material satisfaction is not enough. Man is not content with his limitations on the spiritual level; and he grows bored. Man has proved himself unable to master the technical development of modern civilization by spiritual means. We no longer know for what we are striving. . . . In America people are trying to escape from these problems. The popularity of the *Kon-Tiki* book is a consequence of this.'

But the Kon-Tiki fever cannot be explained simply as a phenomenon of our time. Up to this very day, half a generation after the voyage, a vigorous demand for the book continues. It has become a classic. Perhaps one of the reasons is that it contains a strong element of the mystery of nature, the attraction of the sea, the urge towards the unfathomable, which the sea represents. What wonders shall we encounter if we venture out towards the horizon and beyond? What is hidden in the depths of the sea? Technological miracles like satellites and electronic brains naturally arouse our admiration, but they find no place in our emotions. The desire to return to a primitive life will always exist in most people. Its peace, its

N

quiet, combined with the whistle of the wind in the rigging, the rhythm of the sea—readers of the book are able to experience all this, and we are certainly entitled to say that the author has managed for a short time to carry them back to nature.

The strong appeal of *Kon-Tiki* to our dreams and our love of adventure, and the exciting narrative itself, are not enough, however, to explain a success of such dimensions. The wave of enthusiasm that followed in the wake of the book and the film would undoubtedly have been far less remarkable had it not been for a final and decisive quality: the inspired determination behind the achievement. The voyage was not a whim of adventurous boys. There was a theory behind it. The leader of the expedition was a scientist who was not content with sitting at his desk and quoting the words of others from books and periodicals, but one who himself went out and risked his life to prove what others had thought impossible.

The waves of success that radiated from the *Kon-Tiki* raft encompassed Thor's five companions, as well. Thor had promised them in advance a post-expedition bonus if his planned lecture tour paid off all his debts, but as this prospect did not look very bright, they each were given a copy of the lecture film to use for their own benefit. As Knut Haugland wrote later:

'He did not forget those of us who had made the raft voyage possible. We all got recompensed far beyond what he had promised. Besides, he kept in touch with each of us in the ensuing years, and he was never slow to give us help, whether he had been asked or not. That he himself, in the first years, lay under a heavy burden of debt and had to live on loans, was of minor importance to him.'

Perhaps the expedition came to mean most to Herman Watzinger. He was an engineer specializing in refrigeration, and the almost incredible abundance of fish in the Humboldt Current gave him an idea. He and his family moved to Peru where he began to develop industries based on offshore fisheries, and where he soon became Norwegian consul general. He later expanded and built cold-storage plants for fish throughout Latin America. He also started a great Norwegian fishery in Chile.

Knut Haugland, too, had his life changed by the raft voyage. Although he continued his military career as a major in the Norwegian Army, he finally became involved with museum work full time. He had been the driving force behind the preservation of the *Kon-Tiki* raft, and subsequently became director of the Kon-Tiki Museum. The new modern building, raised adjacent to the structure housing the *Fram*, Nansen's polar schooner, was opened in 1957. In addition to the *Kon-Tiki* raft mounted in a marine setting which occupies the central hall, additional exhibits include material explaining the theory behind the expedition, as well as the findings from Heyerdahl's subsequent visits to the Pacific. Haugland developed the modest exhibit into the most popular museum in Norway, with an annual attendance of more than a quarter of a million and the entire profit goes to a fund for students.

Erik Hesselberg issued his own version of the expedition, a humorous book of cartoons with hand-lettered text that was translated into numerous languages. After extensive lecture tours in German-speaking countries, he bought and personally refitted a small boat and set sail for Mediterranean ports where he lived for years with his guitar and paintbrush. He has, in recent years, been employed as the decorator of various Kon-Tiki restaurants in many countries and as consultant at international exhibitions where models of the raft have been displayed.

Bengt Danielsson's participation in the raft voyage, too, was decisive for his future. In Lima, before departure, he fell in love with a girl in the French Embassy, and at the end of the voyage he fell in love with Tahiti. He returned to Lima, married the girl, and settled with her in Tahiti. He revisited Raroia three times, first to complete a study of social life on the island for his doctorate. Since then he has established himself with his small family in Tahiti, where he became the Swedish consul and has published a great number of books, all with subjects drawn from the South Seas. Recently he has been appointed Director of the National Ethnographic Museum in Stockholm.

Torstein Raaby, Lieutenant 'Pettersen' in Finnmark, was the one who made the best use of the lecture film. A record number of engagements in Switzerland enabled him to complete his training as an engineer in a local college, but he lectured in many other countries, from Sweden to the Congo and Angola, until he finally settled down as civilian radio engineer employed by the army in Norway. For two years of this period he directed the Norwegian radio station on the remote Jan Mayen island in the arctic. In 1964, as the radio operator of an unsuccessful private sledge expedition to the North Pole, he died in the frozen wastes to the north of Canada.

While Thor's *Kon-Tiki* companions could still be traced through their activities in different corners of the world, he himself suddenly disappeared from the scene. As the Kon-Tiki fever rose to its climax, and offers from advertisers, radio, and television flowed in to his Oslo address accompanied by a deluge of fan mail, the author and his wife seemed to have sunk into the earth. Reporters phoned, telegraphed, and searched in vain. What had happened? Had the man really fled from his success, or, a London newspaper asked, was this typically Nordic behaviour, *à la* Garbo?

Chapter 15

COLD SHOULDERS

ON the heathery hills of Dartmoor, not far from the famous prison, stands the Hound Tor Inn, a little stone cottage with a thick-thatched roof. In the spring of 1952 there were only two visitors staying there, a Norwegian couple who had registered with the difficult name of Heyerdahl. It was true enough that they wanted to escape the heartless glare of the limelight, but their main reason was to find time and peace to complete the last pages of *American Indians in the Pacific*, due for publication in the late summer of that year. Apart from two of their young anthropologist friends in Santa Fé, no scholar had yet cared to read the large manuscript, but with the success of the popular book there was no difficulty in finding an international team of publishers willing to print this scholarly mono-graph, which had the subtitle, 'The Theory Behind the Kon-Tiki Expedition.'

The couple spent all day and much of the night in their room, working with books and manuscripts by the light of kerosene lamps in front of an open fireplace. They were so busy that the whole spring went by without Thor finding time to go to the nearest town for a haircut. Finally Yvonne took the scissors and cropped it herself. When the book was ready for the printers they moved to the Hyde Park Hotel in London, where Thor visited the barber of the hotel.

'Excuse me for asking, Sir', said the barber, 'but where did you last have your hair cut?'

'Dartmoor', Thor answered briefly.

The barber pursed his lips.

'That's just what I thought, Sir. The style is typical.'

The delivery of the fifteen pound manuscript to a London post office for shipment to the Stockholm printers represented one of the greatest moments of relief in Thor's whole life. Fifteen years had passed since he had initiated work on this extensive thesis after his return from Fatu Hiva. Since the raft voyage, he had taken advantage of every spare minute adding to the text by sticking on new material with tape to such an extent that Yvonne, who was doing the typing, almost despaired when handed sheets twelve to fourteen feet long. He had been driven to working so desperately hard because the scholars who had refused to read his manuscript were now the very first to criticize him publicly for having published a popular book before he had presented his scientific evidence. Most of their criticisms appeared in the daily press, and over and over again he had been forced to break off his work on the manuscript in order to defend himself.

Few who followed Thor's self-defence through the press in various parts of the world had any real knowledge of the background of the controversy. The majority did not realize that the raft had ploughed not merely across the Pacific, but also through an ocean of conventional thought, breaking the calm surface of Pacific research. Proof that a balsa raft could actually reach the South Sea islands from South America annoyed many scholars. It cut away the foundation of a considerable number of accepted conclusions and dogmas. So far science had unanimously agreed that Polynesia lay far beyond the reach of the many remarkable cultures of pre-Columbian South America. With the success of the raft voyage, anthropologists and biologists alike were suddenly forced to revise their comprehension of a whole series of fundamental doctrines. Their reactions to the Kon-Tiki concept, therefore, were not so unanimously enthusiastic as those of most literary book reviewers. Actually, Thor was trapped in a post-expedition whirlwind that he had never anticipated.

Let us consider in retrospect what happened when the news of the successful expedition was brought to the attention of the scientists.

They had so far ignored the New World as a potential source of the prehistoric culture and domesticated plants and animals on the East Pacific islands. Typically, the leading Polynesian authority, Sir Peter Buck, had written: 'Since the South American Indians had neither the vessels nor the navigating ability to cross the ocean space between their shores and the nearest Polynesian islands, they may be disregarded as the agents of supply.'

What then did the same scholars have to say *after* the Kon-Tiki expedition?

The first reaction came from the same Sir Peter Buck in an interview with the *Auckland Star* of New Zealand. It was immediately taken up by the international press and presented like the introduction to a wrestling match: 'THAT "KON-TIKI RAFT BUSINESS" MAKES SIR PETER BUCK LAUGH', wrote the *Auckland Star* in big headlines, and continued:

'. . . it was too bad that Sir Peter was off on an expedition of his own to Kapingamarangi (in the Carolines) when a handful of young Norwegian scientists climbed aboard a balsa log raft a while ago to challenge the widely known Buck theory of the Polynesians' beginnings. Now back on his own beloved native soil, Sir Peter makes rebuttal.

' "That Kon-Tiki raft business?" He threw back his head and roared with laughter. "A nice adventure", Sir Peter commented. "But you don't expect anybody to call that a scientific expedition. Now do you?"

'The noted anthropologist, a brawny as well as brainy man, waved his arms like a wrestler about to wade into an opponent. And warmed up to his argument.

' "Those Norwegians", he said, "want us to believe their pre-Inca Peruvians were doing a bit of coastal fishing and got picked up by the Humboldt Current. And eventually wound up alive and safe somewhere to father the Polynesian race." He roared with laughter again. And rubbed his ear reflectively. "No fisherman I ever saw had woman aboard. And by their own theory the landings were made on uninhabited islands—so who exactly was going to mother our Polynesian peoples?" '

Thor was astounded at this reaction from a scholar who, as much as Thor himself, ought to be interested in the practical result of the balsa raft experiment. He answered with a rebuttal appearing only in the Scandinavian press that the same objection might equally well have been used against an arrival of *Asian* sailors, or did the Asian men perhaps know of other ways of procreation? Moreover, the Spanish discoverers of Peru had expressly recorded the capture of Inca women on board the first balsa rafts encountered at sea.

Buck's comment became known all over the world; Thor's answer did not. But he had the support of a young American lady, who wrote in a letter to *Life* that she would gladly demonstrate the possibility of populating Polynesia from South America if Mr Heyerdahl would take her with him on a second voyage by raft.

The next attack came in an Oslo paper by the noted American anthropologist, Professor Ralph Linton, who had assisted Thor in disposing of his Marquesas collection in New York during the war. Linton was among those who had tried to make Thor abandon his planned raft expedition, saying it would never succeed. Now he stated in an interview that the theory was invalid 'because the balsa tree, which is one of Heyerdahl's most important proofs, did not grow on the western side of the Andes.' Thor replied in the same paper:

'*Before* the Kon-Tiki expedition it was said that neither the Indians nor we could accomplish such a transoceanic journey *because* the raft was made of the light and porous balsa wood. . . . *After* our voyage has been accomplished, it is now said that we managed it *because* our raft was made of balsa wood, a kind of wood which is suddenly supposed to have been unknown to the Indians on the west coast of South America.'

Moreover, he referred to a number of botanical and historical sources which proved that the balsa tree grew both in the northern and eastern part of the Inca empire. Linton did not reply for several years, then conceded in an issue of the *American Anthropologist* that Heyerdahl's 'practical demonstration that balsa rafts could have drifted to Polynesia indicates that there may have been two-way traffic.'

In the autumn of 1949, soon after Buck's and Linton's interviews, the 29th International Americanist Congress opened in New York. This congress is normally held every other year for specialists on peoples and cultures of aboriginal America. At the 1949 congress, which Thor did not attend, an exhibition called 'Across the Pacific' was arranged by the archaeologists Gordon Ekholm and Robert von Heine-Geldern. It showed among other things that the special fish hooks made of bone, mussel shells, and stone taken by the Polynesians on their migrations were practically identical with the types found among the ancient civilizations on the Pacific coast of North and South America. Not even remotely similar fish hooks were to be found in Indonesia or Southeast Asia.

This important substantiation for Thor's theory was ignored by his opponents, even by those who argued in support of a transoceanic migration, as they had defended a movement in the opposite direction of the *Kon-Tiki* drift. A Danish authority, Professor Kaj Birket-Smith, was interviewed by a Copenhagen paper when he returned from the congress. He said that the experts had agreed that the Kon-Tiki expedition should not be mentioned. The interview was published in Denmark under the heading: 'KON-TIKI EXPEDITION TO BE KILLED BY SILENCE.' A few days later, however, brilliantly coloured posters of the *Kon-Tiki* raft were distributed throughout Copenhagen: the Danish edition of the *Kon-Tiki* book was forthcoming.

It was just about this time that the Kon-Tiki fever was spreading through Europe. The enterprise could not be killed by silence.

In Sweden, where Thor's success was the greatest, he also encountered his bitterest opposition. The Pacific botanist, Professor Carl Skottsberg, known for his early work on Easter Island, was no believer in the tactics of silence. To the contrary, instead he reviewed *Kon-Tiki* as if it were a scientific treatise, a strategy later repeated by scientists in other countries. While admitting, in the leading Gothenburg daily, that the raft voyage was a feat and the book describing it a magnificent chronicle, he stressed that the sailor Heyerdahl was no true scholar; his readers were not to take his scientific assertions seriously. Heyerdahl referred to Easter Island in

Kon-Tiki, he said, although he had admittedly never been there, but he, Skottsberg, *had* been there studying the flora. He could, therefore, point out that Heyerdahl's proposal of how the giant statues might have been erected was erroneous, and so were the given measurements pertaining to these monuments. Before writing his narrative the young man ought to have read the scholarly volume on Easter Island by the French ethnologist, Alfred Métraux.

Thor came right back in the same newspaper with the information that it happened to be precisely in Métraux's volume that he had read of the suggested method of erecting statues; and as to the dimensions of these statues, they had been taken from Skottsberg's own travel report!

To get out of this embarrassment, the old botanist resorted to Latin. Without giving any further explanation he wrote in a brief note that *Hibiscus tiliaceus*, *Thespesia*, and *Triumfetta* represented botanical proof that the human migration must have come from the direction of Asia, and he added that the discussion was now closed on his side.

What the professor could not very well know was that his young opponent was just then completing a detailed botanical study for one section of his yet unpublished *American Indians in the Pacific*. Thor was able, therefore, swiftly to reply that none of these three plants were valid as proof of human voyages, as all three had seeds capable of overseas propagation without human aid; and moreover, one of them, *Hibiscus tiliaceus*, had been just as common in ancient South America as in Asia.

Skottsberg refrained from any further comment, and when he finally reappeared in the same paper, eight years had elapsed. He had then revised his own botanical evidence and, as we shall see later, gave Thor full support.

On Skottsberg's withdrawal from the original discussion, a young Gothenburg archaeologist, Stig Rydén, immediately took up the challenge in the same paper. Heyerdahl had referred to the South American ruins of Tiahuanaco in his book he said, but the only authorities with thorough knowledge of that cult site were Rydén himself and the American archaeologist, Dr W. C. Bennett. According to Heyerdahl's theory, a legendary sun-king, Con-Tici *viracocha*, together with his white and bearded people, had once abandoned that site and left for the Pacific. Rydén maintained that there was no such legend in existence; it was pure invention. The local Indians, he said, were just as 'red' and beardless as all other Indians. He added that the 'beard' of the Tiahuanaco god whose

35. Thor and Torstein with a dolphin.
36. (*next page*) After 101 days at sea, the raft was shipwrecked on a reef in Polynesia.
37. (*next page*) All hands safe, the crew waded ashore on an uninhabited island.

38

39

40

41

head had been copied on the sail of the *Kon-Tiki* might just as well have been meant to represent a nose ring.

In his reply Thor produced documentary evidence showing that the legend was recorded by the first Spaniards who came to Tiahuanaco, and he also quoted such well-known historians as William Prescott and Friedrich von Humboldt. 'The story of the bearded white men finds its place in most of these legends', Prescott had written of the Incas; and von Humboldt had stated with regard to the Tiahuanaco ruins: '. . . at the arrival of the Spaniards the natives attributed the construction of them to a race of white and bearded men who inhabited the ridge of the Cordilleras long before the foundation of the empire of the Incas.' The head on the *Kon-Tiki's* sail was, moreover, copied from a drawing of a stone statue which Bennett, the authority referred to by Rydén, had found in Tiahuanaco. It was, in fact, Bennett himself who had made the original drawing and described the statue as an image of a bearded man.

The Gothenburg newspaper polemics continued for weeks, but Thor successfully defended himself against all assaults and had the last word, a comedown Rydén was never to forget. Bennett, however, did not personally enter the controversy until Thor's scientific volume was published two years later. He then wrote an otherwise critical book review in the *New York Times*, in which he admitted: 'The quantity and quality of the material which Mr Heyerdahl has assembled are too great to be ignored. Henceforth, American contributions to the Polynesian cultures will have to be considered.'

While the controversy filled pages in the Gothenburg paper, an attack was launched elsewhere that hurt Thor so deeply he nearly gave up the fight. He was still in Stockholm working at high speed to complete the movie version of the *Kon-Tiki* film. One night when he returned dead tired to his hotel, the Finnish News Bureau phoned him from Helsinki and wished to know what answer he could give to a serious accusation in *Nya Pressen*, one of the larger newspapers in the Finnish capital. Professor Rafael Karsten, a leading ethnologist in Finland, had charged Thor and his companions with fraud under big headlines: 'THE KON-TIKI HUMBUG.' Maintaining that Heyerdahl's theory was pure nonsense, the professor quoted some alleged comments from Thor, and claimed that the raft that

38. (*previous page*) Back in Europe. From left: Herman, Thor, Knut, Erik, and Torstein. Bengt was still in the United States.

39. (*previous page*) Yvonne assists Thor with proofreading in the Hound Tor Inn on Dartmoor.

40. The documentary film, *Kon-Tiki*, was a success in spite of its technical imperfections.

41. Acting as a guide, Knut Haugland (left) escorts Queen Ingrid of Denmark (second from left), King Olaf of Norway (fifth from left), and King Frederik of Denmark, through the Kon-Tiki Museum.

had crossed the Pacific was not at all an Inca type balsa raft. According to
Heyerdahl himself, Karsten wrote, the raft 'was specially designed in such
a way that it could turn bottom up and still carry on equally well'.
Karsten concluded: 'If half of what is related in the *Kon-Tiki* book is true,
then it must be regarded as a miracle that the voyagers ever came through
the adventure. But as is well known, miracles are not very common.'

Thor was so dumbfounded at what the Finnish News Bureau told him
on the telephone that he could think of no answer except to insist that he
had never said or written what Karsten had quoted.

The professor, however, countered with a new article in which he
categorically insisted that he had taken his quotations direct from the
Kon-Tiki book.

For the first time in Thor's many years of struggle for his theory it seemed
as if his work, still unfinished, had fallen in ruins around him. He had been
publicly labelled as a fake by a respectable professor, and half of his
Kon-Tiki book had been denounced as a lie. He soon learned that Karsten's
offensive statements had immediately spread to other countries like fire-
brands. 'KON-TIKI UNMASKED' was front page copy in other Finnish
papers. 'CAUSE CELEBRE IN THE SCIENTIFIC WORLD: KON-TIKI VOYAGE
HUMBUG, SAYS FAMOUS FINNISH SCIENTIST', was one of the many headlines
in Sweden. 'IS THE KON-TIKI THEORY A PUBLICITY STUNT?' asked Danish
papers. 'HUMBUG—HUMBUG!' was repeated like an echo by the press in
Norway.

Thor felt incapable of fighting back. For a few days he felt as if he was
walking in a daze. His own horizons seemed to grow narrower, and he
could see and hear nothing but Karsten's accusations of dishonesty. He was
unable to concentrate on a suitably reply, and for the first time he could
not sleep at night. Wherever he went these insinuations against him turned
up as a topic of conversation.

It was some days before he recovered enough to be able to prove in an
article in *Svenska Dagbladet*, a leading Stockholm newspaper, that *Kon-
Tiki* did not contain the passages Karsten claimed to have found there,
and that the professor had completely misquoted him. He pointed to the
fact that he and his five companions had risked their lives to prove that a
balsa raft could cross the Pacific from east to west. Karsten might sit
comfortably in his armchair and theorize about migrations against the wind
and current, but Thor demanded that he should at least accept the outcome
of the *Kon-Tiki* voyage as truth.

Karsten replied in the same paper. He now denied having ever used the
word 'humbug'. The headline 'THE KON-TIKI HUMBUG' had been originated
by the editorial staff; he himself had entitled the article 'THE SO-CALLED

KON-TIKI EXPEDITION IN THE PACIFIC'. Nor had he ever used expressions like 'sheer nonsense' about Thor's theory. This, too, was an invention of the newspaper reporter, he asserted.

Soon afterwards Thor's companions on the raft wrote an open letter to Karsten in *Nya Pressen*. They demanded that he either specify the false-hoods in Thor's book, or publicly withdraw his accusations. Karsten's answer was appended to the published letter. He had said nothing about lies; he had merely written that it was a 'miracle' that the Kon-Tiki expedition had been successfully carried through. 'This does not mean that I have accused Heyerdahl of lying. On the contrary it means that I accept the fact, even if I, like most other readers, consider it almost as a miracle.' Karsten's various *dementi* were never printed in other papers, and few were ever to learn that he had dissociated himself from all charges of dishonesty. Some papers, however, carried a note to the effect that the professor had given his solemn assurance that if Thor ever published any scientific work, he, Karsten, would return to pronounce judgement on Heyerdahl's 'brainless' theory.

While the newspaper attacks were raging around him, trying to nullify the scientific value of his expedition, Thor received a letter that served as a valuable stimulus. The world famous Swedish explorer, Sven Hedin, wrote:

'I follow your progress and your scientific work with great excitement and warm interest, hoping that you will thereby succeed in crowning your valiant and admirable Viking expedition. Where great deeds are done one may always be sure to become a target for the claws of the ravens of jealousy and doubt. But that means so little—and it is part of the game.'

Until that time Thor had had the impression that he was confronting a compact army of opposition in the scientific world. Gradually, however, he learned that he had allies of whose existence he was not aware.

One evening in the autumn of 1949, while the adverse wind blew at its worst from the Scandinavian press, he was invited by Dr Carl Mannerfelt, General Secretary of the Swedish Society for Anthropology and Geo-graphy, to his home outside Stockholm. There he met Professor Olof Selling, one of Sweden's youngest and most promising scientists, who was himself an expert on the Pacific and had carried out extensive field-work in Polynesia. Selling's speciality was prehistoric vegetation in Oceania, and he was, therefore, an authority on winds, currents, and the contribution of human migration to the conveyance of plants. He was particularly systematic in his work and had built up one of the world's largest card indexes on the tremendous literature of Polynesia, which was to be of immense use to Thor.

The conversation in Mannerfelt's home also came to be of considerable importance, not only for Thor, but also for the two other scholars who later on became his close friends. It was here that Selling was introduced to Thor's extensive scientific material before it appeared in print. He was quite overwhelmed, and later wrote: 'Hence the history of Polynesia was drawn up against a firm geographical background: the circulation system of the Pacific Ocean.'

Professor Selling saw through the agitation directed against the *Kon-Tiki* leader. There was ample evidence that some opponents had distorted the facts and all of them had intervened too soon, striking at a novice before he had brought out the work he had announced. Selling now challenged the opposition in a well-documented article that showed how Thor's theory of the drift from Southeast Asia via Northwest America to Hawaii was strongly supported by discoveries of prehistoric weather conditions he himself had described in his doctoral thesis on pollen deposits in early Hawaii. He next wrote a powerful *Criticism of the Kon-Tiki Criticisms*.

It may have been that Dr Mannerfelt, as General Secretary of the Swedish Society for Anthropology and Geography, had a definite plan in introducing the two young Pacific scholars. It seems very likely that Selling's positive reaction was a major reason for Thor being invited immediately afterwards to lecture before that exclusive Swedish society when no other scientific institution had yet cared to hear his opinion.

It caused quite a sensation when the society gave the controversial adventurer an opportunity to present the evidence in favour of his theories before a scientific audience, to be followed by an open discussion.

The lecture which took place on September 23, 1949, resulted in a unanimous resolution from the society that the Retzius Medal for 1950 should be awarded to Thor Heyerdahl 'for organizing and carrying out the Kon-Tiki expedition with a scientific scope'. This was perhaps to become the most important event in Thor's scientific career, since it broke for the first time his opponents' chief weapon: their assertion that the raft expedition was undertaken merely for the fun of it.

A less fortunate ethnology professor was so indignant at this award, that the day before the official announcement, he wrote in one of the Stockholm newspapers:

'It seems rather niggardly to hand over a silver coin worth about 9.75 to one who has earned four million by his voyage.'

Selling immediately replied in the paper that the second figure was entirely fictitious for the expenses of the expedition had only recently been recovered.

Three years had passed since the expedition without any scientific recognition for Thor in his own country. So far no institution had let him present anything but a descriptive account of his drift across the Pacific. However, his former professors at Oslo University, Bonnevie, Broch and Werenskiold, had attested verbally and in writing that he was a scholar in the full meaning of the word. Werenskiold, Professor of geography with a profound knowledge of ocean movements and human migrations, wrote in the press: 'Those who do not believe in his results must at any rate bring forward heavy artillery if they are to disprove his theory.'

Shortly after the award of the Retzius Medal, Professor Hans W'son Ahlmann, until then the President of the Swedish Society for Anthropology and Geography, was appointed Swedish Ambassador to Norway. In a press interview held upon his arrival in Oslo, he threw down the gauntlet to his Norwegian fellow scientists: 'Kon-Tiki was a brilliant enterprise. The Swedish Geographical Society feels itself honoured to have awarded Thor Heyerdahl a medal.'

Some months later a request arrived from the Royal Norwegian Academy of Science and Letters for Heyerdahl to deliver a lecture on the scientific motives and results of the Kon-Tiki expedition. Thor accepted, and His Majesty King Haakon announced that he would be present. Fru Alison Heyerdahl was also invited, but Thor's friend Dr Gutorm Gjessing, professor of ethnology at Oslo University, advised the old lady not to go, since two of the linguistic authorities of the academy had promised to demolish Heyerdahl's lecture. But Gjessing's warning had no effect on Fru Alison.

Naturally Thor laid the greatest stress that evening on his opponents' strongest argument, the language. He admitted that the linguists had discovered a distant but indisputable relationship in language proving that once, in the dawn of time, the Malay people and the ancestors of the Polynesians had parted company from some common centre in Southeast Asia. The Malays had stepped directly to the shores of their continental archipelago; the Polynesians had navigated by way of Northwest America. The Polynesians had never been Malays, and the Malays had never been Polynesians, but both had come by separate routes to their isolated island groups from somewhere on the Southeast Asian mainland. He maintained that geographical conditions and archaeological finds proved that the Polynesian route of migration had not gone straight eastward against wind and weather, but had followed the great circle and the ocean current via the extreme North Pacific.

After the lecture the chairman of the evening announced open discussion.

Headed by the geographers, some speakers rose and supported Thor. Among them was Professor Gjessing who stated that, as an ethnologist, he had many words of praise, but at the end of his speech he turned, made a gesture towards the two linguists and said that he knew they had some very strong objections. The great hall grew silent, and one could feel the suspense. Finally the King turned round to see what had become of the opponents. Then one of them, an international authority on Asian languages, slowly rose. He said that since Heyerdahl maintained that the later immigrants into Polynesia had roots in Southeast Asia, his personal objections to Heyerdahl's theory were eliminated.

'But what do *you* say?' he added, turning to opponent number two before he sat down.

The other hesitantly rose to his feet.

'I agree with my colleague', he said, and sat down.

The King threw an amused glance at Thor, and when His Majesty left the hall at the end of the meeting, Fru Alison marched triumphantly after him.

Shortly afterwards, early in 1951, Thor got two new academic awards, the Mungo Park gold medal from the Royal Scottish Geographical Society and the Prix Bonaparte-Wyse in gold from the French Société de Géographie. Later in the year His Majesty, the King of Norway, appointed him Commander of the Order of St Olav, and the Norwegian Geographical Society invited him for the first time to lecture before its audience and elected him an honorary member while the president of the society hung the distinguished St Olav's Order around his neck.

The support that Thor had so far experienced from academic circles had mainly emanated from scholars representing the geographical and biological sciences. Anthropologists throughout the world still refused to accept him as a proper scholar. He struggled, therefore, to finish his scientific manuscript, which he thought would convince even the most sceptical among the anthropologists.

As the documentary film *Kon-Tiki* in the years 1950-51 began to espouse Thor's cause in cinemas around the world, he personally stopped all further lecturing, and rarely even took time to attend an important première. When he arrived in Paris on the opening night of his film, a former Gothenburg student, the noted French ethnologist Alfred Métraux, had just stirred up some new opposition. In a French scientific periodical he had represented Heyerdahl as an adventurer without professional knowledge, and during an interview immediately before Thor's arrival Métraux

had even got the Parisian newspaper *Carrefour* to brand Heyerdahl as a
'*mauvais savant*', a bad scientist. Métraux, a leading world authority on
the Easter Island stone statues, maintained in the interview that there was
no resemblance between the statues of the Polynesian islands and those of
prehistoric South America, as Heyerdahl had written in *Kon-Tiki*. The
press met Thor at the airport with a copy of the paper, and wanted his
immediate answer. He gave no answer. He only asked to meet this new
opponent face to face.

Next morning he was taken to Métraux's office in UNESCO. With
Métraux was Dr Walter Lehmann, a specialist in South American
archaeology at the Musée de l'Homme in Paris. A third person, the
representative of *Carrefour*, sat ready with pad and pencil.

As soon as the discussion started, Thor opened his briefcase and took out
a set of printer's proofs of *American Indians in the Pacific* running to over
eight hundred pages. He showed his startled opponents a series of illustra-
tions proving the resemblance between monuments, buildings, and fishing
tackle of South America and the islands of Polynesia. In his replies to the
questions put by the two experts, he was able to refer to more than a
thousand specific sources cited in the text. The two scholars had less and
less to say.

In the end Thor took the offensive. He placed a stack of photographs
of stone statues in front of the two experts. 'Since you are among the
world's leading authorities on this subject,' he said, 'you ought to be able
to tell me without hesitation which are South American and which are
Polynesian.'

Lehmann eagerly grabbed the photographs to start sorting them into
two groups, but soon hesitated and pushed them across to Métraux: after
all, this was *his* speciality.

Métraux sorted the photographs with the greatest ease. 'These are from
Polynesia and those from South America', he said confidently.

'No!' Thor burst out triumphantly. 'You have put statues from both
areas in each pile. When even you—as an expert—fail to tell the difference,
you must admit that there is a resemblance.'

Métraux looked at his watch and suggested with a smile that as they had
now been talking for two hours, it was time to go down to the UNESCO
bar and have a drink.

The next day a large picture of Métraux and Heyerdahl with wine
glasses lifted in a toast appeared in *Carrefour* with the caption: 'A. Métraux
half convinced by Thor Heyerdahl.' After a detailed report of the meeting,
the article described the dramatic stone statue test and admitted: 'Truth
compels us to say that the experts became embarrassed. In this little game,

they erred as frequently as they stood the test.' The article ended by saying that it was necessary to modify the conclusions reached during the first interview with Métraux. The specialists had realized that Heyerdahl was also an erudite person, and Métraux had been forced to admit that he must be recognized as a genuine scientist.

Métraux's colleague and close collaborator during their work on Easter Island, the Belgian archaeologist Professor Henri Lavachery, was among the more cautious experts who waited to judge 'the Kon-Tiki theory' until the scientific material had been published in full. He later commented in an interview referring to Thor's first appearance on the international scene:

'At that time we were all convinced by the traditional theories, and even I myself never considered the possibility of a movement the other way, so it was quite natural for us to hold onto the classical point of view. It was a pleasant surprise for me when Mr Heyerdahl appeared with his new theory, because he awakened Science from its stagnation; it was like a stone thrown into a frog pond.'

American Indians in the Pacific was published in London, Chicago, and Stockholm on August 12, 1952. The Gothenburg paper which had led the Swedish opposition sent a copy to Alfred Métraux for review. Métraux now wrote:

'Heyerdahl, who has become one of the most popular heroes of our time, now draws the attention of the public to a new achievement. This explorer, who greatly deserves the fame which he enjoys, has rightly been hurt by the contempt to which he has been exposed. He has modestly asked that judgements should not be passed until he had published the work in which, supported by proof, he was to present his ideas. He has kept his promise. Anyone who opens this volume of 821 pages cannot fail to be dazzled by the overwhelming knowledge which he displays. If Thor Heyerdahl had not prepared us in advance for the feat, one would have asked oneself how it could have been possible for a single man to read so many works in so few years, make extracts of them, and present the result of the investigations in a true collection of facts from the sciences of ethnology, archaeology, linguistics, botany, geography and history. I know few men who could master such an achievement. . . .

'It is only proper that Heyerdahl stresses how fragile the foundation is on which we base our hypotheses concerning the original home of the Polynesians and the route they followed to populate Polynesia. The uncertainty is shared by many ethnologists who, while not questioning the Asiatic origin of the Polynesians, declare that they can find no trace of them on the continent from which they were supposed to have come. . . .

'Since Heyerdahl and his brave companions succeeded in crossing the Pacific on a raft, we are compelled to admit that such an achievement could have been accomplished as well by a Peruvian chieftain about the fourth century.'

The appearance of the large volume also gave Professor Selling an opportunity to come back in the Swedish press: 'This book is a remarkable work, epoch-making in the fullest sense of the word, a scientific master-piece. . . . The literature on the Pacific peoples can show no work in which the comparisons are so comprehensive and detailed. Ethnological science, from a regional point of view, has never before been the subject of so extensive a revision.'

When *American Indians in the Pacific* was published in England, the *Sunday Times* of London wrote: 'The author displays a wealth of erudition and he marshals an immense body of diversified evidence for his theories. . . . He has written a valuable, curious and even exciting work.'

Actually, this was a work of such dimensions that few got further than glancing through it before the 30th International Americanist Congress opened in Cambridge a week later. Even before the book was published, however, it was obvious to all of Thor's many opponents that the Kon-Tiki theory could not be killed by silence. There was, therefore, no other course than to kill its author, and a better slaughterhouse than the Americanist Congress could hardly be found for such a purpose. Consequently it was decided to invite him to the Cambridge Congress and give him an opportunity to put forth his views. The young revolutionary would then be faced by an anthropological execution squad composed of his main opponents from all over the world, who would presumably mow him down with deadly arguments. Few doubted that it would be his first and last encounter with a congress of international experts.

Even a declared well-wisher among the Norwegian scientists, Professor Gjessing, wrote in an otherwise favourable review: 'The author may still go to the gallows when in August he defends his views at the International Americanist Congress in Cambridge.'

There was no lack of signs predicting a battle. Reporters were there from all over the world, and from the time of his arrival Thor realized that he was regarded as an outsider. Among the two hundred participants from thirty countries, there were many who looked inquisitively at him. Others met him with a cold or tolerant smile. Although his face was known to everybody through his film and the press, none of them knew Yvonne. She was standing chatting with a group in the corridor when one of the party suddenly said: 'Let's turn our backs. Here comes Heyerdahl.'

o

Another time she was talking with a Swedish ethnologist, Professor S. Linné, when a senior member of the congress came up to them and said in a very friendly tone to Linné: 'Forgive me for not having greeted you before, but I thought you were Thor Heyerdahl.'

After several such incidents Thor did not look forward very optimistically to his lectures. Those of the congress members who delivered any speech at all usually gave only one. The maximum number allowed for each participant was three, and Thor had put his name down for three: 'Aboriginal Navigation in Peru', 'Objects and Results of the Kon-Tiki Expedition', and 'Some Basic Problems in Polynesian Anthropology'.

The chairman nominated for the session in which Thor was to speak proved to be Professor Kaj Birket-Smith from Denmark. In his mind's eye Thor saw the headline in the Danish paper after Birket-Smith's return from the previous Congress: 'KON-TIKI EXPEDITION TO BE KILLED BY SILENCE.' On the day of Thor's speeches everyone was waiting for the showdown. The corridors were crowded and many newspaper reporters were present, which also seemed to annoy the scholars.

Two other speakers were on the programme before Thor. Their topics were of so specialized a character that only a sprinkling of people had taken their seats in the lecture hall. It so happened that the one who was to have spoken immediately before Thor failed to show up. According to the schedule this should have meant a break of half an hour before Thor's appearance. Birket-Smith, however, rose from his chair, looked across the nearly empty rows of seats, and immediately called on the next speaker—Thor Heyerdahl.

Yvonne and Thor looked at each other, deeply disappointed that hardly any of the Congress members would hear the lecture he had prepared so thoroughly, and in which he had put such trust. Thor walked slowly up to the platform and began to speak. In the great auditorium, facing only a dozen or so indifferent listeners, he felt as if he was talking to himself; even Yvonne had unexpectedly disappeared.

For a few minutes Thor went ahead with his lecture. Then suddenly the big door flew open and in poured a swarm of people with Yvonne at their head. There was such a hubbub of voices, banging of seats and scraping of feet that Thor had to put down his paper and wait for quiet. Finally the auditorium was overfilled. People were standing along the walls and crowding the doorways. At last there was silence. Camera lights flashed. Thor took up his speech where he had left off, but immediately there were calls from the audience that he must start from the beginning.

Chairman Birket-Smith told him to start again, which he did, and now to an extremely attentive audience. Most of them were visibly surprised at being confronted not with a rough and bearded adventurer, but with a neat young man who chose his words with academic skill.

After the lecture Birket-Smith thanked him for what he called an extraordinarily interesting report. He then declared the floor open for discussion. Only quite uncontroversial questions were asked and Thor left the platform to loud applause.

His two remaining lectures were delivered together the next day without an intermediate break. His opponents, who had recovered from their surprise, had warmed up for a more penetrating discussion this time, yet no fight ensued. In fact, the first who requested permission to speak was the noted Canadian anthropologist, Professor Ruggles Gates. He stated that the latest results in the field of blood testing were a strong confirmation of the speaker's view. Thor had no difficulty in replying satisfactorily to others who had a few already familiar counter-arguments, and when the chairman finally closed the question period, a reporter from Oslo telegraphed to his paper that 'the well-known Danish scientist, Professor Kaj Birket-Smith, previously not one of the warmest defenders of Heyerdahl's theories, thanked the speaker and stressed the unusual importance of his researches.'

During the Congress the famous French ethnologist Paul Rivet refused to meet Thor, and would not attend any of his three lectures. Afterwards he asked the Congress to pass a resolution that Thor's theories were wrong. This was rejected on the grounds that a proposal concerning papers read could not be accepted from one who had not been present.

Toward the end of the Congress there was a cocktail party held among the glass cases of the Cambridge University Museum. Thor was greatly surprised when a quiet American, his face wrinkled with smiles, came up and shook him by the hand. It was Dr Samuel Lothrop, of Harvard University, the one who first had maintained in writing that a balsa raft could never cross the Pacific, and whose treatise had led Thor to undertake the voyage. Dr Lothrop congratulated him heartily and sincerely, both on his expedition and on his lectures.

'I have just made a model of the *Kon-Tiki* raft', he said with a grin. 'It is standing on the piano at home.'

On the day following the Congress, the important Finnish paper, *Hufvudstadsbladet*, contained a review of *American Indians in the Pacific*, signed R.K. Thor immediately thought that these initials stood for Rafael Karsten, who had promised to attack his 'brainless theory' whenever it was published. The article began:

'Thor Heyerdahl has survived his first ordeal by fire since the publication of his great volume on "the theory behind Kon-Tiki." He has just delivered his three lectures at the Americanist Congress in Cambridge before the most competent audience conceivable. On the whole his critics remained silent, and contented themselves with admitting that he had made very important contributions to science.'

The favourable Finnish review proved to be written by somebody other than Karsten. From the old professor himself there came not a word. Finally the Finnish Academy of Sciences took the initiative and invited Thor to meet Karsten at a round table discussion attended by Finland's most prominent authorities in the pertinent fields of science. Thor went, but Karsten refused to take part, in spite of strong pressure from both the Academy and the Norwegian Embassy. When asked by the press why he declined to meet the person he had formerly criticized in writing, he replied:

'I am not going to involve myself in any further polemics on this question. Has the world still not had enough of Kon-Tiki?'

The round table discussion which opened in a cordial atmosphere, developed into an informal get-together for a valuable exchange of information. Everyone present regretted Karsten's absence, but on the following day Thor was invited alone to Karsten's home. Here he met his hitherto most violent opponent, an old gentleman in a rocking chair who had laid down his weapons and wanted only a friendly and peaceful chat over a cup of tea.

A few days after the meeting in Cambridge, the 4th International Congress of Anthropologists and Ethnologists took place in Vienna. Yvonne and Thor, like many others who had attended the proceedings at Cambridge, decided to go by train direct to Vienna. But just before their departure, they were warned by a friendly Austrian scholar that things would probably be rather unpleasant there for Thor. Another of his earliest opponents, Professor Robert von Heine-Geldern, had been appointed Vice-President of the pending Vienna Congress. He had always been openly antagonistic to 'the Kon-Tiki theory.' Well before Thor's scientific volume was published, Heine-Geldern had tried to tear the theory to pieces in an article in the *Geographical Journal*, the organ of the Royal Geographical Society of London, but Thor had won the round with his unexpectedly powerful rebuttal in the next issue. Now in his capacity as vice-president of the forthcoming congress, Heine-Geldern was in a position to fight back. Thor's Austrian informant said that the vice-president had written a new violent attack against Heyerdahl and the Kon-Tiki theory in a special pamphlet to be distributed free to all Congress members at the opening session.

The prospects of an enjoyable time in Vienna immediately crumbled.

Thor recalled with pleasure his previous visit, but at that time Heine-Geldern had been in America. Thor had been invited to lecture before the Vienna Anthropological Society, where his ideas had been met with great interest. Professor Wilhelm Koppers, later president of the Vienna Congress, had even proposed the formation of a committee for the advancement of studies of pre-Columbian migrations, the committee to consist of Koppers himself, Heyerdahl, Paul Rivet, and Heine-Geldern. On his return this news had made Heine-Geldern furious, and the committee was never formed. There was a special reason for Heine-Geldern's violent reaction. During his years in America he had met considerable resistance from the anthropologists, because he was a declared advocate for the 'diffusionist' views, or the so-called Vienna school, whereas nearly all American anthropologists subscribed to the 'isolationist' view. The diffusionists maintained that cultural characteristics were developed in one place and spread by migrations of people to distant parts of the world, while the isolationists believed that similarities between cultures in widely separated places were the result of independent evolution brought about by climatic similarities or the uniformity of the human mind. The *Kon-Tiki* crossing of the Pacific had, to Heine-Geldern's mind, punctured the isolationists' case, but had also delivered a hard blow to the theory of the Vienna school, which had visualized a trans-Pacific migration in the very opposite direction of *Kon-Tiki*'s drift.

After learning of the ambush that awaited him, Thor acted with lightning speed. He cancelled their railway tickets, and he and Yvonne caught the first plane for Vienna. Upon landing he headed straight for Heine-Geldern's office at Vienna University, and politely asked the Professor for a copy of his already printed critical comments. He found the old scholar to be a slightly stooping but vigorous person who turned his intelligent eyes upon him with surprise. Then he beamed contentedly from behind his spectacles and fetched a copy. Thor next asked to be allotted sufficient time during the congress session to reply to the vice-president's attack. This Heine-Geldern refused. If Heyerdahl had wished to speak at the Congress he should have signed on as a lecturer at the time he was invited to attend. Now it was too late.

Outside Heine-Geldern's office he was stopped by two of the Professor's students. They were shocked to learn that the visitor would not be given an opportunity to defend himself. Shortly afterward, a delegation of students asked Thor if he was willing to meet their Professor in an open debate if they could arrange one under the auspices of the Congress. Thor at once agreed, and they went to the Professor. They returned visibly disappointed: Heine-Geldern had refused.

On the sly the students arranged a meeting with another elderly ethnologist, Professor Dominik Wölfel. Thor joined them all in a corner of an old and abandoned underground wine cellar. Wölfel declared that he sympathized with the theory that the ancient civilizations in Peru and the South Sea islands had a common origin. He had come to this conclusion through his study of weapons and cranial trepanation in the Pacific area. He had in fact pointed out this relationship in one of his publications, but he had not taken any stand as to the direction of the transfer until he became persuaded by the Heyerdahl theory. By the light of a dim lantern the young and the old scholar exchanged mutually useful information, while the students gathered close around them and spoke with lowered voices. It was like a secret meeting in the Roman catacombs at the time of the persecution of the Christians.

That night Thor lay thinking, trying to co-ordinate the information he had received in the wine cellar. In the morning his plan of defence was ready. First he went to Professor Bleichsteiner, the director of the Vienna Ethnographical Museum. He was very helpful and gave him permission to answer Heine-Geldern in the museum's forthcoming year book.

Thor next approached the editor of this year book, Dr Etta Becker-Donner, who was herself a specialist in South American ethnology. He was much surprised when she put into his hands a pre-Inca raft model she had recently brought back from a desert grave on the Pacific coast below Tiahuanaco. But when Thor asked about answering Heine-Geldern in an appendix to the year book she shook her head. The year book had already been printed and would be on sale in the lobby when the Congress opened in three days' time. Thor was well aware of this, but asked permission to put an insert in every copy, if it could be ready in time. The editor agreed with a smile; she could not imagine that there was time enough left.

It was already Friday afternoon, and on Monday morning the Congress was to open. Thor took a taxi to Ullstein Verlag, the publishing firm that had just had a great success with the *Kon-Tiki* book in the German-speaking countries. After a meeting with the publisher and the directors of the printing plant, he was promised that the pamphlet would be ready on Sunday evening if they got the manuscript early on Sunday morning. Then he returned to his hotel and allowed himself a full night's sleep before going to work.

On Saturday morning he started on his reply to Heine-Geldern's attack. From the Professor's point of view, it proved unfortunate he had written his critique so long before Thor's scientific volume had been published. All Thor had to do now was quote from his own volume, where all

Heine-Geldern's arguments had already been refuted in advance. The Professor, who had never been in Polynesia, had gone through a great many books selecting instances of winds blowing contrary to the *Kon-Tiki* drift, and with these references as the basis of his argument, he said that a voyage from Asia in primitive times was feasible. Thor, in his reply, stressed that all these instances represented exceptions from normal conditions, and that by using such a method of selection, one could prove as well that there were so many hurricanes in Polynesia that it was dangerous to live there.

From eight o'clock on Saturday morning until three o'clock on Sunday morning, Thor worked continuously on his article, which he delivered when the printing office opened less than three hours later. The manuscript was written in English, and the printers were all German-speaking, which caused considerable trouble in the proof stage. During the whole of Sunday Yvonne drove back and forth with corrected proofs. That evening an insert was placed in each year book.

On Monday morning Thor was among the first to arrive in the flag-decorated Congress hall, where he was welcomed by the Congress president, Professor Koppers, and the vice-president, Heine-Geldern. He took the opportunity to hand each a fresh copy of his reply, then found himself a place in the hall beside Yvonne.

Heine-Geldern was pale with rage as he walked up to his place underneath the flags on the stage. Yvonne later described how many of the venerable scientists in the hall had behaved like giggling schoolboys, whispering and nudging one another in an effort to get some of the spare copies she had brought with her in her capacious handbag.

Professor Heine-Geldern had difficulty in forgetting this episode at the Vienna Congress in 1952. For several years he continued to make bitter comments in the newspapers about everything that Thor undertook. But in 1960 they arrived at an unexpected armistice. Heine-Geldern had been appointed president of the 34th International Americanist Congress, which was to be held in Vienna. Because he knew that Thor, in the lecture he was to deliver, would inveigh against a common opponent, the American ethnobotanist, Dr E. D. Merrill, he wrote personally to Thor, issuing him a hearty welcome.

For nearly a generation Merrill had been the most pugnacious adversary of the diffusionists. He was one of the leaders of the isolationist view, and the strong opposition to the Vienna school was to a great extent his work. For many years specialists all over the world had allowed themselves to be influenced by Merrill's opinion that America and the rest of the world had not a single cultivated plant in common before Columbus crossed the Atlantic. They accepted this as proof that human beings had never immigrated into or emigrated from the civilizations of America before the Europeans arrived. Had they done so they would certainly have taken with them some of their most important means of life, cultivated plants, and planted them on the other side of the ocean.

Thor maintained in his lecture in Vienna that the logic in Merrill's arguments could be likened to the water in a barrel. It all ran out if only one stave was removed. At the time when Merrill's point of view was initially accepted, the barrel was apparently whole, but in the time that followed, historians and botanists had pulled away one stave after another, so that now it was time for modern research to realize that the barrel was empty. With quotations from Merrill's own works, he showed how the ethnobotanist had revised his own thinking year after year. Merrill had gradually been forced to admit that the sweet potato, the coconut palm, and the gourd, and probably also the cotton plant, the banana, and other plants, did prove that there had been cultural contact between America and Polynesia before the Europeans arrived. In Merrill's last book, which rounded out his life's work, the Kon-Tiki expedition was repeatedly referred to, and obviously represented his most difficult stumbling block. A sketch of the *Kon-Tiki* raft even appeared as a vignette to his index. The old botanist had at last upset what remained of his barrel by stating that there had been a two-way contact between America and Polynesia. 'We may admit', he wrote, 'that natives of South America may have reached some of the Pacific islands on balsa rafts. That there were occasional and accidental associations between the peoples of Polynesia and America, and even occasional ones between the American Indians and the eastern Polynesian islands, actually must be accepted.'

Thus, one of the most prominent defenders of isolationism had been driven into retreat. And what was more, after Heyerdahl's lecture, Heine-Geldern, as president of the Congress, went up on the stage and admitted that the sea route from early Asia to America had perhaps gone with the Japan current north of Hawaii, as Heyerdahl maintained; and he even thanked Heyerdahl in front of the audience for his fine contribution to Polynesian research.

Why was there so much emotional reaction to a seemingly harmless migration theory? Perhaps the best answer to this question was given by Professor Kristian Gleditsch, president of the Norwegian Geographical Society, in a newspaper article on Thor Heyerdahl's cause:

'A man who presents a new scientific hypothesis must of course be prepared for criticism and opposition.

'A man who risks his life to prove his theory must be prepared to call down the special wrath of armchair geographers.

'A man who, in our age of specialization, combines arguments drawn from at least ten different sciences is inevitably the target for the Olympic thunderbolts of the specialists. More often than not, he has even deserved it, for no one can master all the sciences at the same time. And yet, from time to time, someone must try to combine the results of the different sciences and weigh them one against the other.

'A young man who, without having passed all the regular examinations, proves that a long list of distinguished professors have been wrong, cannot count on any mercy. No one likes to lose face. . . .

'Thor Heyerdahl has challenged conventional thought, he has challenged all those who had expressed themselves with a bit too much confidence on the balsa tree and on ancient Peruvian navigation. He has challenged all the specialists, all those who know so much and had arrived at explanations that *almost* fitted. Worst of all—he has found a simple solution for a beautifully complicated problem. The Polynesians had become a Gordian knot. The man with the sword will never become popular with all those who diligently and patiently weave doctorates and stipends from different thread-ends.'

Chapter 16

THE BEWITCHED ISLANDS

WITH the gruelling work on *American Indians in the Pacific* finished, Thor at last felt that he was entirely through with the Kon-Tiki expedition, and that a chapter of his life had come to an end. After six years of continuous work he decided to take his first short holiday, and he and Yvonne joined Professor Selling and the Mannerfelts on a trip to Corsica. Carefree days in a primitive Corsican fishing village, the friendliness of the village people, and the simplicity of life blessed by the Mediterranean sun was just what they needed to counteract the hectic pace of recent years. The wholesome change of setting prompted Yvonne to propose a fine for any of the three young scientists who mentioned one word that had any connection with scientific terminology. They all agreed and lived up to it happily. For Thor this pleasant introduction to the Mediterranean world would become of lasting importance several years later.

The peaceful life did not last long. Only two weeks after the publication of *American Indians in the Pacific* something happened that threw Thor headlong into new adventures in a far-off corner of the world.

It actually began at the Vienna congress in 1952, when Thor met Dr Alfred Métraux for the first time since their dramatic encounter in Paris. On that previous occasion Thor had confused Métraux with a group of pictures of Pacific stone statues. Now Métraux told about a surprising photograph of another stone statue that he had seen not long before in the American Museum of Natural History in New York. It depicted a large stone head recently discovered in the Galápagos group, the cluster of Pacific islands on the equatorial line some six hundred miles off the South American coast. According to the scientists, man had never set foot on these islands prior to the arrival of the Spaniards. Métraux claimed, however, that this stone head strongly indicated pre-European occupation. He added that the sculpture was strikingly reminiscent of the statues on Easter Island, and for this reason he was convinced that it must have been the Polynesians rather than the South American Indians who had been visiting the Galápagos.

This information was so fascinating to Thor that he decided on the spot to go to this remote island group in search of the mysterious stone head and other possible remains from hitherto unknown pre-European visits.

The historic fact that the Galápagos group was uninhabited when discovered by the Europeans had been used as an argument against Thor's migration theory. If South American balsa rafts had sailed as far as to Polynesia, it had been argued, why then had their crews not found the Galápagos which lay much nearer to the South American coast?

It was maintained that there were no archaeological remains in the Galápagos group, and that no human foot had trodden its soil before Bishop Tomas de Berlanga discovered it in 1535. But when Thor began to check the existing literature in search of a documented source for this assertion, he found that the various writers went around in a circle quoting each other, without any archaeologist having ever been ashore for actual investigation. The islands had seen numerous visits by geologists and biologists, among them Charles Darwin in the *Beagle*, but no anthropologist had taken the trouble to go there, because they had all been convinced that the South American balsa rafts were incapable of keeping afloat across the six hundred miles that separated the islands from the mainland.

Thor had heard first-hand descriptions of the arid Galápagos group since he was a schoolboy, and he realized that such an inhospitable world of lava and cactus was little suited for permanent aboriginal habitation. Thus the group might very well have been discovered and known to the early seafarers from the mainland without anybody settling there permanently. He remembered how one of his own teachers in primary school had once left Larvik with an expedition of intrepid local pioneers who wanted to try their fortunes as colonists on this unexploited island group. They had come back disappointed: water shortage and other problems had forced them to abandon 'the Bewitched Islands'. The latter nickname had been given to the Galápagos group by the early conquistadores and British buccaneers who had tried to land there. If they steered towards the mountainous islands in the evening, they could wake up in the morning to find they had vanished. They did not realize that their ship had been carried off by the Humboldt Current, which encircles the Galápagos at great speed on its way from Peru to Polynesia.

A few weeks after the Vienna Congress, in the autumn of 1952, Thor was off once more to America. In New York the archaeologists of the American Museum of Natural History verified that Métraux had given

an accurate description of the photograph of the newly discovered
Galápagos statue. The picture had only been on loan to the museum,
but nobody doubted that the sculpture was genuine. The photograph had
been taken by an American botanist, and Thor finally tracked him down
in Boston, where he got a chance to inspect the picture personally. When
he saw the photograph of the big coarse stone face emerging from the
underbrush with lichen on the tall wrinkled forehead, the last remaining
doubts left him too, and the botanist firmly reasserted that he had made
this discovery in the Galápagos. He even drew a sketch map showing
the site of the monument in the interior of Floreana, one of the southernmost islands in the group. Thor wasted no time in engaging two professional archaeologists for his expedition: his old friend from Sante Fé,
Dr Erik Reed, head of the archaeological division of the United States
National Park Services, and Arne Skjölsvold, a young and promising
Norwegian archaeologist recommended by the University of Oslo.
In January 1953, the three met in Guayaquil on the Pacific coast of
Ecuador.

In the expedition diary which was initiated on January 8th, Thor wrote:
'The plan and purpose of the expedition is to carry out the first archaeological survey on the Galápagos islands in the hope that evidence may be
found to show that the group was known even to pre-European people.'

The skipper of a little coastal vessel bound for Santa Cruz Island by
way of Panama was persuaded to take the three men along, and in
exchange for a considerable sum of money, agreed to set them ashore
on the out-of-the-way island of Floreana. One late afternoon at the end of
January, they landed on Black Beach, Floreana.

Early the next morning the three explorers made for the interior of the
high island, following a steep and narrow trail aided by the crude pencil-
drawn sketch map. It was as hot as an oven under the equatorial sun and the
climb was hard, so when they finally reached a shady cave, Erik and Arne
threw themselves down to recover their breath. Thor went on by himself,
and was suddenly confronted by the stone head in the photograph. Large
and grotesque, with much of its surface covered by moss and lichen, it
gazed at him from between the foliage. But a single glance at the image
was enough to make Thor's heart sink. This was just a natural moss-
covered stone that resembled a wrinkled face with a prominent nose.
To increase the resemblance to a human head still further, someone had
quite recently added the outlines of eyes and mouth. Without revealing
his bitter disappointment, Thor went back to the others and said quietly:

'Come and see how a camera can lie.'

It was a most embarrassing affair. Here he had brought two professional archaeologists halfway around the world to one of the most remote places on the globe, only to be confronted with a practical joke.

They heard someone working in the brush nearby and discovered a man hoeing a fruit and vegetable garden. He told them that he was Heinz Wittmer, a German, who with his wife and two children were the only inhabitants of the island. They had lived a Robinson Crusoe existence for years in the wilderness. Wittmer admitted, with an innocent smile, that he himself had touched up the stone to amuse his children. He had even been present when the two American scientists had photographed the 'statue', but when he had seen how delighted they were with their discovery, he had not had the heart to tell them the truth.

Thor had to fight hard not to show that he was deeply depressed, and one thing was certain: he would not leave the Galápagos without making an all-out effort to find traces of pre-European visits.

After a few days of futile exploration of the inner mountains and coastal cliffs, something happened which more than compensated for the initial disappointment caused by the stone head. When Thor asked the Wittmers if they had ever encountered old potsherds or other prehistoric remains during their digging in the fields, they replied that they had often seen fragments of ceramic vessels in the ground, most of them in the chicken run, where the hens had kicked them up out of the earth.

Could it be possible? The three explorers asked Mrs Wittmer to take them there. They found a recent rainstorm had dug a small ravine through the chicken run, and stuck to the sides were potsherds and other remains of early Indian activity on the site. Arne dug carefully in the soil and produced an Inca flute of terra-cotta. He picked the soil out of it with a straw, put it to his mouth, and for the first time in centuries its piping notes sounded through the air.

On their way to Floreana, Thor had arranged with two natives from the island of Santa Cruz to come for them in their fishing smack before a certain date. They were then to take the men around to other islands of the group where pre-European Indians might have been ashore. Their method of selecting spots for archaeological investigation was simple and direct. They tried to visualize where the Indians would have chosen to camp or settle during their visits to the islands. The coastline was for the most part made inaccessible by precipices and by black and rust-red rocks and pinnacles. In only a very few places did the highlands drop gently towards the coast to form some sort of bay with a narrow landing beach. They went ashore in every place where primitive seafarers could have made a landing and there they searched for a suitable camping ground.

It turned into an exceedingly interesting trip, not only because of new archaeological finds, but also because the animal life on the islands and in the seas surrounding them was so remarkable and of so many varieties. On land there were large colonies of giant multi-coloured iguanas looking like young crocodiles. Giant tortoises, called *galápagos* in Spanish, from which these islands got their name, were once common, but now extremely rare. These two types of giant reptiles were the only land animals prior to European arrival. But the early Spaniards and British buccaneers had brought cats, dogs, donkeys, and pigs to the islands. Their descendants now ran wild. There was also plenty of bird life, including a large variety of remarkably tame finches in all colours, and also penguins, pelicans, and graceful red flamingos. The sea was thronged with easily caught fish, and occasionally a shark was spotted deep down in the clear water or a giant ray would shoot into the air and strike the surface with a noise like a cannon shot. As the small expedition boat passed along the coast a large number of sea iguanas and sea lions slid into the water and disappeared, and occasionally a huge sea turtle would jolt from a beach into the ocean.

Thor, who had by now trained himself to be a strong, long-distance swimmer, often dived into the midst of a school of curious sea lions. Once he threw himself on the back of a giant turtle to try to catch it, but it dived and drew him down into the depths until he had to let go. Another time, wearing swimming goggles, he was searching for rare creatures underwater in the crevices along a large block of lava. He saw something moving slowly in the shadows close to his face: the ugly twisting head of a moray eel, its evil eyes set on him and its mouth open for attack. He moved away in a hurry, for he knew from his year on Fatu Hiva that this huge eel is just as dangerous as a shark, and can easily cut off an arm or a leg with a single bite.

Everywhere he went he took his film camera as he was particularly keen to get good pictures of the iguanas. Of all the animals on the islands they were certainly the most interesting. To see them scurry off into the underbrush or draw themselves lazily across the blocks of lava like brilliantly coloured, fringed dragons was like stealing a glimpse into the past, when their ancestors, the giant saurians, were rulers of the animal kingdom on earth. The marine variety blew foam through their nostrils like the fiery dragons of fairy tales.

One day in the noon hour, when Thor had fallen asleep on a shelf in a cool, shadowy cave, he was awakened by something touching him. He turned over and looked straight into a bearded and dark shiny face with sparkling eyes. It was a female sea lion which had been so attracted by this blond man that she would not go away despite all his attempts to get rid of her. Finally he turned over on the other side and went back to sleep, leaving the furry mammal lying against his back.

The male sea lions could be vicious, but the females were humorous, often as tame as domestic animals, and full of fun. When Arne played his harmonica on the beach in the evenings, they would come ashore in throngs, wriggle up close to his legs and stay there, quietly blinking their eyes.

On the large but uninhabited Santiago Island, Thor and Arne, with their two guides, set off towards the trailless interior, hoping finally to get some pictures of the giant tortoises. Erik remained behind, preferring to pursue another line of activity. Because whalers, sealers, fishermen, and other casual visitors had for centuries carried out wholesale slaughter for food and oil, the giant tortoise was nearly extinct, but occasional specimens were still to be found among the cactus forests on the approaches to the inland volcanic craters. The little party had filled their canteens from the water container in the boat before they started. The day was burning hot. It was a hard climb, and lava blocks and giant cacti made any progress slow and cumbersome. With the equatorial sun straight overhead, the sweat poured from them, and soon mosquitoes and horseflies attacked in great swarms. Thor and the elder guide tried to economize with their sparse water supply, but soon had to share with the two others who had already emptied their canteens.

Their thirst was almost intolerable. Towards evening Thor was the only one who had a few drops left in his canteen. Suddenly black clouds began to form around the inland volcanoes, followed by a downpour. They spread out their tent on the ground to collect the precious drops, and soon it was a pond. As the water was polluted from the dirty canvas, they poured it off to make a cleaner second catch. No sooner had they spread out the clean canvas than the rain stopped as abruptly as it had started, and they were left without a supply. Around them all the rain water had been immediately absorbed by the porous lava ground. Arne found a single hollow in a rock holding a little muddy water, and carefully scooped it up and filled his canteen. But to disinfect it, he poured so many chlorine tablets into it that the water became undrinkable.

The men struggled on, their tongues almost stuck to the roofs of their mouths, and when they pitched camp that night, the only topic of conversation was water—the normally unappreciated blessings of plain water.

The following morning they were strongly tempted to return to the coast at once, but since they had not as yet seen any of the tortoises, Thor talked them into going farther into the cactus forest. Soon they heard a strange sound. It came from among the large and spiny cactus trees and sounded like wind forced out of a large pair of bellows. 'Galápagos', said the guides, and explained that when the giant tortoise is scared by the approach of man, it withdraws its head and limbs into its shell, pressing out the air with an audible noise. Searching where they had heard the noise, they came upon a gigantic tortoise hidden inside its high and vaulted shell which was almost as big as a bathtub. Nearby some smaller ones were chewing on cactus leaves.

This led the men to remember that the cactus is in a way a living water tank. They cut off a few of the thick leaves, removed the thorns and hard green skin, and found a white watery mass, something like the inside of unripe watermelon. They chewed and sucked out the liquid and discovered the taste was not unpleasant, but it had an astringent effect on the throat. When Thor had filmed the tortoises, the four men had one single thought in their heads: to go back to the water supply on the boat. The journey was almost torture, and when they finally reached the boat, Arne threw himself face down in the tank and, in spite of all warnings, drank like a madman. When he stood up, eyes closed and mouth wide open, he looked like a marble fountain. The water was spouting out of his mouth until he was just as empty as he had been before he started drinking.

By looking for camp sites near landing areas that would have attracted primitive raft voyagers, the three explorers, in the course of a couple of months, had discovered four pre-European habitation sites on three of the main islands. It was soon apparent that the arid Galápagos group, in all probability, had never housed any permanent settlers until modern man came with concrete water tanks. Yet coastal Indians from Ecuador and Peru had made frequent calls long before the rise of the Inca Empire, and the various prehistoric visitors had used the same traditional camp-sites. The expedition encountered, among ancient flint scrapers and other remains, more than two thousand prehistoric potsherds representing at least a hundred and thirty-one different jars.

The ancient Indians very rarely broke a jar, so the quantity of broken jars suggested frequent visits throughout the centuries. The scarcity and often complete absence of surface soil prevented vestiges of less enduring materials, like wood, bone, or cloth, from being preserved, whereas flint scrapers and ceramics are everlasting and can only be broken into smaller fragments. The early South American Indians had made pottery vessels of different shapes, colours, and consistency, at different cultural epochs and in different places along the mainland coast. Thus many of the potsherds serve as real 'fingerprints' when analysed by a trained archaeologist who wants to know in what period and place the jar was manufactured.

It was therefore a moment of great excitement to the three men when, after pitching camp on an aboriginal habitation site, they ran across identifiable black Chimu pottery with frog or wart patterns as soon as they scraped the ground with their trowels. On the same site they also came across the familiar polychrome pottery characteristic of the period when the Tiahuanaco culture expanded from the highlands down to the coast of north Peru, long before the time of the first Inca. In one area scattered with prehistoric potsherds and once cultivated American Indian cotton now growing wild, they found a primitive pre-European type of chalkstone spinning wheel.

When the little expedition was finally picked up by a visiting Ecuadorian naval ship, and the black cones of the Bewitched Islands sank into the ocean, Thor's thoughts went back to the lonely stone head half hidden in the foliage on Floreana, and the strange combination of circumstances that had led him on an expedition with such a rewarding outcome.

Back on the mainland of Ecuador, Thor took Reed and Skjölsvold on a trip to the jungle coast of the Santa Elena peninsula. There he solved the riddle he had tried in vain to solve on the Kon-Tiki expedition: the use of the *guaras* for steering purposes. It was known that *guaras*, broad, almost sword-shaped boards of hard wood with a handle at the upper end, had been used by the ancient Inca seafarers not only as centre-boards but also to steer the raft. But although a number of experts had been consulted, nobody was able to explain the principles of *guara* steering. The ancient secret of the Inca navigation method was lost, and modern scholars were convinced that a balsa raft could only sail before the wind like *Kon-Tiki*.

An Ecuadorian amateur archaeologist, Emilio Estrada, took Thor's party to see some coastal Indians who were still fishing from small rafts of three logs. They knew that until the turn of the century their forefathers had *navigated* huge balsa rafts carrying many tons of cargo to and from Peru, irrespective of the winds and currents. They told Thor that the whole secret was knowing how the *guaras* should be lifted and dropped in correct sequence and in relation to the sail. With the Indians' help, Thor and his friends built a small balsa raft of the *Kon-Tiki* type, and with Estrada, they let themselves be blown out on it into the Pacific by an offshore wind.

This little trip became an unforgettable experience even for Thor. At first a number of wrong manoeuvres with the *guaras* resulted in the raft turning entirely around and drifting on into the ocean as before, only stern foremost. This was exactly what had happened so often on the

P

Kon-Tiki five years earlier. But then suddenly they discovered how, by a simultaneous manipulation of sail and *guaras*, they could stop the turning of the raft and set the course of the bow in almost any direction they wanted, as sharp into the wind as any regular sailboat. After a 101-day drift on *Kon-Tiki*, it was a great and delightful experience for Thor to suddenly see their burgee at the masthead fluttering with the wind in the direction opposite to the raft's drift forward. They were tacking against the wind! The Incas had thus been able to steer around any reef and land on the sheltered side of any island! With one man pulling in the guy ropes of the square sail and another merely raising or lowering a *guara*, Thor and his companions swung their balsa raft around, and when they came about they tacked against the wind back to their starting point on the beach. Such leading authorities on South American archaeology as W. C. Bennett, S. K. Lothrop, Junius Bird, and Gordon Ekholm also turned up to get a first-hand report on the results of the Galápagos expedition.

They were all invited to the New York apartment of Dr Lothrop, where Thor noted Lothrop's model of the *Kon-Tiki* standing on the piano in the living room like a kind of scientific 'Oscar'. All those assembled were amazed when Thor disclosed the truth about Wittmer's stone head, but still more so when he opened a suitcase full of dirty bags containing Galápagos potsherds, which Lothrop emptied on the big mahogany table. Here was something that they could all recognize and accept as evidence of pre-European activities in the oceanic Galápagos group.

Two of the world's leading experts on aboriginal pottery from the coast of Ecuador and northern Peru, Dr Betty Meggers and Dr Clifford Evans, then examined the material in the Smithsonian Institution in Washington. The results were published in *Archaeological Evidence of Pre-Spanish Visits to the Galápagos Islands*, a monograph by Thor Heyerdahl and Arne Skjölsvold issued by the Society for American Archaeology. Thus the range of ancient South American civilization was pushed out for the first time to the oceanic islands in the Pacific, six hundred miles or more from the nearest mainland, and it was proved that the coastal Indians had gone on voyages just as extensive as those the Norwegian Vikings made when they discovered Iceland.

The news that the Heyerdahl expedition had found ancient habitation sites on the Galápagos was quickly spread in the press. Heine-Geldern was immediately quoted in a Vienna newspaper, that although he did not know what the expedition had found, whatever it was must be remains left by Polynesian seafarers on their way eastwards to South America. When it was revealed that the finds were sherds of American Indian pottery, he refrained from further comments.

The Gothenburg archaeologist, Rydén, entered the fray once more with an article in an American technical journal in which he tried to negate the value of the Galápagos findings by suggesting that the broken ceramic vessels had probably been left by visiting Spaniards. In a subsequent issue, however, he was put in his place by Dr Evans, one of the experts who had identified the Galápagos material. Evans disclosed that Rydén had never even seen the finds in question, whereas he and his colleagues at the Smithsonian had analysed them and established that they were not only pre-Spanish, but even pre-Inca. From then on there were no further attempts at minimizing the importance of the Galápagos discoveries.

By now a number of American scholars had begun to doubt whether the various New World civilizations had really been as isolated as they had hitherto believed. Lothrop and others had made archaeological discoveries suggesting that there had been direct contact by sea between Mexico and northwestern South America. At the 33rd International Americanist Congress, held in Costa Rica in 1958, the young American archaeologist, Dr Michael Coe, was able to produce clear evidence of such contact by sea between the Pacific coasts of North and South America. He referred to earlier works which had maintained that such voyages were impossible until the Spaniards arrived with European ships, then added:

'These papers were written, however, before the Kon-Tiki expedition and before the find, of pre-Columbian sherds on the Galápagos Islands, 600 miles from the nearest shore. The evidence that primitive navigators could make journeys of such distances on balsa rafts with or without *guaras* has cleared the way for a new interpretation of prehistoric diffusion.'

Chapter 17

THE ROAD TO TIAHUANACO

DURING the years following the Kon-Tiki expedition, Thor had been on the move incessantly, and Yvonne had accompanied him on long and fatiguing journeys, living in cabins, hotel rooms, and flats as the circumstances required. They were on their way to the Galápagos when she discovered that she was expecting her first child, and she returned to Oslo. When Thor came back from the expedition, it was time to find a permanent home. Both of them would have preferred to settle down in the picturesque log cabins at Owl's Creek, but Thor's many activities made it desirable for him to remain in or near Oslo, where he could be within reach of libraries, the airport, and the Kon-Tiki Museum. After a long search they happened to find a beautiful early eighteenth-century farmhouse surrounded by enormous trees, an antique among the modern blocks of flats in Oslo's residential district. This was a home after Thor's own heart. With all the respect for antiques and relics of the past that had been nursed in him since his childhood days in Larvik, he began to restore and renovate the old buildings.

About the same time, in May 1953, Princess Margaret of Great Britain paid a formal visit to Norway, and Thor was asked to show her around the Kon-Tiki Museum. Afterwards, at a royal luncheon in the Canadian legation, Lady Wright, the wife of the British Ambassador, asked if Thor would escort the Princess in to dinner at a party in the British Embassy that evening. He accepted, saying he appreciated the honour, but when he returned home he telephoned to add that if it involved any dancing, he regretted that he would have to decline the invitation. Lady Wright assured him that there would be no question of this.

Shortly after the event he wrote me in Larvik:

'Dear Arnold,

'So much has happened recently. For some days I have been wondering whether or not I have written to tell you that Yvonne has given birth to a well-shaped girl. Just what we wanted. Guess if we are happy! . . . By the way, knowing me as you do, you will appreciate a bizarre experience I had the other day. You know I can't dance, never go to dances, and have never even danced with Yvonne. But on May 16th I met Princess Margaret, first at the Kon-Tiki Museum, then at lunch, and in the evening I took her in to dinner at a gala banquet in the British Embassy. I had explicitly told both my hosts and the Embassy that I do not dance. While the Princess and I were sitting in an anteroom after dinner with Princess Astrid and the British Ambassador and his wife, we heard a flourish in the hall. The Ambassador got up and said we must join the others for there was to be an entertainment.

'We went into the great hall, where two hundred guests were standing in close ranks up against the walls. Only Prince and Princess Viggo of Denmark and some of the other royalty were seated. We took our places standing beside them in the front row. I looked round expectantly for the performers. The orchestra began to play a tune with a curious rhythm, and suddenly Princess Margaret took hold of my hands and said:

' "Come, let us dance."

'All eyes were fastened upon us; wherever I looked there were Generals adorned with medals, royalty, and the *élite* of Norway in full evening dress, and there was I—*the only one who could not dance*—expected to perform solo with the sister of the Queen of England! I tried to withdraw my hands and whispered cautiously that I could not dance.

' "Oh, just try", said the Princess and drew me on.

'I protested that I hadn't any idea what dancing was; had never tried it since I was forced to when I was eight years old. But she insisted, and the more I drew back, the more she kept holding me and, of course, I couldn't start fighting with her in public. In a low voice I tried desperately to explain to her that I was in serious trouble. Everyone was watching us excitedly. As a last attempt I said that I only danced the hula-hula and Indian war dances.

' "All right," she answered. "Either you dance the samba with me, or I dance the hula with you!"

'Smilingly she put her arm around my neck. The battle was lost. I braced myself as if for a parachute jump, pushed the Princess in front of me onto the great dance floor, and all by ourselves we started moving, I hoped in time with the music. Now that we had gone that far, both the Princess and I were nearly choking with laughter, and most people were so much occupied with looking at our faces and trying to hear what the joke was, that perhaps they forgot to look at our feet. We danced the samba and the waltz and another dance I don't even know the name of, but I danced all three in the same way, and the Princess refused to let me go until the music stopped and we could sit down to listen to the *real* entertainment, supplied by professional actors.

'So now I must begin to take dancing lessons. Never another experience like this!

'But Princess Margaret and I parted the best of friends. Today I have the unusual task of sending to H.R.H. Princess Margaret Rose, Buckingham Palace, London, the score of the Norwegian student song, "Mens mannen var ute efter öl" ("While the husband was fetching beer")! Can you beat that? We sang it and she thought it so amusing that I had to promise to get the music for her. . . .'

The next week Thor took his first voluntary lesson at the dancing school he had so thoroughly scorned as a boy. Soon afterwards he got a letter from Princess Margaret, thanking him for the score.

'When you said you couldn't dance', she wrote, 'I didn't believe you, and I still don't, for we swept round the floor with the greatest ease and rhythm.'

In August, 1954, Thor was invited to the 31st International Americanist Congress, in São Paulo, Brazil. Due to his success at the previous Congress, he was elected one of the honorary vice-presidents, and went as the official representative of Norway. Yvonne accompanied him. He was to give a preliminary report on the Galápagos expedition and show samples of the pottery found there.

The first person he saw when he went up to start his lecture was Dr Paul Rivet, the elderly French ethnologist who had demonstrated against Thor by staying away from his three lectures at the Cambridge Congress. Now Rivet was sitting in the front row right below the lectern. When Thor began speaking he took out a newspaper, turned the pages and started reading. Thor paid no attention, but he noticed that the Frenchman kept looking up to see if the speaker was annoyed. As Thor calmly proceeded, Rivet folded his newspaper with a rustle that was heard all over the hall, rose to his feet, marched up the central aisle and went out. A little later he came back, sat down and opened the paper again. This time no one would say that he had stayed away! Afterwards, when the audience gathered around the fragments from the Galápagos, Rivet vanished.

After the lecture Thor was talking in the anteroom with a friendly young Argentinian student, Rex Gonzales, who was anxious to introduce him to his countryman, the noted ethnologist Professor J. Imbelloni, even though the latter was antagonistic to Thor's theory.

'There he comes', said the Argentinian.

An elderly man was slowly descending a broad flight of stone steps. The young man stopped him and tried to introduce Thor. Imbelloni ignored Thor's outstretched hand and said in an expressionless voice: 'You must have made millions out of your voyage.'

Then he calmly continued going down the steps.

Years later, when the 37th International Americanist Congress was in Argentina, this same young student, now Dr Rex Gonzalez and the leading Argentine archaeologist, as president of the Congress, invited Thor to organize and direct a symposium in which a number of international scholars presented evidence supporting voyages to and from America before Columbus.

Upon the termination of the São Paulo Congress, the official delegates of the various nations had been invited by the Brazilian government to go by air into the interior, where there were very primitive Indian tribes. During the Congress, however, the president of Brazil committed suicide, and because of the period of disorder that followed, the authorities thought it wiser to cancel the trip. Thor and Yvonne decided to go into the jungle by themselves.

At the Congress they had met Wilma Schultz, an intrepid woman who had been on frequent expeditions with her ethnologist husband into the interior of Brazil. She agreed to act as guide. They flew inland to Anápolis by a regular commercial flight. There they hired a single-engine plane, which was so small that the pilot refused to carry their provisions and camping gear; all they were allowed to take with them was a rifle, a fishing rod, and plastic dolls for bartering with the Indians.

They flew over the jungle to Santa Isabel, a small Indian village on the bank of the Araguaia, a tributary of the Amazon. There they engaged two Carajá Indians, Irua and Uriala, to take them by dugout canoe down river and further into the jungle to the village of a primitive tribe. They set off at a rapid pace and were soon completely enclosed by the dense, dark blanket of foliage, which constitutes the river jungle in the interior of Brazil.

The torrid heat made them tired and apathetic. At first the three white people were careful to strain the muddy brown river water through a handkerchief, then boil it in a saucepan the Indians had brought along. The next day they drank the water right after filtering it, and on the third day they were so adjusted to life in the jungle that they did as Irua and Uriala did—dipped their cupped hands into the water over the side of the canoe and gulped down the cocoa-like mud.

At their first stop, as soon as they jumped into the water to pull the canoe ashore, the muddy bottom below their feet was suddenly alive with twisting, hideous disks, some the size of plates, others as big as large dishes. These were river rays, repulsive creatures that sped away with a great splash. While Irua and Uriala cleared a site for the camp, the other three felt so thoroughly roasted by the tropical sun that they lay down as they were in the muddy shallows next to the beach. Next Irua lighted a fire and set up a grill of interwoven twigs. Uriala cut a fishing rod, threw out a line, and began to pull in piranhas. Seeing this, the three in the water hurriedly got up on land. Though small, the piranha is probably the greediest creature in the world. The natives are far more afraid of it than caymans and boa constrictors. With teeth as sharp as needles, it tears the clothing, skin, and flesh off its victims; a little shoal of piranhas can reduce a great ox to a skeleton in a few minutes. Like sharks, they are attracted from great distances by blood in the water. Piranha, however, grilled above the fire was really delicious.

On their journey farther down river, they saw some pirarucus, a huge fish that can measure fifteen feet or more in length. Brightly coloured parrots and screaming bands of monkeys played about in the foliage overhanging the banks of the river.

When evening came, they pulled the canoe up on a sandy beach in a bend of the river and lay down with their feet almost in the water, so as to keep an eye on possible dangers emerging from the jungle wall behind. Out of the dark water, pairs of luminous balls appeared. Caymans, the alligators of the Amazon region, were staring at the strangers on the shore. Now and again the pairs of eyes glided slowly along the surface, submerged and vanished completely, reappearing in a different place, their gaze always fixed on the shore. None of the brutes showed any signs of approaching, and finally the five weary people went to sleep, including the Indian who should have been keeping watch.

In the middle of the night they were all alarmed by a cry of terror. For a moment a wave of panic ran through the jungle, then the sounds and the excitement died away. For a long time Thor lay watching the starry sky and the glowing eyes of the caymans until he fell asleep again. With the dawn he was awakened by a slobbering sound. An ugly, ratlike beast as large as a wild boar was lapping water from the river. It really was a kind of wild rat, the capybara, the largest rodent in the world.

After two days' paddling the group arrived at a sandbank that formed a long promontory into the river, and there lay a village of low huts made of leaves. As they approached, an old man, completely naked, was standing on the bank. When he saw there were females in the canoe he

42. Princess Margaret is an attentive listener.
43. (next page) Thor Heyerdahl receives the Vega Medal from the King of Sweden.

ran to his hut, and shortly reappeared wearing a European belt around his waist. When the canoe stopped, a swarm of naked natives poured out and crowded round them with troublesome curiosity. But Wilma Schultz had friends there from a previous visit. She was greeted with joy by the chiefs, Variha and Dihaoa, who immediately painted her face red with a black circle on each cheek, a sign of honour to all who had been admitted to the tribe.

There followed a festive meal of fish, turtle, and manioc roots, all roasted in the ashes. Afterwards, Thor and his companions politely refused to go to bed in one of the miniature sleeping-huts, since they were already overcrowded and, instead, hung up their Indian hammocks in a grove behind the village. They were not to regret this, for in the moonlight that night they witnessed a performance so strange that afterwards it seemed like a dream.

They had been asleep for an hour or two when they were awakened by rhythmical mutterings and chants. Shadowy figures moved with a rustling sound back and forth across the sandy ground next to them. Immediately afterwards two young girls, stark naked and obviously in great terror, ran past the hammocks like gazelles. Then two more appeared, or perhaps it was the same pair, and so it went on—girls in pairs running past them, while the macabre chorus of mutterers continued their song. When the moon rose higher, four fantastic figures could be seen on the sandbank. Side by side they tottered and hobbled around in a curious witchlike dance. On their heads were Ku-Klux-Klan-like hoods which were made of layers of straw and fell almost to the ground, so that only the wearers' bare arms and feet protruded. These animated haycocks and the young girls must have had superhuman powers of endurance, for the dance went on the whole night, and was so exciting that the visitors were not able to sleep till morning.

The next day, Thor was unable to get an explanation of the significance of the strange dance. The natives reacted strongly to all questions and would say nothing, although the four men were willing to show off their costumes.

Later, the chief Variha and another native, both great hunters, invited their guests to go with them on a hunt for caymans. Wilma refused, but Yvonne and Thor were eager to go. Before they set out at about midnight, they were scratched on the arm with a sharp, comb-shaped bone implement till it drew blood—to bring them luck in the hunt.

44. (*previous page*) Yvonne's first encounter with the jungle Indians in the interior of Brazil.

45. (*previous page*) Dancing witch doctors at the Araguaia River.

46. Thor Jr, Thor, Yvonne and Anette before the journey to the 'Navel of the World'.

The natives brought spears and axes with them, but in case of emergency, Thor took his rifle, and they started off through the primaeval forest. They followed a narrow path for quite some distance until they reached a lake, cut off from the river by the dry season. Here, in the undergrowth, the hunters had hidden a dugout canoe so narrow that a grown man could barely force himself down into it. One had the feeling that the least movement would capsize the slender log. It was, however, longer than it first seemed to be, and with its thick bottom it proved remarkably steady and glided through the water at a surprising speed.

Suddenly a big dark body came up close to the side of the canoe, snorting like a sea monster. It was more than twelve feet long, and resembled a whale. Soon two others appeared next to it, letting out windy sounds.

'*Boto*', said one of the Indians calmly.

Dolphins! Right in the middle of the jungle! It is one of the great curiosities of the animal kingdom that dolphins have been able to find their way from the ocean far up the huge Amazon River and its tributaries, and gradually acclimatize themselves to life in fresh water. One particular kind now lives confined in jungle lakes that are connected with the rivers only when the water rises in the rainy season. Thor was just as surprised when they were all bombarded by cold, wet projectiles that came sailing out of the darkness along the banks, where the moonlight did not penetrate the dense foliage. Flying fish in the interior of Brazil! There seemed no end to the wonders of this jungle lake locked in the heart of South America.

To Yvonne and Thor this hunt by night was a unique adventure. Chief Variha stood in the bow of the canoe, his muscles rippling in the moonlight as he waited ready with the spear. In the stern sat the native paddler, axe by his side, and amidships were Thor, his rifle across his knees, and Yvonne, whose job it was to sweep the surface of the water with a flashlight. If its beam was caught and reflected by two flashing dots in the darkness, they could be sure their prey was at hand.

They neared the middle of the lake. Yvonne swung her flashlight, and all of a sudden a pair of eyes glowed ahead of them. Variha straightened up and slowly raised his arm. The spear flew through the air and struck right behind those balls of fire. Variha slowly drew in the line while the paddler cautiously worked the unsteady canoe toward the struggling cayman. Thor put the rifle to his cheek, took aim and squeezed the trigger. Nothing happened. The mechanism was stuck, completely plugged by sand.

'The axe!' he shouted to the paddler, who passed it to him.

He swung the weapon above his head and struck the brute straight between the eyes. This single blow seemed enough, so they paddled to shore with the cayman in tow. Variha grabbed the tail, Thor threw his arms round its powerful neck, and together they dragged it a good way up on the shore, a safe distance from the other caymans. Later, they would come back for its precious skin.

The hunt procedure was then repeated, but this time it was the paddler who used the axe. On the third occasion things did not go off so well. It took a long time to track down a new quarry, and then Variha was unsuccessful with his throw; he hit the cayman, a huge specimen, but in the belly instead of the head. The powerful brute was only slightly wounded. It threw itself round, lashed the water to foam, and snapped savagely with its frothing red jaws, which looked big enough to cut the canoe in two. The line held, but the canoe was tipping and tilting dangerously. Slowly and with great skill the paddler manoeuvered closer to land. On reaching shallow water, Variha leaped overboard with the line and waded ashore. Now he was in a tight spot. If he hauled the cayman ashore it would attack him; if he let it go it might, in its blind rage, turn on those in the canoe. Something had to be done. Thor grabbed the axe, slid quietly over the side and, in muddy water up to his waist, tried to approach the brute from the flank. It turned, lunging and snapping at him with dreadful roars, but each time was held back by Variha's line.

If Yvonne had not been frightened before, she was now. Although the cayman could not reach Thor as long as the spear held, Thor could neither get to shore nor close enough to the cayman to reach behind the long snapping jaws and strike its skull. Now, too, there was blood in the water from the cayman's wound, and at any moment a shoal of piranhas might appear.

Yvonne then did what few could have done. She jumped overboard and attracted the raging brute's attention to herself by shining the flashlight straight at it. This gave Thor the chance to use the axe and he had to strike three times before he killed it.

When they went ashore after the fight to look for the cayman they had caught first, they discovered—with a shudder—that it had disappeared. Only broad footprints leading to the water remained. Thor and Variha had carried a cayman that was merely stunned!

They stayed with the natives on the sandbank for nearly a fortnight, then were taken upriver again to Santa Isabel by Irua and Uriala. On the trip they lived on piranhas and turtles' eggs dug out of the sand. Hunger even drove them to eat cayman's tail roasted in the ashes.

Back to São Paulo, Yvonne and Thor said good-bye to Wilma, who for a long time had to go about in the city with two black circles on her cheeks; the Indian 'make-up' was not easily removed. Then they crossed the continent by plane to Peru, where Thor planned to do some research in museums and in the field.

After some weeks along the coast and in the northern Andes, Yvonne went home to little Anette, while Thor continued by himself southwards through the Cordilleras to Lake Titicaca, which extends from southern Peru into northern Bolivia. This enormous inland lake lies at an altitude of 13,000 feet and is flanked by mountains reaching another 9,000 feet. On the plains around the lake the Tiahuanaco civilization had once had its base long before Inca time. Thor wanted to have a closer look at the numerous ruins and stone statues that were of such importance to his work.

In his solitary wanderings around the lake Thor came across some Indians making boats of bundles of *totora* reeds. He learned from personal experience that these peculiar boats, resembling rafts, had a marvellous buoyancy and seaworthiness. He sailed with some of the fishermen out to the Island of the Sun, where, according to the Inca legends, Kon-Tici *viracocha* had originally lived before he founded Tiahuanaco near the south end of the lake. Kon-Tici's white and bearded men of the Island of the Sun were not only known as *viracochas*, or 'sea foam', alluding to their white skin and seamanship, but were also called *Ringrim*, or 'Long-Ears', because they had artificially lengthened their ear lobes, a style that was later adopted by members of the Inca nobility. The Spaniards knew them as *orejones*, which means 'long-ears'.

The Aymara and Quechua Indians around the lake were remarkably cautious when the talk touched on the fair-skinned *Viracocha*, but it soon became evident that everywhere in the region the ancient legend about the *viracocha* people still survived. One of the old Indians said to Thor to explain the word:

'You are a *viracocha*.'

Thor was particularly fascinated by the ruins of Tiahuanaco, with its enormous Akapana pyramid, the Gateway of the Sun, the remains of raised temple terraces where the walls were built of splendidly hewn and fitted blocks of up to a hundred tons, and a variety of large stone statues in human form. Previous observers had pointed out that the oldest form of statue was represented by some realistically carved kneeling giants, two of which had been moved in modern times to the doorway of the village church where they still knelt piously gazing up to heaven. Deeply absorbed by these strange sculptures of the vanished *viracocha* artists, Thor had no idea that he would later come across their close counterpart on the nearest Polynesian island.

The 'birdman' was an important symbolic motif in Tiahuanaco. Men with hook-beaked birds' heads and wings were carved in relief round the image of Kon-Tici *viracocha*, which adorned the façade of the Gateway of the Sun. When Thor came to an isolated mountain village to the southeast of the lake, he found that the birdman tradition still survived. The Indians had got roaring drunk on chewed and fermented *chicha* and were dancing a 'birdman dance' with large artificial wings tied on their backs.

On the other side of the lake lay the extinct volcano Kapia, with the main stone quarry of the *viracocha* people. Enormous hewn blocks had been shipped from here over the stormy lake to Tiahuanaco. There were many still lying abandoned near the ruins of a wharf. The Aymara Indians of the locality still referred to the site as 'The Road to Tiahuanaco'. The conical mountain next to the loading berth bore the curious name 'The Navel of the World'. Thor made detailed notes in his journal of everything he saw and heard.

One night before he went to sleep in a boat on the lake, he started to make some notes in his diary. He wrote the date, October 6, 1954, then paused. There was something familiar about that date. He had to laugh as he suddenly remembered that it was his fortieth birthday.

From the various sites around Lake Titicaca he visited all the other pre-Inca cult sites where there were stone statues, from Bolivia in the south through Peru to Columbia in the north. These South American field studies were to prove of great importance in his future work and plans.

Chapter 18

THE NAVEL OF THE WORLD

On a winter's evening in 1955, a green Buick stopped in front of the gate to my Larvik home. Yvonne had driven Thor from Oslo for a short visit to his father, and before returning they called to see us. From the expression on their faces I could tell that they had great new plans to reveal. As they sat together on the sofa in front of me, a brief remark from Thor brought back to my mind words he had uttered as a fifteen-year-old schoolboy towards the end of the 1930s. 'It's not only in geography that we can make discoveries', he had said then. 'There are still many great challenges in the world, among other things the mystery of Easter Island.'

Now, twenty-five years or more later, he was sitting in my home saying:

'Arnold, I am going to tell you something which is still a secret. I am planning a new expedition—this time to Easter Island.'

Then he briefly sketched the background of his planned enterprise. He wished to realize his old dream. What was more, now he had a working hypothesis to guide him: he was convinced that the founders of the mysterious Easter Island culture had been the *viracocha* people who had left Tiahuanaco.

He told me that only two archaeological expeditions had ever gone to Easter Island. In 1914 Katherine Routledge had arrived in her own sailing yacht *Mana*, to lead a British private expedition to survey and map everything she saw above ground. Twenty years later, a Franco-Belgian expedition arrived, and the noted Belgian archaeologist, Professor Henri Lavachery, examined the hundreds of rock carvings and petroglyphs. He was accompanied by Thor's old acquaintance, the French ethnologist Alfred Métraux, who collected oral information from the islanders for a study of Easter Island's ethnography. None of them had undertaken stratigraphic archaeological excavations, for no one had ever suspected that the barren soil of the treeless island had anything to hide. Furthermore, everybody had been convinced that Easter Island, of all Pacific islands, must have been the last to be inhabited as it lay farthest away from Asia, the supposed source of all Pacific migrations.

Thor, however, had an opposite approach to the problem: of all the Pacific islands, Easter Island lay nearest to South America and Tiahuanaco, and he thus suspected that this particular island had been occupied early, perhaps before any other land in Polynesia. The natives themselves called their island 'The Navel of the World'. This poetic name itself was most suggestive to Thor who recalled its use around Lake Titicaca. Why, of all the thousands of Pacific islands, should this tiny speck next to Peru be considered the navel of the island world? To him the answer was obvious: Just as the navel was the link to the mother, Easter Island, with its extreme eastern location, would once have represented the navel of the islands because it had been the natural link to the motherland—Peru.

Thor now wanted to take a team of professional archaeologists to this island. But lonely Easter Island had communications with the outside world only once a year, when a warship from Chile, whose protectorate the island was, anchored off the unsheltered coast for a week. One week was, of course, insufficient time for worthwhile archaeological excavation, and to be left ashore for a whole year with a full expedition would be too risky if the experts were correct in their claim that it was futile to dig in the local soil. To work on Easter Island he would need his own ship, manned by a first-class crew, and equipped with everything necessary for his plan to be realized. This would be a most expensive project, but he was willing to stake his whole fortune and even more, and he did not intend to ask for any grants or other financial support. He would try to get the Crown Prince of Norway as patron of the expedition, to facilitate obtaining official documents and digging permits from foreign countries.

'But', I argued, 'you have never been on that island, and as far as I know it is nothing but a barren and windswept lava islet in the midst of the ocean. Suppose you find nothing by digging?'

'That would of course be embarrassing', he replied. 'That's exactly why I want a ship of my own. If we find nothing there we can at least proceed to other islands where I have actually seen ruins and stone statues half buried in the jungle.'

From experience I knew better than to argue further against his expedition plans. During the months that followed I had casual glimpses of Yvonne and Thor, who were now completely absorbed in hectic preparations. The *Kon-Tiki* voyage had been a primitive expedition. At that time the scarcity of dollars had been the principal obstacle. This time most of the money was already available, but in spite of his raft experiences Thor still knew very little about regular seamanship. What was needed to equip a modern ship with its crew for a full year? He did not know, so he had to learn, and he threw himself into the task with heart and soul.

Consulting his old shipping friend Wilhelm Eitrem of the Fred Olsen Line, he hired a 150-foot Greenland trawler, the *Chr. Bjelland* for a year, and had it converted to a tropical expedition ship. He next carefully selected and signed on a captain and a crew of twelve, a doctor, a photographer and, most important of all, a team of five professional archaeologists, three of them from the United States, one from Norway, and one from Chile.

All the scientists needed special equipment; so did the cameraman and the doctor, who was fully prepared to perform surgery. But more complicated still was the complete supply of spare parts for ship and engine. Everything from anchors and propellers to radio, radar, and machine parts had to be carried in duplicate, since there was no store or machine shop within thousands of miles of the area where the expedition vessel was to operate. The strangest cargo was stowed on board: the bulky bodies of frozen steer, cases of canned food and chemicals, digging gear and frogman's equipment, three tons of dental plaster for making casts, fresh water supply for a year, a jeep, a smithy, a carpentry shop, a good thousand yards of dress material, and a hundred and fifty pounds of fish-hooks for barter and payment for native labour, as well as untold quantities of drums, canvas, tents, ropes, sacks, boxes, bundles, and suitcases. Nothing must be forgotten and, as the ship's captain, Arne Hartmark, told me later, nothing *was* forgotten. The way in which Thor tackled his preparations was described by the captain in a letter he wrote to me:

'The common feature of all Heyerdahl's activities and achievements is the masterly planning, which has developed from prominence to per-fection. It may safely be said that Heyerdahl's planning reached perfection in connection with the Easter Island expedition. I myself was fortunate enough to be involved in the planning from an early stage. As skipper of the expedition ship I was responsible for the safe transoceanic voyage and for the security of the ship during the stay.

'I had actually formed an opinion of my own as to how everything was to be arranged, but I was soon to discover that Heyerdahl had in advance thought of all the problems. Thus there was hardly anything left for me to do but to O.K. all plans of his that came within the field of my responsibility. His brilliant preparations actually overlapped further into my professional sphere than I liked at first, but gradually I just had to surrender to his superior knowledge and logical reasoning.

' "I believe this is where we ought to anchor", he would say as we bent over our charts while still in Oslo, "this promontory ought to be facing east-south-east while those two rocks fall on a line." And then he confidently put a cross on the chart. In some irritation I objected that it might depend on the anchoring-ground and on the weather gods' allowing us to drop anchor just on that spot. But this was before I had learned to know the expedition leader well. He at once took down the right book from his shelf and opened it—it seemed to me blindly—at the page where it stated in print that exactly where he had put the cross there were thirteen fathoms of water and a first-rate holding ground. "And of course you know the prevailing winds", he said. "If we draw a line from the point here to the anchorage, you will see that we are lying sheltered from the normal southeast trade winds. Besides", he added with a sly smile, "it was here, in Anakena Bay, that King Hotu Matua made his first landing on Easter Island, and Hotu Matua knew all about seamanship—which reminds me, we must take with us a flat-bottomed boat which will permit us to land with the Pacific swells on the shallow beach. Have a look at Routledge's description of the sandy beach in the Anakena Bay. Can you imagine any better camping place—with the ship anchored straight in front of the doorway of our tents?"

'At this stage I found it difficult to form any opinion about Hotu Matua's seamanship; but I had to surrender to Heyerdahl's logical arguments.

'And so it came about that we ultimately anchored in Anakena Bay, where Heyerdahl, three months before, had drawn a cross while sitting in his home in Norway. With thirteen fathoms of water we lay safe with our little ship.'

'Everywhere is the wind of heaven; round and above all are boundless sea and sky, infinite space and a great silence. The dweller there is ever listening for he knows not what, feeling unconsciously that he is in the antechamber to something yet more vast which is just beyond his ken.'

Thus had Katherine Routledge described her impression of the place in her book, *The Mystery of Easter Island*, and Yvonne and Thor felt exactly the same as they stood by the rail, gazing towards land, on the October evening in 1955 when their ship anchored in the lee of the island. In one of the two lifeboats on the upper deck sat Thor Junior, watching this legendary place fading into the twilight. He was sixteen years old and had been signed on as a deckhand. The rest of the expedition also stared towards land until the darkness of the night obscured all further vision.

Most keen on getting ashore were perhaps the five archaeologists: Edwin Ferdon of the Museum of New Mexico, an old friend of Yvonne and Thor's from Santa Fé; Arne Skjölsvold, Thor's companion on the

Galápagos expedition; and the newcomers, Dr William Mulloy and Dr Carlyle Smith, professors of archaeology at the Universities of Wyoming and Kansas respectively, and Gonzalo Figueroa of the University of Santiago, the official representative of Chile.

The only member of the mixed party who was missing on deck was two-year-old Anette, from whom Yvonne had not been able to tear herself away for a whole year. She was sound asleep in her berth, but before she was put to bed she, too, had caught a glimpse of grass-covered undulating hills and stark precipices which rose from the sea ahead of the bow. She had even pointed to the big 'dolls', the huge stone statues which could be seen scattered over the slopes of an extinct volcano.

The captain of the little vessel beamed with satisfaction; he had safely brought his passengers and cargo halfway around the world to this lonely speck in the immense Pacific Ocean, known to modern man as Easter Island just because it was Easter day when the Dutchman Jacob Roggeveen discovered it in the year 1722.

Why had this tiny islet attained its worldwide fame?

Thor gave an answer in his subsequent book *Aku-Aku*: 'On this remote island, east of the sun and west of the moon, mankind once had one of its most curious ideas. No one knows who had it, and no one knows why.... They landed there, whetted their stone adzes, and set about one of the most remarkable engineering projects of ancient times. They did not build fortresses and castles, or dams and wharves. They made gigantic stone figures in man's likeness, as tall as houses and as heavy as boxcars, and they dragged them in great numbers across country and set them up erect on huge stone terraces all over the island.'

As darkness fell on the little ship and only the scent of soil and dry grass made them feel that land hovered from the depths a stone's throw away, Thor gathered the men on the aft deck and gave them an advance description of the island on which they were to land the following day. He told them that if anyone expected to step ashore among palms and hula dancers they would indeed be disappointed. The present Easter Islanders were probably as civilized as anyone on board; they were all Catholics, had a church, a school, and a hospital, although no shops or cinemas. They probably dressed and behaved like anybody else.

According to local tradition two different races had originally lived together on this island, the 'long-ears' and the 'short-ears'. The long-ears had forced the short-ears to work on their large statues and stone con- structions, until one day the latter revolted and massacred nearly all the long-ears, burning them in a large ditch. Since the present island population was decended from the surviving short-ears, they would hardly possess any memories that would throw light on the riddle of the enormous statues, but the local natives might still prove useful for manual labour in the planned excavations.

Next morning the ship, with Kon-Tiki's head on the funnel and her colours flying, glided round the island to Hangaroa village, where the entire population lived. They were all assembled on the rocks ashore as the expedition ship dropped anchor off the unsheltered coast. One person stood out from the crowd—the island priest, sixty-eight-year-old Father Sebastian Englert, one of the most impressive personalities Thor ever met.

Father Sebastian came to mean a great deal both to Thor and to the final results of the expedition. He knew the native population better than anyone else; they were his children, and there existed between them a high degree of understanding and trust. Thus his counsel and support became of the greatest value to the team of archaeologists and seamen.

Thor was rather astonished to learn that he was already known and expected on Easter Island. Everyone had heard of his raft voyage across the Pacific, and respectfully addressed him as 'Señor Kon-Tiki'.

'It must take an infinite amount of courage to set out on such a raft trip', said Father Sebastian.

'Not courage', Thor replied, 'but confidence.'

The islanders themselves felt greatly honoured that Señor Kon-Tiki himself had come to investigate the history of their island. Everyone was anxious to help him—and to do business. They crowded around him, producing sacks of weird wooden figures and small models of the island statues, some meant as gifts and some to barter for clothes and shoes. A few of the carvings were so cleverly made that the sailors could not decide whether they were really old or not without aid of the scientists. The best wood-carver was the native mayor, Pedro Atan. He looked like a pale Arab with a small moustache, and Father Sebastian said that he and his brothers were the only natives who could claim direct descent through the paternal line from the last surviving long-ear. Before long, it would become evident that the mayor possessed strange information which had been passed on from father to son and kept as a family secret through many generations.

After a formal but most friendly reception by the Chilean governor in his bungalow near the village, the expedition members returned to the ship, and sailed eastwards from Hangaroa to the uninhabited side of the island, where they dropped anchor according to Thor's cross on the chart in front of Anakena Bay. By means of a special pontoon raft, the equipment was carried ashore through the surf to a shallow white beach. Thor then led his men straight for the level ground behind the huge prehistoric temple wall where he knew from Routledge's book that Hotu Matua, the first legendary king of the island, had once lived. The house foundation wall of beautifully cut and fitted stone, as well as a curious five-sided stone oven, were still visible in the low grass. Thor marked out a camping site in front of a fallen stone giant's head, and soon green tents sprang up, forming a peaceful little village in Hotu Matua's temple square.

During the first days, the archaeologists went out in different directions on reconnaissance tours. The island appeared even more barren than the books had suggested. Near each corner of the triangular island, and occasionally in the interior, the land rose towards the craters of extinct volcanoes, ring-shaped crests on naked cones gazing vacantly up into space. The fieriness of the volcanoes had long since vanished; they seemed to have settled down to eternal rest, gently robed in a thin carpet of grass and ferns and with a sky-blue lake half covered by reeds at the bottom of some of them.

One of these water-filled volcanoes, Rano Raraku, was particularly curious, for it was here that the long-eared sculptors had once had their workshop, the enormous quarries where the large statues had been wrought from the crater walls. In these long-abandoned quarries, solid rock, by the hundreds of thousands of tons, had been cut away, carved into gigantic stone men, and carried off to all parts of the island. Everything suggested that the activities in the quarries had been suddenly interrupted. More than a hundred and fifty unfinished statues, in all stages of work, lay abandoned in the niches of the crater walls at the foot of the volcano, and scattered about in the rubble from the quarries. Hundreds of others finished in every detail lay face down next to their temple platforms all over the island. Most of these showed signs of having been deliberately overthrown in earlier times.

Indeed, the surface of the island abounded in impressive prehistoric remains, but nearly all had been previously recorded and described. These visible remains were not the target of Thor's investigations.

Not long after camp had been set up, Yvonne suggested unrolling the canvas wall on the windward side of the mess tent. 'There is dust coming in through the mosquito net', she said. With her finger she drew a distinct line along the bookshelf.

Dust! Thor took a closer look. In a few hundred years a pretty thick layer of dust would have accumulated. Just because the island had no forests, wind and weather eroded the surface of the hills and sent an almost invisible but continuous shower of dust over the lowlands. Maybe, then, digging would be worthwhile after all, as the most ancient remains might have been buried by silt and wind erosion.

Excavations were started next to the tents, following the successful method used in the Galápagos. Instead of a pickaxe and spade, the men used little mason's trowels, with which they scraped their way down into the ground, a fraction of an inch at a time, so as not injure what might be found. The earth scraped loose was next shaken through fine-meshed netting leaving anything of interest on top. The depth was noted exactly, as the deeper one went, the older the findings were.

No sooner had the first piece of turf been removed than a discovery was made: part of an old stone bowl. Next obsidian spearheads, stone adzes, and bits of fishhooks made of human bone and of beautifully polished stone came to light. When they had got a foot down into the earth beside Hotu Matua's oven, they found another five-sided oven of the same type, and two feet further down, still another. The natives were highly perplexed: according to tradition, King Hotu Matua had been the first to land on their island, and his oven was thought to be the one they always knew above ground. How then could there be other ovens like his deep down in the earth?

After the initial excavation at Hotu Matua's site, the archaeologists spread out to different parts of the island.

Ed Ferdon later wrote about this procedure:

'After we had had sufficient time to make some surveys of the island, Heyerdahl called all of us archaeologists into the mess tent for a meeting. At that time he told us outright that we were to talk over the archaeology of the island among ourselves and to choose *our own* projects. He explained that the archaeological work was our problem alone, and that regardless of what excavations we might choose to make he would see that we were supplied with labour and tools. I further recall that he finally added that if we found something that supported his hypothesis he would be most happy, but that the main job was to determine the culture history of Easter Island. Please believe me when I say that he could have saved himself considerable money and bother had he chosen to direct the archaeological programme himself as a co-ordinated effort. Instead, he chose to give us absolute freedom.'

Thor himself was engaged in a thousand tasks. The everyday activities of the expedition had to be organized, and he never missed an opportunity to inspect and supervise the progress in the field, or to draw out every bit of available information from Father Sebastian and the natives. With his rare ability to penetrate the native mind, he soon learned to understand the mentality of the Easter Islanders and to reason and react like them.

The natives took Thor, and Erling Schjerven, the photographer, to a large number of volcanic caves. Many were known to everybody, whereas others were difficult to find, their entrances being hidden in the cliffs or blocked by stones. Some had gaping openings and one could just walk right in, but others, probably used during periods of war, had extensive underground passages, with narrow man-made entrances constructed in such a clever way that an intruder would have to wriggle down like a worm, feet first and arms over head. These fiendish shafts usually ended in small dark chambers, but occasionally opened into a whole series of other caves following each other like pearls on a string.

Cave exploring was neither easy nor free from danger. There was the chance of getting stuck deep down in the crevices, or having the exit blocked by loose rocks, or disturbing one of the numerous scorpions hiding in the darkness of the rocks. On one occasion Thor overturned a single boulder sealing a cave entrance and thus uncovered fourteen of these hideous creatures. While going down a particularly long shaft, the photographer had claustrophobia, another ever-present danger.

The archaeologists investigated the floors of those caves which showed signs of artificial masonry. In most of them the roof was so low that one could only stand if doubled up. The former inhabitants had dropped their refuse where they sat, and the floor had often risen toward the roof. Burned shells mixed with fish, bird, and turtle bones lay packed in the compressed floor surface. Even rats and human beings had been on the menu. Otherwise there was nothing to be found apart from the fragments of the common bone and stone fishhooks, bone needles, and crude stone implements. The ancient occupants of these refuges must have had a remarkably primitive culture. This didn't make sense. How could a people with such an inferior culture be identical with the creators of the gigantic statues and cyclopean walls that had made the whole world marvel? These were achievements requiring a high degree of artistic development, engineering skill, and organization of mass labour.

Perhaps the natives were correct that two different people, the long-ears and the short-ears, had co-existed on the island. According to tradition, the statue-making had ended twelve generations ago when the indigenous long-ears had been burned in the Poike ditch, and the natives were filled with stories of how their own short-ear ancestors had pulled down the long-eared statues and lived on alone, until the white man came, through a terrible period of family feuds and cannibalism.

Father Sebastian was thoroughly convinced that the native traditions were founded on facts, and that the archaeological remains all over the island clearly indicated that this was so. He pointed to the well-known fact that Roggeveen, on his voyage of discovery, reported having found a mixed race on the island and recorded that there were unmistakable remnants of a white race. Father Eugenio Eyraud, the first European to settle ashore, had also been surprised to find completely white people with red hair among the dark ones. The mayor, Pedro Atan, said with pride that many of his long-ear ancestors were as fair as he, and he pointed to the red hair which was still a prominent feature of his family.

One day Father Sebastian offered to show Thor *Ana o Keke*, the holy bleaching place of the *neru* virgins. These were specially chosen young girls who, in old days, were confined in a deep cave to become as pale and white as possible for special religious festivals in honour of the fair predecessors.

The visit to *Ana o Keke* was a dramatic experience. Following Father Sebastian and a native from the village, Thor climbed along the upper edge of a windswept precipice that dropped vertically into the sea where the easterly waves were beaten to white foam as they rose against the feet of the cliffs. On a narrow ledge in the vertical wall Father Sebastian, in his white cassock, stooped down and crawled on his stomach through a hole smaller than the door of a dog kennel. He beckoned the others to follow.

Inside this rathole entrance the cave expanded into a room some five feet high and large enough for a dozen children to be seated along the walls, which were covered with curious signs and figures. Here the poor *neru* virgins had lived for weeks, perhaps months, waiting for their skins to turn white enough for them to perform for the people.

Father Sebastian pointed to a small hole in the rear wall and said jokingly that by crawling through it Thor could get four hundred yards farther into the rock. He had done it himself but was not going to do it again. At one point the tunnel was so narrow that a man could only just force his way through, and inside there lay human bones and teeth, as in an ordinary burial cave. It was a mystery to him how anyone could have carried a dead person in there, for it was impossible to push a corpse in front, and to drag it was to bar the way back for himself.

Thor persuaded the native to follow him, and crawled in through the hole. Farther in, the roof rose sufficiently for them to run for short distances to save time. The flashlight was miserable, and for safety's sake Thor carried a stump of candle and a box of matches. The tunnel gradually grew narrower once more; they were soon forced to move ahead on hands and knees, and finally to lie flat on their stomachs and worm their way along under the rock while ice-cold mud soaked their shirts and trousers.

Thor almost regretted having started when he reached a place where for about five yards, he had to manoeuvre himself through a passage half filled with water and so narrow that he had to force in his chest to prevent getting stuck. But if Father Sebastian had done it, they too should be able to manage. Inch by inch they squeezed their way ahead until they were through the needle's eye and reached the part of the cave where the remains of skeletons lay.

At last the cave ended in a smooth, steep and slippery slope leading up to a hole in the roof. Thor scratched his way and found a bell-shaped dome, probably caused by a bubble of volcanic gas at the time the lava was molten. He found a candle stump left behind by Father Sebastian. Thor tried to light it, but it would not burn. There was something wrong with the matches too.

He felt the sweat streaming down his face; the air was bad. Thor hastily slid down the slippery slope to his mud-caked companion who was waiting for him and they retraced their steps. They tried to joke a bit, but it was easier to keep silent.

When Thor had forced his way through the horribly narrow section for a few yards, he began to wonder why he had not yet reached the end. But his brain was strangely weary, and he just shoved and shoved to get his body through the vice. Then he saw in the faint glow of the flashlight that the tunnel in front suddenly took a little upward bend. With all his might he forced himself a little farther forward and tried to look up through the hole in a cramped position. Then he saw to his terror that it was impossible to get past this bend.

'We can't get any further', he shouted to the man behind, the sweat pouring from his face.

'Go on, Señor. There isn't any other way out', was the reply.

Thor forced himself another fraction of an inch further, with his head twisted on one side to find room in the narrow gap between the rock surfaces, and with his chest in a devilish squeeze. Then he saw, by turning the light upward, that the hole above was much smaller than his own head: it was absolutely impossible to get through.

He immediately put out his light to save the battery. Thinking was possible in the dark. It felt as if the entire mountain rested on his back.

'Go back', he shouted. 'This won't work.'

The native flatly refused. There was no other exit, he insisted.

What could possibly have happened? Had the roof collapsed after they had passed this section on their way in? If so, how long would they survive with this shortage of oxygen before the others would realize something had happened?

Once more Thor shouted that they *had* to crawl backwards, but by now the native behind him had become panic-stricken, and tried desperately to force Thor on by pushing his feet.

'Go back, go back!' Thor shouted again, and kicked out with the sole of his foot. That had some effect. Inch by inch they forced their way backwards into the cave, one little jerk at a time. They went slowly, afraid of getting caught by the head between the rocks, for it would not yield to pressure as the chest did.

In *Aku-Aku*, Thor wrote:

'Suddenly there was more space above us. I understood nothing: I was quite muddleheaded from the bad air. Could we have got right back to the skeleton place? I used my flashlight again and saw two openings in front of me: the right-hand one went slightly uphill. This was where we had gone wrong; we had crawled to the left instead of up to the right. I called to the native, but he only went on, as if in a stupor, shoving himself backwards.

' "Here it is!" I cried, and crawled forward again into the left-hand entrance, the native following me automatically. Our voices sounded very queer in the cave. The passage grew narrower and narrower again. This was ghastly. At last I used my light and saw ahead of me the same impossible little hole as before. Then I realized that my brain was no longer functioning clearly: I had crawled into the wrong hole for a second time, although I knew perfectly well that it was the other hole I should have taken.

' "Go back!" I groaned.

'And now all our actions seemed purely mechanical. We forced ourselves out again backwards and I thought of only one word: right, right, right. When we saw the two passages again I crept mechanically into the right-hand opening, and soon we could raise ourselves up, we felt gusts of cold, fresh air in the tunnel, we were able to crouch and crawl, and finally we came out of the last hole and into the snug cave with the inscriptions on the walls where our friends were sitting waiting for us. It was heavenly to push oneself out of the cliffside, out into the roaring wind. Heavenly to meet again the blinding sunshine and the unlimited space stretching from the precipice sheer below us into the unbounded blue immensity of sea and sky.

' "Did you give up?" Father Sebastian asked eagerly, laughing heartily at our appearance.

' "No", I said. "But it is understandable that skeletons may be left in a cave like that." '

When the archaeologists were given a free hand to select their own sites for excavations, Arne Skjölsvold chose to investigate the statue quarries of Rano Raraku. With the ship's crew and a large team of natives he began to dig around the giant stone heads standing erect at the foot of the volcano. Centuries of sand and gravel blown from the quarries above had buried some to the neck and others up to the nose, but digging revealed that they all had enormous bodies extending far down into the ground. The tallest of the standing figures were nearly forty feet high, or as tall as a four-storey house, all in one block of stone weighing up to eighty tons. The longest, which lay unfinished and aslant on the side of the volcano, was sixty-nine feet long, or as tall as a seven-storey building. Some of the statues had curious symbols carved on their bodies. All of them represented male long-ears with earlobes hanging right down to their shoulders, thin lips, and sharp projecting chins suggesting beards. All were carved as legless busts with long arms and slender figures meeting under a protruding belly.

Digging at Rano Raraku had barely been initiated before a series of interesting discoveries were made. Skjölsvold's team uncovered a particularly old and hitherto unknown stone giant that lay deeply buried in centuries of silt. It was unlike the other statues, which were all carved according to one standard pattern. Thus, while the others were tall, slim, columnar busts with hands in low relief at the base, this had a fully developed body with complete legs, sculptured in a kneeling position. His head was quite round with a peculiar goatee beard, his hands were placed on the protruding knees, while his fat backside rested on his upturned heels.

This was exactly the kind of statue Thor recalled so well at Tiahuanaco, which Dr Bennett had identified as the oldest type there. The fact that this local specimen correspondingly dated from the earliest period on Easter Island was evident from its discovery at the foot of the oldest section of the quarries, and from the depth at which it had been buried. Here, then, was the hitherto missing link between the oldest types of stone statues in Tiahuanaco and those on the nearest inhabitable island in the Pacific. The other statues of Tiahuanaco and Easter Island were younger and their different styles the result of subsequent independent local evolution.

Later, other strange statues of types so far entirely unknown on Easter Island were excavated by Mulloy and Ferdon: a four-sided column carved from red stone representing a man and some flat, rectangular stone heads without bodies. They, too, conformed closely with characteristic statues from Tiahuanaco, which Bennett had also placed with the kneeling figures as the earliest local types.

The riddle of the Easter Island statues included three further problems which had caused much speculation and theorizing among previous investigators: how had these colossi been carved without metal tools? How had they been transported for many miles from the Rano Raraku quarry to all parts of the island? And how had they been raised on their high temple platforms by a stone age people without mechanical devices? Thor had read many strange hypotheses as to how these statues had reached their present sites. One of them suggested that they had originally stood around the crater, but had been flung in all directions by a volcanic eruption. The still-current belief of the Easter Islanders was that the statues 'went of themselves'. They had walked of their own accord.

One day Thor brought up the question with the mayor, Pedro Atan, who calmly replied that he knew how it had all been done. He said that although nobody else knew it, he and his brothers, who were descended from the long-ears, had preserved the secret which had passed from father to son for twelve generations, from the time the long-ear Ororoina had escaped from the pyre in the Poike ditch. He seemed so sincere, Thor did not know what to believe.

'But why, if you know how, why didn't you tell all the people who have been here and asked long before us?' Thor asked sceptically.

'No one asked *me*', the mayor replied proudly.

When Thor asked if he could carve a statue in the Rano Raraku quarry, he remained silent for a while, then he said: 'It shall be done, señor. How long is it to be?'

'Medium-size, fifteen to twenty feet.'

On the night before the work was due to begin, the mayor, his brothers, and two other long-ears took part in a peculiar ceremony. Some wore bird-men paper masks with long projecting beaks. They sang a strange and exotic tune, beating time on the ground with their feet rhythmically: this was the stonecutters' ancient song which no foreign ears had ever heard. The next morning they started work in the quarry. They first collected a quantity of the hard basalt picks which still lay abandoned and scattered on ledges and the ground. Then the mayor outlined the size and shape of the statue-to-be on a smooth rock face. Splashing water from gourd containers on the rock at intervals, to soften it, the six natives hammered away at the mountainside with their picks held like daggers in their hands.

They worked in time with the rhythm of the stonecutters' song of the night before. For the first time in centuries the clink of picks resounded from the wall of Rano Raraku. The mark left by each single stroke was hardly perceptible, but as the days passed the contours of the resting giant began to be clearly visible on the rock wall. There could be no doubt left: this was how the carving had been done. With two teams working in shifts it would take a year to complete a statue, said the mayor, and calculations based on the progress of work proved that he was right.

Thor now wondered if this remarkable native would be able to raise a finished statue. He offered to pay him one hundred dollars on the day the largest statue at Anakena stood in its place upon the temple wall. The mayor said it was a deal.

The night before another and different ceremony took place. This time twelve men turned up, all decked with leaves and boughs. They began to sing and dance to the rhythm of a foot-drum buried in the ground, while an old hag sat with her eyes closed and led the choir with shrill voice.

As the first rays of the sun hit the tents the next morning, the twelve natives were all set to begin their work. The statue lay with its head down a slope and with its base four yards from the stone platform from which it had once been overturned. The giant measured almost ten feet across the shoulders and weighed about thirty tons. Its face was buried deep in the ground, but the natives thrust the tips of three long poles beneath it, and while three or four of them hung and heaved at the end of each, the mayor lay flat on his stomach and pushed small stones under the huge face. Occasionally there was a faint suggestion of movement in the giant when the men got in an extra good heave. When evening came, the head had been lifted a good three feet from the ground, while the space beneath was packed tight with stones.

Next day two of the poles were pushed under one side of the giant, which now tilted almost imperceptibly. Then the poles were moved to the other side, and it, too, tilted up slowly. All the time, stones were pushed in and under. On the ninth day the huge figure lay face down on the top of an elongated stone tower, the highest part of which was nearly twelve feet above the slope. The men could no longer reach the poles; they had to dangle from ropes made fast to the ends of them. And still the prone giant had not begun to slant towards a standing position. At this stage the natives began using the poles to jerk the statue, feet first, towards the huge elevated slab on which it was to stand. Next the poles were inserted beneath the forehead of the colossus, and for the first time, they began to work the giant into a sloping position by building the stones up even higher, but only under the face and chest.

On the eighteenth day, the thirty-ton giant stood erect on its old foundation. The loose stone pile was now removed, and there the colossus stood, a terrific monument to primitive ingenuity, gazing out over the camp across the temple square, just as it had done in times long forgotten.

Thor now had an answer to his first and third question. The second one remained. How had these monoliths been moved from Rano Raraku to the most distant corners of the island? The mayor was willing to demonstrate this too if he had enough helpers. Thor had two oxen slaughtered, and invitations to a great feast in Anakena were then sent to the natives of the village. The natives came in crowds by foot and on horseback, and after the feast, sated and jubilant, took their places on a long stout rope which was made fast around the statue's neck. It was established that 180 natives with full stomachs could drag a twelve-ton statue across the plain on wooden skids. The last of the three questions had been answered.

One day Father Sebastian reminded Thor of the well-known traditions about the Poike ditch, and suggested that the area should be tested archaeologically. According to the still vivid legends, when the short-ears revolted, the long-ears sought refuge on the precipitous Poike Plateau. They dug a huge trench, two miles long, separating this eastern headland from the rest of the island. The ditch had been filled with tree trunks and branches, ready to be set ablaze if the enemy attacked. However, in the dark of the night, and with the help of a traitress, the short-ears managed to outflank the position, and thus the long-ears had been driven into their own ditch and burned alive.

Every visitor to the island had heard this legend, and all who had written about the mysteries of Easter Island had mentioned it. Vestiges of the ancient ditch were still clearly seen. Katherine Routledge had been doubtful and had come to the conclusion that the depression was a natural geological depression which the long-ears might have used in self-defence. Métraux, however, was convinced that the depression was not only natural, but that it had inspired the natives to invent the whole story of the long-ears and the short-ears. A professional geologist had also seen the ditch and concluded that it was a natural formation originating in pre-human times by the joining of two different flows of lava.

Thor did not content himself with guesswork. He approached the problem the simplest and most natural way: he sent a team to dig in the ditch under the supervision of Professor Smith. In all the test holes dug at intervals along the ditch the same observations were made. A good six feet below the mustard-yellow earth surface a broad red-and-black stripe was discovered. Charcoal and ashes in thick layers! There *had* been a tremendous pyre inside this ditch. Systematic excavations were now started, and it was established that the defensive ditch had been artificially cut into the rock. It was constructed with a rectangular bottom, twelve feet deep, about forty feet wide, and nearly two miles long across the hillside. Slingstones, carved slabs, and worked obsidian were found down in the ditch. A laboratory analysis of the radioactivity of the charcoal revealed that the pyre had burned about three hundred years before, which to a remarkable degree confirmed the date Father Sebastian believed, calculated on the basis of the native tradition. The Easter Islanders were proud: they had known what they had been talking about, but the foreign experts had not believed them.

Fresh life had been breathed into the story of the long-ears, both in the village and in the camp at Anakena.

The Poike ditch had given rise to new speculations. It was now ascertained that a fierce fire had raged all along this artificial trench almost three centuries ago. But where could the long-ears have found wood enough for such a gigantic pyre on this island? The remarkably barren nature of the landscape had been stressed by visiting Europeans ever since the time of discovery. Could it be that Easter Island, like all other Polynesian islands, had been originally covered by forest, and that man destroyed it prior to European arrival? There was only one way of finding an answer to this question: collect identifiable pollen deposits by borings in the bogs around the crater lakes.

Not far from the Poike ditch the Rano Raraku crater rose above the plain like a giant bowl enclosing a sky-blue lake partly overgrown by a green bog of floating reeds. This bog would be ideal for pollen boring, and if the island had ever been wooded, pollen of trees would be found in the samples. According to the palæobotanists, fossil pollen would be preserved for thousands of years in bogs like this, and each plant has its own characteristic pollen form which can be identified by the pollen experts.

Thor waded all over the heaving bog to locate solid areas where he could sink his twenty-four foot long pollen bore into the deep layers of turf and mud. Hundreds of stratified soil samples were put in test tubes with formaldehyde and sealed.

Microscopic analysis of the Easter Island samples were later to show Thor's suspicion was well-founded. The Swedish pollen expert, Professor Olof Selling, found the samples to be filled with thousands of pollen-granules from extinct trees and shrubs. The quarry of Rano Raraku had originally been covered by groves of palms, the pollen of which filled every cubic inch in the lower levels of the bog. Even a coniferous species known only in South America had grown on the island. At a certain level in the deposits, numerous soot particles suddenly appeared in the samples, and from this level upward the pollen deposits decreased rapidly, and many species disappeared completely. It was obvious that the original vegetation had been destroyed by fire. Before the fires had started to devastate the forests, there was no pollen of freshwater plants in the stratified deposits, but the immigrants who had lit the fires had brought with them two useful freshwater species and planted them in the crater lakes. Here was an indication of the direction from which man had arrived, for the two aquatic plants existed only in South America and in no other part of the Pacific Ocean. One was the South American *Polygonum acuminatum*, used as a medicinal plant both in the Lake Titicaca area and on Easter Island; the second was the highly important *totora* reed.

On Lake Titicaca the Uru Indians built their houses and boats from bundles of the tall *totora* reed. So did the Easter Islanders, who had a legend to the effect that this freshwater reed had been introduced and planted in their crater lakes by their ancestor hero, Uru. When the archaeologists, working independently in various parts of the island, discovered pictures of crescent-shaped reed boats among old ceiling paintings in ceremonial stone houses or incised on stone statues and walls, four old brothers proudly claimed that they knew how these reed vessels had been built. Encouraged by Thor, they went down to the crater lake in Rana Raraku and cut and dried *totora* reeds. They first each made their own *pora*, a tusk-shaped bundle of reeds used as a sort of raft for swimming about in the open ocean. In this way their ancestors had swum to the bird islet off the coast in search of eggs. This peculiar one-man boat had been a characteristic feature of the coastal Indians of Peru for centuries.

The old men next tied several of the tusk-shaped bundles together to form a broad, boat-shaped, two-man boat whose bow and stern were drawn out in a long point sticking up in the air, and in this they confidently paddled into the open sea. Once upon a time, legend said, their ancestors had tied together reed bundles in such great quantities that the largest reed ships could carry 400 men, and the prows and sterns of these ocean-going vessels were turned up like a swan's neck. Their descriptions, and the ancient drawings and ceiling paintings, corresponded closely to the huge reed ships Thor had seen depicted on ancient jars in pre-Inca Peru, and the ingenious reed boat launched by the old natives through the surf in Anakena Bay strongly recalled the smaller reed boats he knew so well from his experiences at Lake Titicaca.

Referring later to the two useful aquatic plants, the *Polygonum* and the *totora* reed, Thor's former opponent, the Swedish botanist Professor Skottsberg, wrote in a most favourable review of Thor's subsequent expedition report: 'Both are undoubtedly American. It is difficult to understand how they could have spread across thousands of miles of ocean without human aid. When therefore the author advances the idea that his Peruvian immigrants brought with them tubers of the extremely useful *totora* reed and planted them, it sounds to me like a most satisfactory explanation.'

As work progressed all over the island, bits of new information were uncovered and could be fitted together like pieces in a puzzle. Independent of each other, all the archaeologists reached the same basic conclusion: Easter Island's pre-European history consisted of three distinct epochs which were now called the Early, Middle, and Late Periods. With this important discovery the history of Easter Island began to gain in depth.

The earliest visible evidence of large scale activity on the island was carbon-dated to about A.D. 380. The first settlers ashore had brought with them the two aquatic plants from South America and planted them in the crater lakes. To make clearings for their settlements and stone quarries, they burned down the existing virgin forest, since they arrived as expert stone sculptors and masons with little or no appreciation of wood. Unlike any other Pacific island tribe, but like several South American peoples, they built their houses from stone thatched with *totora* reed. They constructed their cyclopean temples from huge blocks cut and fitted with the same highly specialized technique, otherwise unique to the pre-Inca civilization from Tiahuanaco, and the adjacent regions of the Andes. They carved strange kneeling statues and rectangular pillar images like the earliest sculptors in Tiahuanaco and, like them, they had been sun worshippers because their temple walls were astronomically oriented to the annual movements of the sun. At the beginning of the second millenium A.D., the Early Period seemed to have had an abrupt end.

The Middle Period began with violent destruction and the rebuilding, according to an entirely different plan, of all the Early Period structures. This abrupt change of religious and architectural concepts may have been due to a local social revolution, but more probably to the arrival of a second immigration, very likely from the same general area. The characteristic features of the Middle Period culture were the substitution of a peculiar bird-man cult for the previous sun worship, and the construction of *ahu*, or solid stone platforms, designed solely for strength as their entire purpose was to carry rows of uniform statues from the Rano Raraku quarry. All the large stone statues of the type hitherto known, those that had made the island famous, belonged to this second period.

This Middle Period was brought to a sudden end about A.D. 1680 with the victory of the short-ears at the Poike ditch, and all activity in the quarries ended once and for all. The long-eared *ahu* images were pulled down, and spear points and other weapons became the most important local products. The last epoch, the Late Period, was typified by warfare, destruction, and cultural degeneration, and when the Europeans finally arrived in 1722, they found a population of war-ridden Polynesians, among them some white and bearded men, a few with artificially extended earlobes hanging down to their shoulders.

Who, then, were the stone carvers who had been annihilated by the Polynesians on Easter Island? Mulloy's and Smith's excavation of stratified temple walls disclosed that it was the very earliest structures which were sun-oriented and carved according to the specialized Peruvian technique, and distinct from any known practice in all the rest of Polynesia. Skjöls-vold compared his kneeling statue with a specimen from Tiahuanaco, and wrote in his technical report: 'As we have pointed out, the similarity between this Tiahuanaco statue from South America and our specimen is so great that it can scarcely be put down to chance, but must be ascribed to a close relationship, which implies that there is a connection between these two examples of ancient stone sculpture in the Andes and on Easter Island. . . .'

Ferdon made a special study of the numerous circular and boat-shaped Easter Island stone dwellings which the expedition discovered and which were carbon-dated to the pre-European period, and he showed that they represented house types unknown in any other part of Polynesia, but were characteristic of the aboriginal cultures in early South America. He also excavated a solar observatory and a ceremonial village of peculiar stone houses on top of the Rano Kao volcano, where typical American Indian motifs, like the weeping-eye symbol, the double-bladed paddle, crescent-shaped reed boats with sails, and hook-beaked bird-men were painted on the slabs of ceilings and walls. All around this ceremonial village, crouching human figures with birds' heads had been carved in relief on the lava blocks. He stressed in his report that the entire ceremonial village with its bird-man cult was utterly non-Polynesian, whereas it showed intimate relationship to the ancient cultures of Peru.

Thor was no longer in doubt: the legendary white and bearded long-ears, who had sailed into the Pacific after deserting their original cult centre in Tiahuanaco, had not been lost at sea, but had landed safely in Polynesia, and established their new kingdom on the Navel of the World.

The natives were greatly impressed with the archaeological discoveries made by foreigners in their own soil. They looked on in wonder as un-known stone giants and other strange finds were extracted from the depths of the earth. They began to feel that locating these invisible pagan remains involved magic. The barely concealed superstition of the Easter Islanders gradually flared up in full blaze, and whispering about Señor

R

Kon-Tiki's supernatural gifts began. Perhaps he was one of their own ancestors who had now come back to erect old statues and restore their island to its former greatness. Whoever he might be, this fair visitor from the North had a powerful guardian spirit, an *aku-aku*, who gave him a superhuman insight in all that lay beyond human understanding.

The first unexpected reaction was that some of the natives made secret trips to Thor's tent at night, bringing him objects of great interest. They would have to have kept these things stored in secret hiding places. Anything left in their homes was immediately stolen, theft being considered a skill rather than a crime in the local culture pattern. Thor was not to show their gifts to other natives on the island because the disposal of such ancient objects was taboo. With the stories that accompanied the queer gifts, Thor began to see the first faint outlines of a secret world that had so far remained impenetrable for all visitors to the island.

Even Father Sebastian, who had lived on the island for over twenty years, was unaware of the extent to which the pagan beliefs founded on ancestor worship still existed in the minds and thoughts of the local population. He knew that superstition was strongly ingrained in the members of his congregation, but then, superstition was present among the citizens of modern cities as well. Father Sebastian had often heard of the existence of secret family caves filled with pagan objects: small sculptures and figurines in wood and stone and ancient wooden tablets covered with a form of long-forgotten hieroglyphics, locally known as *rongo-rongo*, which neither the natives nor modern scientists were able to read. Although the old priest was convinced that such secret storage caves still existed, he had written in his own book on Easter Island: 'The secret of the exact situation of the cave entrances is buried in the graves with the last survivors from the olden times. . . .' So when he heard what Señor Kon-Tiki had to say, he was astonished.

Señor Kon-Tiki had a great deal to say. He had learned of the existence of caves filled with family relics and known to only one or two chosen individuals within the family. The entrances to these family caves might be right on the plain, hidden under a slab covered by grass and sand, or be concealed in the rock face under some almost inaccessible precipice above the sea. Powerful ancestral *aku-akus* guarded these caves and punished unauthorized intruders who tried to enter and steal the contents. Before entering, even the rightful owner had to conciliate the *aku-aku* with the *unu takapu* ceremony which involved the consumption of the little tail on the rump of a hen, freshly baked in an earth oven not too far from the cave area.

In other words, Easter Island was two different worlds. There was the visible world on the surface: the volcanoes, the stone giants, the church, and the daily life. And then there was the hidden underworld: pitch dark caves filled with demons, symbols, skeletons, and witchcraft. Many of the skeletons were those of ancestors whose bodies had been carried into the family cave under the cover of darkness, whereas others were those of old and sick relatives who had crawled into the cave by themselves when they knew they were ready to die. There were many curious sculptures hidden there: skulls, boat models, bird-men statues, fantastic animals and distorted monsters, and statues of women carrying children or fish on their backs, all carved from volcanic rock.

Thor was eventually introduced to a whole series of secret family caves, but not until the island population had recovered from the serious epidemic that followed the visit of the warship.

The expedition had been on the island for four months when a ship appeared on the horizon. It turned out to be the *Pinto*, a Chilean warship paying her annual call to the island, bringing supplies for the people and— the inevitable *cocongo*, a sort of influenza. On board the vessel were Chilean Professors Ottmar Wilhelm and Gustavo Peña with a group of archaeology students who had come to see the excavations.

During a visit to the mayor, Peña heard about Señor Kon-Tiki's powerful *aku-aku*, which conjured forth the most remarkable things from the depths of the earth. At first the professor paid little attention, for he knew that the mayor was a braggart, but when the mayor really became excited he gave the impression that the grass of Easter Island grew upon a solid mass of art treasures, and that there was no end to all the things Señor Kon-Tiki's party had dug up. He quite forgot to mention that all they had found of real value underground were ruins and giant statues, all of which were still left in place.

Professor Peña could not but believe that the *Chr. Bjelland* was full of excavated treasures and museum pieces. He communicated by radio with the Chilean Minister of Education, who gave him authority to confiscate all the expedition's archaeological finds. This was a great shock to Thor and his colleagues. He had obtained Chile's formal permission to dig on Easter Island through the Norwegian Foreign Office, and had even been to Chile himself to settle all problems before the expedition left for the island. Did they now have to give up everything, every splinter of bone and every sample of charcoal? They protested violently, and finally Peña agreed to a meeting to discuss the matter. Meanwhile the news had spread to the natives. They came to Thor trembling with anger and assured him that no one could take from him what he had received as gifts or bought from them. The mayor was profoundly distressed, and realized that all this was his fault.

The meeting was held in Father Sebastian's little study. After considerable discussion that did not seem to lead to any acceptable solution, Thor proposed that the expedition archaeologists be permitted to take with them to their respective laboratories all the excavated material, complete their analyses, and publish the results. The Chilean specialists could then choose what was of interest for their museums. Peña found this proposition reasonable. Thor then asked him if there were any restrictions on the articles brought to him by the natives.

'That does not interest me', said Peña. 'I haven't come here as a customs official. The things you have bought from the natives we all could have bought. What concerns us is what you yourself have found in the earth, for no one has dug here before you.'

At this an agreement was drawn up and a delicate problem was brought to a happy conclusion.

When Thor left Father Sebastian's little bungalow after the meeting and got into the jeep, he noticed a figure standing motionless in the darkness near him. It was Lazarus, one of his close native friends. He told Thor in a whisper that he had overheard everything, and that if Thor had not won, he would have run to the mayor and returned with two hundred men. Further down the road Thor came upon the mayor, visibly agitated, standing outside his own garden gate. When he heard that nothing was to be taken away from Señor Kon-Tiki after all, he straightened up and thumped himself briskly on the chest.

'Ha! he said triumphantly, 'Our combined "aku-akus!"'

The year's supply of flour, sugar, and other commodites were brought ashore at Hangaroa in the *Pinto's* launch, which took back large bales of wool from the Navy's sheep ranch on the island. Then, about a week later, the warship sailed away, and life returned to normal, but the *cocongo* now began to spread. Father Sebastian and all the natives fell ill, some of them very seriously. The mayor's grand-daughter died and he himself developed pneumonia, which was nearly fatal. When he finally recovered, the illness had left him a sadly changed man. He had previously promised to take Señor Kon-Tiki to see his own family cave where quite marvellous things were supposed to be stored. After his illness he invented endless excuses, and even tried to deceive Thor with a collection of newly carved copies. Obviously the misfortunes in his family since the *Pinto's* visit were interpreted by the mayor as signs of the wrath of the 'aku-akus', because he had disclosed intimate secrets about his family cave.

However, his youngest brother, Atan Atan, was not so easily frightened, and decided to take Señor Kon-Tiki to see his own smaller cave. He was a good Christian and thought it best if the whole responsibility was transferred to a protected museum. During a small ceremony, he presented Thor with the symbolic 'key' to his cave—a grinning death's-head of lava with horribly realistic features—then took Thor to his inland cave one dark night, and finally gave to him all the strange sculptures it contained. Now Señor Kon-Tiki had all the responsibility for keeping these pagan images, and Atan Atan felt that he was a completely free man. Besides, he had received a generous reward. He was no longer in doubt that what he had done had brought good luck, so he went to his wife's brothers, Andres and Juan Haoa, and suggested they do the same with their cave.

Andres Haoa was willing in principle to let Thor have the 'key', but it was not his to dispose of; his father had given it to his brother Juan, a hard man, who was much annoyed when he learned what his brother was suggesting. Atan Atan proposed, then, that he, Andres, and Thor all try to persuade Juan, and one dark night they went to Juan's little whitewashed hut outside the village. As soon as Thor entered the room he realized that this could be an ordeal. Atan and Andres stepped modestly aside, and Thor was left face to face with Juan, known as the Wizard, a tough-looking man with black stubbly beard and piercing dark eyes, whose fanatical expression revealed a stubbornness and mental strength far beyond anything Thor had ever experienced. Behind him stood a slightly older, equally tough-looking man, who stared at Thor with a hostile expression. He was the arbitrator and judge in the family Haoa's affairs and bore the ancient title of *tumu*.

Juan the Wizard gave Thor a penetrating look with half-shut eyes and said intensely like a man in a trance:

'Watch my "aku-aku"! This is the "aku-aku's" house.'

'I know,' said Thor. 'I can see.'

The man brushed his answer aside and stepped towards him.

'Show me your "aku-aku's" power!'

Thor went two inches nearer till their chests all but touched, then took a deep breath to be equal to the situation.

'If your "aku-aku" is as powerful as mine', he said, putting the same note of contempt into his voice, 'you can send him out through the door. Send him out across the whole island. Ask him if the island is changed. Ask him if everything has not become better. Ask him if old walls and buildings have not reappeared, and unknown statues risen up out of the ground. When you get your "aku-aku's" answer, I'll ask you: Do you need any more proof of my "aku-aku's" power?'

Juan the Wizard seemed to accept the answer as valid. He turned quickly and marched out of the room. In a few minutes he came back with a light flat parcel under his arm, and a heavy basket in his hand. Both were made of plaited *totora* reed. He gave the flat parcel to his brother, who laid it on the table, and stood motionless before Thor. He fixed him intently with his eyes, still holding the basket, which presumably contained the 'key'. Thor also stood motionless, with an expression of utter indifference. Juan suddenly turned to Andres and gave him the basket. Andres handed it to Thor who accepted it, thanking Juan for giving the 'key' first to his elder brother as Atan had coached him to do before the meeting. Juan then pointed to the parcel on the table.

'What is inside this parcel?' he demanded. 'Show me your "aku-aku's" power.'

Staring, tense, and expectant, all four of them stood round Thor. He racked his brains. The parcel was too flat and light to contain anything of wood or stone. Taking it for granted that it had been removed from Andres's cave at the same time as the 'key', he thought of the feather work the natives had often brought him—copies of the feather hats and long strings of feathers used for dancing by their ancestors. Perhaps there was something of this kind in the Haoa cave.

'My "aku-aku" says "con pluma"—with feather', he said cautiously, trying not to be too specific.

'No!' snarled the Wizard, crouching forward like a cat about to spring. 'Ask your "aku-aku" again!'

It had suddenly become uncomfortably hot in the room. Atan, who had arranged this encounter, wiped away the beads of sweat and looked desperate. Tumu and Andres seemed menacingly suspicious and slowly came nearer. Thor had intruded into the most inflammable recesses of their private lives. If anything happened, nobody knew where he was. Nowhere in the world were there so many hiding places in which a man could disappear without leaving a trace.

He thought again. Could the parcel contain *tapa*—bark cloth?

'Something to wear', he hazarded.

'No! Ask once more, and ask well!'

Atan drew back. The others closed in. As a last resort Thor tried the technique of animal, vegetable, or mineral of the radio programmes.

'A material?'

A queer grunt was the only reply. He was then brusquely asked to open the parcel. It contained an unbound register book full of Easter Island *rongo-rongo* signs. The hieroglyphic ideograms were drawn in ink that had faded with age.

Suddenly it flashed into Thor's mind that the Spanish word 'pluma' means 'pen' as well as 'feather'. He slammed the book down on the table and drew himself up indignantly.

'My "aku-aku" was right! It said "con pluma" and this indeed is written "con pluma"!'

All their faces changed immediately. They looked at each other foolishly. Atan could only stammer:

'Oh, what a powerful "aku-aku" you have!'

'It's a powerful book', Thor said and realized he'd chosen the right adjective. Juan obviously regarded the book as pure magic.

From then on they were the best of friends. Thor was given the basket and the *rongo-rongo* book. Juan the Wizard placed both hands on his shoulders.

'Now we are brothers', he said 'Now we will drink each other's blood.'

Again he marched out of the room as stiff as a post and came back, not with a knife, but with five glasses and a bottle of red wine from the *Pinto*. He solemnly opened the bottle and filled the glasses, and with grave faces the five men drank a brotherly toast.

Six months had passed and the time of departure was at hand, for before returning home, the expedition was to visit all the other islands of Polynesia where stone statues were to be found. In his book *Aku-Aku* Thor wrote about his departure from Easter Island on 6 April, 1956:

'When orders from the bridge brought the anchor chain rattling up from the depths, and the bell to the engine room set wheels and pistons humming and beating down in the ship's bowels, there were few cheerful hearts either on board or ashore. We had been accepted by the little community and become part of it. The green tents had seemed completely at home on the king's site at Anakena. Now the newly erected giant stood in solitude, once more betrayed, staring out over the sun-filled valley where no one lived any longer. He looked so lonely when we struck the last tent that we felt he was asking to be overturned again, nose down in the sand, as he had lain for the last few centuries.

'But the giant of Anakena was of stone, while at Hangaroa we left a giant of flesh and blood. Father Sebastian, bareheaded in his white robe, towered above the swarm of natives down on the quay. We felt that he belonged to the expedition as much as any of us. But he had both feet firmly planted on the soil of Easter Island. He did not stand alone like the giant at Anakena: he stood as the central figure of the living population. ...'

In gratitude for his valuable contribution to the expedition, in the fields of both science and humanity, King Haakon of Norway appointed Father

Sebastian a Knight of the Order of St Olav, and Thor sent him the means
to build a new church in which he could carry on his humanitarian
mission.

Four of the other islands the expedition visited were Pitcairn, Raivavae
and two of the islands in the Marquesas group, the only four areas in the
Pacific other than Easter Island where monumental statues had ever been
erected. It is a strikingly suggestive fact that stone giants in human form
occur only on five islands, all in the very eastern fringe of Polynesia,
directly facing the South American coast. Excavations with carbon-
datings revealed that the Early Period monuments of Easter Island, next
to South America, were centuries older than all the rest.

On all the inhabited islands the expedition doctor, Emil Gjessing, collected blood samples from the purest-blooded Polynesians he could find,
and stored them in the ship's refrigerator for later dispatch by air to the
Commonwealth Serum Laboratories in Australia. Hitherto no expedition
had brought back fresh blood samples from eastern Polynesia so the
genes and mechanism of inheritance could be studied and determined.

On the mountain island of Rapa Iti, the expedition excavated a strangely
shaped mountain summit, which proved to be an overgrown fortified
village with huge masonry walls, moats, and terraces, the largest artificial
structure ever discovered on any Pacific island.

When the expedition vessel returned from the Pacific after a year of
fieldwork, Thor and his team could look back upon the successful completion of the first stratigraphic excavations ever attempted in eastern
Polynesia, with the exception of Hawaii. Carbon-datings were to disclose
that eastern Polynesia, those islands nearest South America, yields archaeological vestiges of early occupation which antedate previous scientific
assumptions by at least a thousand years.

47. The giant statues of Easter Island had subterranean bodies. The tallest was as
high as a four-storey building.
48. (*next page*) It took eighteen days for twelve natives with stones and poles to
raise a fallen statue.
49. (*next page*) Unknown gods lay hidden in the soil.

48

49

51

Chapter 19

A CHANGE OF WIND

ON the way home from Polynesia, Thor left the expedition ship as it passed through the Panama Canal, and with Yvonne and little Anette took the first plane to Denmark, where the 32nd International Americanist Congress was about to open in Copenhagen.

As soon as he reached Europe he was met by reporters who told him that British and Norwegian newspapers had accused him of unjustly laying claim to the honour of having discovered how the Easter Island statues had been transported and erected. A brief press release from the expedition had referred to the mayor's practical demonstrations, whereupon the head ethnologist at the British Museum, Mr Adrian Digby, had protested in *The Times*. He claimed that the mayor's method had already been discovered and described by the Routledge expedition in 1919. The reporters now asked Thor for his comments.

Thor, who had a high respect for Katherine Routledge and carried her book in his luggage, turned to the page where she had concluded: 'No statues were, therefore, found of which it could be said that they were in process of being removed, and the mode of transport remains a mystery'. With regard to their erection, she had suggested that the statues probably were 'hauled up on an embankment of earth made higher than the pedestals and then dropped on them.' Everybody had to admit that this theoretical method had nothing in common with the technique the natives had demonstrated for Heyerdahl. When Digby met Thor at the Copenhagen Congress, he was the first to admit that he had been too rash in his accusation, and he apologized for the fuss he had caused. He later offered his wholehearted assistance when Thor went to London to analyse the important Easter Island collection stored in the British Museum.

Two further surprises awaited Thor at the Copenhagen congress. He found that his old antagonist, Paul Rivet, had announced a lecture on the inflammable topic of 'white' aborigines in pre-Columbian America, and

50. (*previous page*) Father Sebastian, the uncrowned king of Easter Island, was awarded the Order of St Olav for his valuable assistance to the Norwegian expedition.
51. Back home in Oslo, Yvonne unpacked the strangest of souvenirs.

everyone expected that he would challenge Thor's contention that the legendary 'white and bearded' natives had actually existed in the New World before the Europeans came there. Thor took a seat in front to be prepared to defend his view. Rivet noticed his arrival and flashed him a strange, inscrutable smile. To the surprise of the audience, and of Thor most of all, Rivet began by quoting Heyerdahl's arguments in *American Indians in the Pacific*, after which he devoted the whole of his lecture to presenting concrete evidence that such fair-skinned and bearded Indians had really been observed in various parts of America by the first Europeans to arrive.

There was also a new name on the programme, Dr T. Barthel, a German ethnologist and cipher expert, who produced the sensational news that he had deciphered the *rongo-rongo* writing on Easter Island. All previous attempts of the experts to interpret these ideographs had failed, and Alfred Métraux had finally maintained that it was not a real script. Now Barthel asserted that he had solved the problem and could read what was written on the tablets. According to the inscriptions, he said, the very first immigrants had come to Easter Island about the year A.D. 1400, probably from the island of Raiatea, near Tahiti. The text on the tablets, said Barthel, thus disproved the Heyerdahl theory.

Two Russian ethnologists, Drs Knorozov and Butinov, opposed Barthel, and had a completely different opinion about the *rongo-rongo* script. Thor noted that neither they nor Barthel had produced a single translated quotation. He rose to his feet and said that he had just come back from Easter Island with archaeological evidence that the local settlement had taken place at least a thousand years before the century of A.D. 1400 which had been mentioned by the speaker. His expedition had also visited Raiatea and had found nothing at all to suggest a migration from that island. Barthel was visibly surprised at finding Heyerdahl in Copenhagen, and he said curtly that he was no archaeologist, so could not discuss this point. He had merely made known what he had 'read' on the hitherto undeciphered tablets. He promised to publish the text of his translation in the near future.

Barthel's claim of having deciphered the hieroglyphic writings of Easter Island whose text allegedly contradicted Heyerdahl's theory got wide publicity in the world's press. After the Copenhagen Congress Barthel went to Oslo, where he, as Thor's guest, was invited to study the paper manuscripts with *rongo-rongo* given to Thor by Juan Haoa and other natives. He became so interested in these native documents that he decided to go to Easter Island on the next Chilean warship in the hope of finding further folklore of the same kind. In the meantime, he had written a long report for *Scientific American*, in which he repeated that he had deciphered the *rongo-rongo* script, and that it 'seems to disprove conclusively Heyerdahl's theory of an arrival from Peru'. Yet he still did not give any exact translation of the tablets.

'Hamburg University is now publishing a complete account of my translation of the tablets to date', he wrote. When the Hamburg publication finally appeared, it proved to be a voluminous collection of tables and lists filled with signs, letters, and numerals, but the most careful reading of the text failed to locate any translation of a single tablet.

Eight years after Barthel's appearance at the Copenhagen Congress, Mulloy, Skjölsvold, and Smith, in an issue of *The American Anthropologist*, challenged him to present the translation of one tablet, as this would suffice to check its accuracy by comparison with signs on the other existing tablets. Barthel never replied.

The Russian scientists continued to join in the controversies over the undeciphered Easter Island *rongo-rongo*. A year after the Copenhagen Congress, the Leningrad ethnologists, Knorozov and Butinov, unexpectedly assailed the genuineness of Thor's *rongo-rongo* manuscripts, which no one but Barthel had so far seen. The Russians now maintained that Heyerdahl had been deceived by his native friends, and that the manuscripts they had given him were mere copies of a sign-lexicon made up by the French Bishop Jaussen in Tahiti in the last century. Their statement reached the foreign press in a distorted form: 'Russian scientists accuse Heyerdahl of plagiarism', read the front page headlines in the main Oslo paper.

Simultaneously two Norwegian ethnology students used this opportunity to make a fresh attack on the Kon-Tiki expedition. To navigate a raft was very easy, they wrote in the same paper; with his Peruvian centreboards Heyerdahl should have been able to avoid shipwreck in Polynesia had he not wished to dramatize the incident. Just at this time Thor was sick with Asian flu which that winter had struck the greater part of Europe. Run down by uninterrupted work on his six-hundred page scientific volume on *The Archaeology of Easter Island*, which was to follow his popular narrative *Aku-Aku*, he became an easy prey to the epidemic. Wracked by fever, and with headaches so intense that he could read with only one eye at a time, he lay in bed trying to write rebuttals to these various accusations, strictly against the doctor's orders. Sheet after sheet went into the wastepaper basket. The illness turned into inflammation of the brain. Thus, this time there was no reply from Thor.

As soon as he was able to get out of bed, in the early spring of 1958, he packed his suitcases, and with Yvonne, Anette, and one-year-old

Marian headed for warmer latitudes. He realized that to have a successful comeback he needed to find a peaceful hideout far from telephone, mail, and the press.

With their happy holiday in Corsica six years ago still fresh in mind, they headed for the Riviera and went to Italy for the first time. Thor found a faithful friend in an Italian taxi driver, Gandolfo, who took the family on daily trips from Alassio into the olive-covered valleys and recesses between the Italian Maritime Alps and the sunbaked coast of Liguria. Failing to find the peaceful spot they were searching for, they had decided to leave the area when Gandolfo parked one day at the foot of Capo Mele and took them on foot up the mountain to Colla Micheri, a drowsy little mediaeval hamlet perched on a ridge high above the Mediterranean, half buried in ivy and pine forests centuries old. Thor lost his heart as soon as he set foot inside this seemingly forgotten and half-abandoned fairy-tale place, and later said:

'I knew straightaway that I had come to stay. Somehow, I had felt rootless since my attempt to return to nature in the luxuriant jungle of Fatu Hiva. When in the tropics, I soon longed for the Norwegian mountains, but if I had been back home for awhile, I found myself yearning for the sunshine and exuberance of the southern latitudes. Here, at Colla Micheri, was everything I had dreamed of, palms and blue sea, pines and orange groves and, nearby, snow-covered mountains sheltering friendly shepherds and vine cultivators from the northern winds.'

Next to the old village church lay an equally old patrician house, its tall windows broken and its roof caved in. Chickens lived under the mediaeval vaults on the ground floor. A tall stone wall isolated this house from the rest of the half-crumbled village, and ran around an old park where a narrow stone tower rose among the old trees on the highest summit. An inscription above the door of the pink church wall commemorated the visit of Pope Pius VII in 1814, when the old Roman cobblestone road that crosses the village *piazza* was the only means of communication between Rome and France. Since then Napoleon had built a new road along the seashore, and the steep, moss-covered Roman road lay as forgotten as the ruined village of Colla Micheri.

There were no difficulties involved in the acquisition of the abandoned estate with its olive groves, the little church, and most of the ruined village. Thor pitched his tent among the old trees and started reconstructing the buildings with the aid of the local people.

Four years were to pass before Thor got his chance to meet his Russian opponents, and thus disprove the accusations of plagiarism in the press.

The Russian Academy of Sciences invited Thor on a visit to the scientific institutions in the Soviet Union. He accepted and took with him his disputed *rongo-rongo* manuscripts. Dr Keldysh, president of the academy and head of all sciences in Russia, gave him a hearty welcome at a solemn reception in Moscow to which he had summoned the department leaders of all branches of research. Thor produced his native *rongo-rongo* manuscripts which were immediately dispatched to the Russian experts at the ethnographic institute in Leningrad.

After a week of lecturing in universities and museums under the auspices of the Academy of Sciences, a round-table discussion was organized in Leningrad for all the leading Russian ethnologists to take up Thor's migration theories as well as his *rongo-rongo* manuscripts. Drs Knorozov and Butinov, who had now had ample time to study the original native documents, withdrew their accusations and asserted, instead, that the manuscripts were extremely interesting. They offered to collaborate with Thor in their analysis and publication, and with the official approval of the Soviet Academy, Knorozov and two colleagues later sent Thor an important contribution for inclusion in the second volume of his private expedition report, which was to be a joint publication by the American School of Research and the Kon-Tiki Museum. Before his departure from Russia, Thor was awarded the Lomonosov Medal by Moscow University.

Two years after this event, the 7th International Congress of Anthropologists and Ethnologists assembled in Moscow. The Russian team now admitted that all efforts at breaking the *rongo-rongo* script had failed, and they stressed that it was useless to base an attempt to decipher the signs on the assumption that it had been written in the present-day language of Easter Island, as Barthel had done. During the Congress, *Izvestiya*, the official government paper, invited Thor to a round-table debate with the leading Russian experts. During this discussion Knorozov asserted that a strong undercurrent of an unknown language was noticeable in the Polynesian speech on Easter Island. What was more, he pointed out that there were only two places in the entire world where script had been arranged in a sequence that was known to scholars as 'inverted boustrophedon'. The two places were Easter Island and—Peru!

Thor was now elected an honorary member of the Geographical Society of the Russian Academy of Sciences.

The original attack launched by the Russian *rongo-rongo* experts had been based on the rash assumption that Thor had published all his scientific evidence in his popular book *Aku-Aku* which had appeared in the autumn of 1957. It was the same thing that happened when *Kon-Tiki* was published. A number of scholars once more rushed to make a premature judgement without waiting for the announced technical report. It was an irony of fate that the same Russian *rongo-rongo* experts appeared as collaborators and co-authors when the large technical report on the Easter Island expedition subsequently was published.

In the United States, the most active of a little group of scientists who still tried to debase Thor as a sincere scholar, was a young American archaeologist who attempted to obtain world fame by writing a pocket-book filled with unreliable information on Polynesia, and more especially on Thor and the Kon-Tiki theory. Attacks of this dubious nature made even less impression on the scholars than on the general public, and Thor's scientific reputation continued to rise in America. He was first awarded the Elish Kent Kane Gold Medal by the Geographical Society of Phila-delphia. In 1960 he was elected a member of the New York Academy of Sciences, which later nominated him as a Fellow of the Academy 'in out-standing recognition of scientific achievement and promotion of science'.

The first volume of the expedition report, *The Archaeology of Easter Island*, was published in the autumn of 1961, with Thor Heyerdahl and Edwin Ferdon as co-editors. The reviewers had nearly seven pounds of strong meat to digest. The report was reviewed in three technical periodicals by Sir Peter Buck's successor, the American authority on Polynesia, Dr Kenneth P. Emory of the Bishop Museum in Hawaii. In *American Antiquity* he opened his review by stating that 'this volume has very significantly advanced Polynesian archaeology', and he ended by concluding that the publication 'becomes a fortunate and essential reference for those dealing with the archaeology of Polynesia'.

The outstanding American archaeologist, Dr Betty Meggers of the Smithsonian Institution, reviewed it in the American *Journal of Archaeology*, describing it as 'one of the most thorough studies ever made in the Oceania region'. She concluded her review:

'It is relevant to note in conclusion that Heyerdahl has made a remarkable contribution to archaeology, not only by overcoming massive resistance on the part of professional archaeologists to recognition of transpacific contact as a legitimate field of research, but by organizing and financing fieldwork by competent archaeologists whose previous experience in no way com-mitted them to his views. The result is not only a major contribution to unravelling the problem of the origin and development of Easter Island culture, but a provocative argument for influence from Andean South America that students of that area can no longer afford to ignore.'

What meant most of all to Thor at this time, however, was a letter from the prominent American archaeologist, Dr Samuel Lothrop at

Harvard, the old authority on balsa rafts. He had read the Easter Island volume, and now wrote: 'As the years go by, I feel more and more inclined to accept your viewpoint without reservations and I greatly admire the scholarship on which it is based.'

Only a few days after the publication of the Easter Island volume, Thor and Yvonne flew to Honolulu to participate in the 10th Pacific Science Congress. Nearly three thousand international specialists in the Pacific area attended, among them Thor's Easter Island collaborators, Ferdon, Mulloy, and Smith. The three American archaeologists presented the main results of the Easter Island expedition, whereupon one of Thor's former opponents, Dr Roger Duff of New Zealand, thanked Heyerdahl from the stage for his contributions to Polynesian archaeology and asked for applause from the audience. He then called on Thor to say a few words extemporaneously.

This gave Thor a convenient opportunity to stress what he had always maintained, but very few had noticed, that the answers to the Polynesian problems were not to be found in Peru alone, but that the roots of a second migration must be looked for in some coastal area of Southeast Asia. He had never denied the arrival of one component element from Asia. It was only the dogmatic ideas pertaining to the migratory *route* from that area he had disputed.

Nobody questioned that the world was round, but still the anthropologists had somehow forgotten that the Pacific Ocean formed a complete hemisphere. The equator is not a straight line on a flat sheet of paper, but it curves across the Pacific in a complete semicircle. The tropical coasts of Southeast Asia and South America represent exact antipoles. Accordingly, to believe that the semicircular equatorial line between Southeast Asia and South America is any shorter than the semicircular route north of Hawaii between the same points, is just as absurd as to speak of a short-cut from the North Pole to the South Pole. The immense ocean surface is equally curved in all directions, and Heyerdahl claimed that when Stone Age people set their course towards empty horizons it soon became the winds and currents that set the direction of any prolonged oversea migration, unless they knew in advance where they were going. The Japan Current by way of Northwest America, and not the equatorial semicircle against the current and trade winds, was the easiest and only natural route from Stone Age Asia to Polynesia.

No one objected to this declaration.

Dr R. T. Simmons from Australia, the leading authority on Polynesian blood groups, then presented the results from his analysis of the blood samples collected by the Heyerdahl expedition. For the first time live blood from eastern Polynesia had been available for a complete laboratory study of all known genes, and among these A-B-O, M-N-S, Rh, and Fy^a pointed directly towards America. None of the blood groups pointed towards Melanesia or Micronesia, and only a high percentage of M agreed with Indonesia, but a high M was equally typical of aboriginal American Indians. This supported the evidence produced during twenty years of Pacific research at the Commonwealth Serum Laboratories in Melbourne, and confirmed furthermore the conclusions already reached by Dr Simmons and three of his colleagues, 'that there is a close genetic relationship between American Indians and Polynesians, and that no similar relationship is evident when Polynesians are compared with Melanesians, Micronesians, and Indonesians. . . .'

Dr Simmons admitted that a few immigrants might perhaps have reached Polynesia from the west, but the Polynesians were connected with the American Indians by much stronger ties of blood than with any tribes in the west. In his opinion, the two possible migratory routes from the New World were those pointed out by Heyerdahl, from Peru and from the Northwest American coast respectively.

The Congress also held an important ethnobotanical symposium, led by the French Pacific botanist Dr Jacques Barrau. He opened the meeting by stating: 'The year 1947 saw two events which, for various reasons, marked the beginning of a new era in Pacific ethnobotany.' These were, he said, a publication by the Oxford University Press, and the voyage of the Kon-Tiki expedition. The Oxford University Press publication was a report by three cotton specialists who had discovered that the cotton plants on each side of the Pacific could be divided into two botanical groups according to their chromosome number. The pre-Columbian Indians of Mexico and Peru had artificially produced cotton species which had the double chromosome number of all Old World species, and it was this cultivated American kind which had been subsequently brought to the Polynesian islands where it grew wild when the Europeans arrived. Thor Heyerdahl's balsa raft crossed the Pacific from South America to Polynesia that same year, Barrau continued, inferring that this demonstration showed how useful plants could have spread to aboriginal Polynesia from the New World. He added: 'I would like to say that his Kon-Tiki expedition forced many of us to reconsider some of the then almost universally accepted dogmas concerning human migrations in the Pacific.'

The old isolationist Merrill had, before his death, raised the question whether America was really the original home of the sweet potato, since this was one of the plants supporting Thor's theory of the pre-Columbian voyages from Peru to Polynesia. Three different specialists—from New

Zealand, Japan, and the United States—therefore took up the question for consideration anew. At the ethnobotanical symposium all three of them announced the same final result: the sweet potato was an American plant, entirely unknown in Asia including Indonesia, or Africa, before Columbus. But before the Europeans arrived, aboriginal agriculturists had carried it over to all the islands of Polynesia, where it was a staple food plant cultivated from Easter Island to Hawaii and New Zealand under its old South American name, *kumara*.

After these encouraging reports, Thor lectured on the origin of the cultivated plants and domestic animals of Polynesia. He showed that in spite of all superficial assertions, neither animal nor vegetable life provides a single example of Polynesian contact with Indonesia or Asia. The Polynesians got pigs, poultry, and most of their useful vegetables by trade with the neighbouring island of Fiji, and there they had also learned to use single outriggers on their canoes. But all these important benefits came from Fiji at such a late date that none of them ever reached New Zealand, which had been settled by the original waves of Polynesian immigrants, and subsequently remained isolated from secondary diffusion such as the acquisition of things like poultry and outriggers. On the other hand, the dog, the gourd, and the sweet potato did reach New Zealand, because they had come with the first immigration from Peru. Voyagers from ancient Peru had also carried the American cultivated cotton plant, the *totora* reed, and a long series of other useful plants to various islands in Polynesia. Thor could demonstrate that together the little Fiji group and America answered every problem of the origin of domestic animals and cultivated plants in Polynesia.

The same Congress organized a Galápagos symposium, where anthropologists joined zoologists, botanists, and geologists for the first time as Thor reported on the archaeological evidence of human activity on these islands in pre-Columbian times.

Thor Heyerdahl's various activities in the Pacific were thus reflected in the most diversified sections and discussions of the 10th Pacific Science Congress.

Prior to the closing session, the participating archaeologists joined at a round-table conference. Here, for the first time, the three men who had brought modern archaeology to the three corners of Polynesia were seated at one table in friendly debate. They were Kenneth P. Emory, who had started the first controlled excavations on his own home island in Hawaii; Roger Duff, who had similarly initiated excavations in his own native country, New Zealand; and Thor Heyerdahl, who had come from the opposite end of the earth to accomplish the first stratified excavations in

S

eastern Polynesia. During this conference a five-man committee was appointed for the co-ordination of further archaeological work in the Pacific, and Heyerdahl was elected as the only European member. He agreed to devote special attention to the Marquesas group, and thus found himself committed to promote further work in the very islands where, as a young man, he had made his first archaeological discoveries.

At the archaeological round-table conference, opinions were divided on the relative importance and chronology of the American and Asian sailings into the east Pacific, but no one denied any longer that the New World came into the picture. Finally a resolution was drafted on lines suggested by Professor Roger Green of Auckland University, in which it was stated that Southeast Asia with the adjacent islands and South America constitute the two main source areas of the peoples and cultures on the Pacific islands. The document was passed on to the Resolution Committee, and was next unanimously approved by the entire Congress.

Thor signed with deep satisfaction: the migration routes from America to Polynesia were now open to scientific thought and consideration.

Two days after the close of the Pacific Science Congress in Honolulu, Thor and Yvonne were in Oslo. They arrived just in time for the three-day celebration of the one hundred and fiftieth anniversary of Oslo University, to which they had been invited as guests of honour. Through its long history, Oslo University had lived up to the rule of presenting honorary doctoral degrees only to foreign scientists, but at this anniversary the title of *doctor honoris causa* was to be bestowed for the first time on a Norwegian scientist—Thor Heyerdahl. With this degree and the previously assigned seat in the Norwegian Academy of Sciences, he had received the highest scientific recognition any scholar in his field could obtain in Norway.

The following year Thor was once more called back to Sweden to receive a new award from the Swedish Society for Anthropology and Geography. On April 24, 1962, the commemoration day of the Swedish *Vega* expedition, Thor was awarded the highest distinction any scientist in his field could attain in Scandinavia: the Vega Gold Medal. Before the presentation the president of the society delivered the following speech:

'When on this day fifteen years ago, Thor Heyerdahl—then a practically unknown Norwegian—added the last touches to his balsa raft and was ready to start his voyage from Callao's port near Lima, many regarded him as an adventurer.

'Even though all of us are fascinated by Thor Heyerdahl's determination, courage and narrative skill, and the immense fighting spirit displayed during the *Kon-Tiki* voyage and subsequent expeditions, it is appropriate for this society to affirm that it is not the feat or the adventure that has induced us to award Thor Heyerdahl the Vega Medal.

'The lines of thought and the ideas which he has advanced were at first considered so radical and daring that he was met with criticisms and objections from older scientists in various countries. But his theories opened new roads, and his fresh ideas flowed through channels which had too long been barred.

'Today we find that the opposition has steadily become more low-voiced and reflective.

'The council of the Society is of the unanimous opinion that the Vega Medal is being given to a highly meritorious scientist, who had constantly probed deeper, and who has ripened into the man who today occupies a central position in the study of archaeology in the Pacific region. . . .

'The value and tenability of the new theory does not only depend on whether it can successfully and logically be fitted into a pattern of already accepted lines of thought. In the long run, an idea shows its worth through the dynamic power which it develops by inspiring others to continued investigations and deeper and more versatile knowledge.

'The archaeological and ethnographic research in the Pacific area is just now more intensive and comprehensive than ever before. No one today can dispute that it is the merit of Thor Heyerdahl.

'I will now turn to the Vega medallist of today, Dr Thor Heyerdahl, and beg him to accept the Vega Medal at the hands of His Majesty the King, for his epoch-making investigations into the history of Polynesia's and Easter Island's early colonization, and for his co-ordinating of the diversified investigations which have led to our understanding of the cultural migrations within the Pacific region.'

On June 8, 1964, Thor was the special guest of the Royal Geographical Society in London for the third time. The annual gala banquet of the distinguished society in the large, gilded hall was well underway when the herald announced the speech of Sir Michael Wright, former British Ambassador to Norway. Sir Michael had this to say:

'Mr President, Your Excellencies, My Lords, Ladies and Gentlemen. Somehow travel and hospitality go hand in hand. It is the proud tradition of this society to welcome and to feast those distinguished explorers and geographers who have escaped being feasted upon themselves by cannibal, shark, rival or critic. The first we wish to honour tonight is the winner this year of our Patron's Medal, Dr Thor Heyerdahl. We welcome him both as a scientist and a man. It has been claimed, and rightly claimed, that the greatness of Winston Churchill lies in the fact that he combines a sense of history with a search for adventure. Of Thor Heyerdahl we may fairly say that he combines a sense of adventure with a search for history. He has, I suppose, done as much as any man of our time to keep burnished the mintage of bold and imaginative endeavour and to fire others to essay bright journeys both of muscle and of mind. He is a man in the high tradition of Nansen, himself awarded the Patron's Medal three-quarters of a century ago. Indeed, the *Kon-Tiki* rests on the shore of the Oslo Fjord side by side with Nansen's vessel. We welcome most warmly Thor Heyerdahl and Mrs Heyerdahl.'

In delivering the Royal Gold Medal, the president, Professor Dudley Stamp, said:

'I now turn to the most important event of this afternoon, the presentation of the Medals and Awards for 1964. This year Her Majesty the Queen, our Patron, has approved the award of the Patron's Medal to Dr Thor Heyerdahl for geographical explorations in the South Pacific Ocean and we are all delighted that Dr Heyerdahl should be present with us to receive it this afternoon. His explorations, the most famous of which was his voyage in 1947 on the raft *Kon-Tiki*, have been by no means purely adventurous enterprises, requiring as they have done great personal courage and endurance. They have been inspired by motives of scholarship and research. Through his various expeditions, including those to the Galápagos islands of 1953 and later expeditions with an archaeological motive to Easter Island and the eastern Pacific, Dr Heyerdahl has added greatly to our knowledge of the historical geography of these regions and of the routes by which, in early times, cultural influences and trade were transmitted. It give me very great pleasure to present our Patron's Medal to Dr Thor Heyerdahl.'

Chapter 20

AN ITALIAN VILLAGE

THE warm fragrance of pine resin and wild spices is wafted towards us through the wide open windows of the old bird-catcher's tower that has become Thor's study at Colla Micheri. The Mediterranean sun blazes down through the crooked branches of the centuries-old pine trees outside, and the air is filled with the twittering of birds and the fluttering of wings. Feathered songsters can now once more come here to rest, for this longtime hunting ground has become a sanctuary, a safe resting place on their flights from the north towards southern lands.

From the tower we can see the snow-capped crests of the Ligurian Alps in the distant north; below us on each side fertile valleys, green with olive groves and vineyards, worm their way inland to drowsy mediaeval hill villages; and deep below and in front, the Mediterranean sea stretches past the wide southern horizon like an inverted companion of the blue sky above. Hidden from sight, at the foot of the steep seaside slope, is the modern world: Italy's *Riviera dei Fiori*—the Coast of Flowers—a narrow fringe of lowland with beaches and fishing villages bustling with temporary sun worshippers. Few escape from the beaches and the coastal asphalt road to discover the unspoiled beauty of the inland mountain world. The village of Colla Micheri, a stone's-throw from modern civilization, lies perched on its mountain crest with the same view and the same visage it had when born in the early mediaeval ages.

Palms against snowcapped mountains and oranges against the blue sea, here a Nordic wayfarer adjusted to tropical life could feel at home.

'Here', he says, 'are also people from whom I have much to learn. These modest shepherds and hill farmers of Liguria are industrious, honest, and wise with healthy roots in a millennial tradition. *They* never need to search for the way back to nature, since they have never lost it. They have fitted some true virtues of modern civilization into their old traditional living pattern. They live their modest life in as intimate harmony with nature as is possible in a time when the world around them has so drastically changed.'

We climb down the winding stairway from the pine-encircled tower and come out into the sunshine. Through a green crest of cypresses we look down across a little terraced vale set like an amphitheatre facing the main valleys below. On the upper terraces Thor has orchards and garden plots, and down below his little fold of sheep is grazing.

'There is immeasurable wealth', he says, 'in owning a piece of live earth where one can go round like a magician, saying: "Here I want an orange tree to appear, here an almond tree, there maize, cauliflower or grapes!" Then everything shoots up into the daylight forcing its way out of the soil with a power so great that the stones are pushed aside. For anyone who works with his pen it is a relief for awhile to wield an axe or a spade. Only then do we feel right through our body—to the very marrow of our bones —how wonderful life is. Then we take part in a great project—a truly worthwhile project: taming nature instead of spoiling her.'

On a hillock down below us the jagged ruins of Castello Romano seem to float upon the valley haze. Down there, amid towers and walls from Roman times, I have found myself a peaceful nest, a moss-grown stone house hidden between laurel trees and giant cacti. An afterglow of a more romantic era hovers over the place, like a reflection of something half forgotten hidden inside ourselves. It brings back childhood memories, with dreams and hopes and castles in the air.

'You've found your way back to nature after all', I say, nodding towards the vineyards and the olive groves on the terraces around us. 'I remember how we used to talk about nature versus civilization. You used to compare civilization to a building.'

'That's what it *is*—a fantastic building. Man has never ceased working at it; but progress has mostly been confined to the technical department, where we are on the way to breaking the bounds of imagination. But we ourselves—the human beings—we have not managed to keep pace. We have only taken a few steps sideways instead of upwards. We have not improved ourselves.'

'But surely we have developed *some* of our gifts?'

'And weakened others. One who seriously probes into man's activities in earlier cultural epochs cannot avoid detecting that we are neither better nor worse than our remote forefathers, neither wiser nor more stupid than they. The fool, the mediocrity, and the genius have existed side by side throughout the ages. The history of mankind is filled with examples of both practical and philosophical intelligence from its very beginning. It is perhaps our greatest error that we always take it for granted that *we* are superior. We feel justified in looking down upon earlier generations, upon other nations, and upon people whose skins are different from ours.'

'But at least we're not cave dwellers or cannibals any more.'

'I once had a friend who had been a cannibal—old Tei Tetua of Fatu Hiva. When he heard that white warriors kill thousands, even millions of their fellow men just to bury them in the ground, this seemed to him the most savage barbarism. Many of the South Sea islands were much happier before we "civilized" them. The people were far more trustful and generous. Both there and among the Northwest Indians generosity was a moral ideal and the one who displayed the greatest willingness to distribute gifts won the greatest prestige in the community. Until the white men arrived. Now they have all become greedy like us and cheat each other as best they can.'

He pauses for a moment before he goes on:

'Of course, the technical progress has given us many benefits, yet it hasn't made us any happier. We build better houses than before, we have softer beds, more practical kitchens, more elegant clothes and coiffures. But do we sleep better, do we love any better, or do we eat with any greater relish? We have our machines to save our muscles and our time. But do we feel any less tired, and as for time saved, don't we rush more than ever? Above all, we have invented the deadliest weapons of all times, but are we any safer than earlier generations?'

We stroll across the open green behind the tower. Yvonne is sitting by the swimming pool, keeping an eye on Anette, Marian, and Elizabeth, three fair-haired little girls who are playing about in the water with shouts of laughter and joy. Children of nature, still happy and safe—for a time.

'You once said that modern inventions—or at least some of them—have been made to make up for the shortcomings of civilization.'

'I still think so. Today the doctors and psychologists are occupied with curing troubles and diseases which are due to our unnatural way of life— congested living conditions, contamination, noise, rush, sedentary work, and overeating. We are just as careless with our minds as with our bodies. We have no time for artless pleasures and quiet moments. The twilight hour has disappeared, and we no longer sit on our doorstep at sunset chatting with our neighbour. We suffer from haste, and we have forgotten how to relax. Fortunately we have developed music and art, which compensate to some extent for what we lost when we gave up life within the very heart of the greatest of all art galleries and music halls: Mother Nature. The day we cut down the last tree and pour asphalt and concrete on the last stalk of grass, we shall be left like orphans in the street.'

'It's no use trying to put back the clock.'

'No, but it pays to check that it doesn't run riot. A wise architect prepares a thorough plan before he begins to build. He asks himself: "How is the final structure going to be?" The greatest enterprise mankind has embarked upon is our unfinished civilization. We are in the midst of building it, but no one has thought about its ultimate shape. There is no plan. People of all nations are running about, adding a brick to the building wherever they find an empty space. But how is the final edifice going to be, what are we making? Is the final goal of man to push buttons for a living? Is it to sit motionless and comfortable in a cushioned arm-chair gazing at a screen which supplies his daily ration of sport, excite-ment, sex, and laughter? If that is our aim, there will soon be nothing exciting any more; nothing really amusing either. Hasn't the time come for the world powers in common fellowship to appoint a committee of practical philosophers to think a little into the future and draw a plan of the world structure we want to build?'

We have passed the garden gate and reached the little *piazza* by the church. Above us a jet fighter leaves its ominous trail in the blue sky. In the white and black pebble mosaic in front of the stairway to the church, a dove is spreading its wings. It has an olive branch in its beak.

The sundial on the gable shows that midday has now been reached, and I read once more its old inscription:

'Can I tell you the time? Of course I can:

It is time to work, for an honest man'—

We exchange a farewell handshake, and Thor goes back to his books, his maps, and his manuscripts in the old bird-catcher's tower. There is still much work to be done.

52. The *Kon-Tiki* is visited by a quarter of a million people each year. From left: Thor Heyerdahl, Prince Philip, Queen Elizabeth II and King Haakon of Norway.
53. (*next page*) Outside the tower of Thor's study at Colla Micheri. Yvonne and her three daughters, Anette, Marian and 'Bettina', and the mule 'Mora'.

BOOKS BY THOR HEYERDAHL

HEYERDAHL, THOR
Aku-Aku: The Secret of Easter Island, 3rd imp 1958, Allen and Unwin Ltd., London.
American Indians in the Pacific: The Theory Behind the Kon-Tiki Expedition, 1952, Allen and Unwin Ltd., London.
The Kon-Tiki Expedition, Translated by F. H. Lyon, 25th imp 1965, Allen and Unwin Ltd., London.
Sea Routes to Polynesia, 1968, Allen and Unwin Ltd., London.

HEYERDAHL, THOR AND FERDON, EDWIN, N. JR (editors)
The Archaeology of Easter Island: Reports of the Norwegian Archaeological Expedition to Easter Island and the East Pacific. Vol I, 1962, Vol II, 1966, Allen and Unwin Ltd., London.

54. (*previous page*) Thor at work on a scientific study.
55. (*previous page*) In the forgotten village of Colla Micheri high above the Italian Riviera, Heyerdahl works in peace. His house is partly obscured in the background.
56. Two old friends meet again at the author's home at Castello Romano, an old Roman stronghold near Colla Micheri.

INDEX

Note: the abbreviation TH is used throughout for
Thor Heyerdahl, Señor Kon-Tiki

Aboriginal Navigation off the West Coast of South America 148
Ahlmann, Prof Hans W'son: quoted 205
Aku-Aku 267, 269, 281; quoted 242, 249, 263
Algonquin National Park, Ontario 106–9
Allen (George) & Unwin Ltd 183
American Indians in the Pacific, revised version of *Polynesia and America (q.v.)* 185; finished and sent to printer 196; published 208; reviews quoted 201, 208–9, 211–12; other refs 186, 200, 207, 218, 266, 281
Ana o Keke see Easter Island
Anakena *see* Easter Island
Angatau 171–2
Animal House, Larvik 25–6
Araguaia river 231–6, *Plates 44–5*
Archaeological Evidence of Pre-Spanish Visits to the Galápagos Islands by TH and Arne Skjölsvold 226
Archaeology of Easter Island, The, edited by TH and Edwin Ferdon: Russian contribution to 269; publication 270; reviews quoted 255–6, 270–1; other refs 267, 271, 281
Artfilm, Stockholm 187–8, 188, 189
Asia, Southeast *see* Polynesian migration theories
Astrid, Princess 106, 229
Atan, Atan 261–3
Atan, Pedro, mayor of Easter Island 243, 247, 251–3, 259–60, 260
Australia 193
Axvall, Sweden 136–7

B.B.C., London: TH's broadcast on Finnmark quoted 125–6, 126–7, 130, 135; other refs 128
Balchen, Colonel Bernt 137, 139, 140, 142
Ball gang *see* Consolidated Mining and Smelting Company
Balsa rafts: in Spanish documents 148; believed incapable of crossing Pacific 148–9, 151; TH determines to prove possibility 149–50, 151; their construction 152, *Plate 29*; Eitrem's opinion 152–3; building of *Kon-Tiki see Kon-Tiki* (raft); TH learns to steer 225–6
Baltimore 97–9
Barrau, Dr Jacques: quoted 272
Barthel, Dr T. 266–7, 269
Becker-Donner, Dr Etta 214
Bella Coola valley, British Columbia: Fougner on 71–2; TH visits 77–9, 80–1, *Plate 18*; Indian's advice on fires 89; other refs 74, 84, 97, 140. *See also* Polynesian migration theories

Bennett, Dr W. C. 200–1, 226, 250; quoted 201
Bethlehem Fairfield Shipyard 97–9, 123
'Bewitched Islands' *see* Galápagos Islands
Beyer, Erik 112, 113, 117, 119
Bird, Junius 226
Birket-Smith, Prof Kaj 199, 210–11
Björneby, Ola 28–9, 31
Bleichsteiner, Prof 214
Boas, Dr Franz 76
Bokförlaget Forum, Stockholm 183
Bonnevie, Prof Kristine 33, 37–8, 42, 205
Bowman, Dr Isaiah 97
Brander, Captain 45, 46, 54
Brazil *see* São Paulo; Araguaia river
British Columbia *see* Bella Coola valley; Kwatna valley; Trail; Vancouver
British Columbia, University of 86, 96
Broch, Prof Hjalmar 33, 38, 42, 205; quoted 33
Brooklyn Museum 99, 150–1
Buck, Sir Peter 197–8, 270; *An Introduction to Polynesian Anthropology* quoted 149
Bustamante y Rivero, Don José 158
Butinov, Dr N. A. 266, 267, 269–70

Callao, Peru 158, 159–60
Cambridge Congress 209–11
Carlyle Smith, Prof *see* Smith, Prof Carlyle
Carrefour, Paris 207; quoted 207–8
Castello Romano 278, *Plate 56*
Chicago University Club 183
Chile 239, 242, 243, 259–60
Chr. Bjelland 240, 241, 259, 263–4
Christensen, Lars 177, 179–80
Churchill, Winston 121, 136, 275
Coe, Dr Michael: quoted 227
Colla Micheri 7, 15, 268, 277–80, *Plates 53–5*
Columbus, Christopher 72, 146, 151, 216, 231, 273
Con-Tici *Viracocha* (Contici) 147, 200; *see also Kon-Tiki* (raft); Polynesian migration theories
Consolidated Mining and Smelting Company of Canada: TH employed by 86–96, *Plate 16*: in 'ball gang' 86–9, 91–4, asphalting team 89–91, research 94–6; *see also* Lepsoe, Robert
Copenhagen Congress 265–6
Coucheron Torp, Liv *see* Heyerdahl, Liv
Criticism of the Kon-Tiki Criticisms 204

Dahl, Colonel Arne 122, 126, 127–8, 128, 129
Danielsson, Bengt: joins *Kon-Tiki* crew 158; on voyage 166, 167, 168, 175, 176, *Plate 34*; later life 195

Dartmoor 196-7, *Plate 39*

Darwen, Charles 17, 219

Dedekam-Simonsen, Yvonne *see* Heyerdahl, Yvonne

Did Polynesian Culture Originate in America? 91

Digby, Adrian 265

Dixon, Dr Ronald 76, 149

Donner, Dr Etta Becker- 214

Dovrefjell 39-41

Duff, Dr Roger 271, 273

Easter Island: TH's youthful interest in 29, 238; expedition to 238-64, *Plates 47-9, 51*
    Ana o Keke caves 247-9; Anakena anchorage and camp 241-2, 243-4, 253, 254, 255, 263, temple and digs 244, 245, 252; Hangaroa village 243, 260, 263; Poike ditch 246, 251, 253-4, 256; Rano Raraku quarries 244, 250-1, 252-3, 254-5, 256; other refs 52, 61, 218; *see also* Polynesian migration theories; Sebastian, Father

Ecuador: in Inca legend 147; balsa logs obtained 157-8; TH learns to steer balsa raft 225-6; other refs 220, 224; *see also* balsa rafts

Eitrem, Wilhelm 152-3, 172, 240

Ekholm, Gordon 199, 226

Elish Kent Kane Gold Medal 270

Elizabeth II, Queen 276, *Plate 52*

Emory, Dr Kenneth P. 149, 273; quoted 270

Englert, Father Sebastian *see* Sebastian, Father

Estrada, Emilio 225-6

Evans, Dr Clifford 226, 227

Explorers Club, New York: TH's election 99; visits before *Kon-Tiki* expedition 153; first showing of *Kon-Tiki* film 180; other refs 150, 162

Fatu Hiva 38, 44, 45-59, 61-5; Omua valley 46-50, 56, 57-8, 61, *Plates 8, 9*; Ouia valley 61-4, *Plates 10-12*; Tahaoa beach 51, 64-5, *Plate 14*; other refs 69, 84, 85, 93, 120, 123, 222, 268; *see also In Search of Paradise*; Polynesian migration theories; Tei Tetua; Victorin, Père

Ferdon, Edwin: on Easter Island 241, 245, 250, 257; quoted 245; co-editor with TH of *The Archaeology of Easter Island (q.v.)*; other refs 187, 271

Figueroa, Gonzalo 242

Finnish Academy of Sciences 212

Finnish News Bureau 201, 202

Finnmark campaign: Red army in Kirkenes 122; TH in Finnmark, based at Kirkenes 125-9, 137-42, *Plates 24-7*; TH's broadcast on Finnmark quoted 125-6, 126-7, 130, 135

Floreana 220-1

Fougner, Judge Iver 71, 78

Fred Olsen Line 74, 83, 85, 152, 240

Free Norwegian Forces: recruiting office in New York 99; TH's training in Canada 100-9, *Plates 19-21*; I-Group *(q.v.)* in Great Britain

Free Norwegian Forces:—*cont.*
    110-6; TH's S.O.E. *(q.v.)* training 117-9, 120-1; Finnmark campaign *(q.v.)* 122-42

Freuchen, Peter 153

Galápagos Islands ('Bewitched Islands'): and *Kon-Tiki* expedition 164, 166, 193; TH's expedition to 218-25, 230; symposium on 273 Floreana 220-1; Santiago Island 223-4; *see also* Polynesian migration theories

Galbe, Jörgen 178, 179

Gates, Prof Ruggles 211

Giaever, John 105; quoted 102

Gjessing, Emil 240, 264

Gjessing, Prof Gutorm 205-6; quoted 209

Gleditsch, Prof Kristian: quoted 216-7

Glittertind 35-6

Goddard, Dr P. E.: *Indians of the Northwest Coast* quoted 72

Gonzales, Dr Rex 230-1

Green, Prof Roger 274

Gunther, Prof Erna 76

Gyldendal Norsk Forlag 157, 182, 183

Haakon, King of Norway, 98, 205-6, 206, 263-4, *Plate 52*

Hangaroa *see* Easter Island

Haoa, Juan the Wizard and Andres 261-3

Harald, Prince 106

Hartmark, Captain Arne: quoted 240-1

Haugland, Knut: first meets TH 121; joins *Kon-Tiki* crew 154, 158; on voyage 165-6, 167, 168, 170, 173, 175, *Plate 34*; ashore on Angatau 172; on Raroia 176-7; after *Kon-Tiki* 179, *Plate 38*; and *Kon-Tiki* Museum 185-6, 194-5, *Plate 41*; quoted 186, 194

Hawaii *see* Polynesian migration theories

Hedin, Sven 188, 203

Heine-Geldern, Robert von: opposition to TH 199, 212-3, 214-5, 226; armistice 215, 216

Hesselberg, Erik: climbing with TH 34, 35-6; joins *Kon-Tiki* crew 154, 159; on voyage 163, 165-6, 167, 168, 169, 170, 175, 176; later life 195, *Plate 38*; other refs 145

Heyerdahl, Fru Alison (mother of TH, *née* Alison Lyng): before marriage 16-17; upbringing of TH 17-21, 23-4, 28-9, *Plate 2*; breakup of marriage 30; Oslo 33, 34; supports Marquesas expedition 41-3; heroism in war 135-6; other refs 39, 69, 70, 98, 161

Heyerdahl, Anette (daughter of TH): born 228; Easter Island 242, *Plate 46*; Colla Micheri 279, *Plate 53*; other refs 236, 265, 267-8

Heyerdahl, Bjorn ('Bamse', son of TH): born 85; christened 97; and Peik 105-6; other refs 86, 95-6, 96, 99, 101, 103, 104, 110, 111, 142, *Plate 21*

Heyerdahl, Elizabeth ('Bettina', daughter of TH) 279, *Plate 53*

Heyerdahl, Liv (1st wife of TH, *née* Liv Coucheron Torp): before marriage 32, 33, 39, 41, 42–3; marriage 43; Marquesas expedition 44–65, *Plates 8, 11, 13, 14*; Norway and birth of Thor 69, 70, 71; Bella Coola 78, 80; Vancouver 82–3, 84–5; birth of Bjorn 85; in British Columbia 86, 88, 95, 96; Baltimore 97, 98; Canada again 99, 101, 103, 104, 106, 110; New York 111; Norway 142, 145; breakup of marriage 150, 182

Heyerdahl, Marian (daughter of TH) 267–8, 279, *Plate 53*

Heyerdahl, Thor (father of TH): before marriage 16, 17; upbringing of TH 19–20, 25, 26, 27, *Plate 3*; breakup of marriage 30; financial support of Marquesas expedition 42–3, *Kon-Tiki* expedition 151, 154; TH visits 182, 186, 238; other refs 33, 69, 98

Heyerdahl, Thor (TH, Señor Kon-Tiki):
Life: birth and childhood 15–32, *Plates 1–3*; Oslo University (*q.v.*) and mountaineering 33–43, *Plates 4–6*; marriage to Liv (*q.v.*) 43; Marquesas (*q.v.*) expedition 44–65, *Plates 8, 12, 14*; writing and Polynesian migration theory (*q.v.*) 69–77, *Plate 15*; Bella Coola (*q.v.*) expedition 77–81, *Plate 17*; stranded Vancouver 82–6; employed at Trail (*q.v.*) 86–96, *Plate 16*; Baltimore 97–9; Free Norwegian Forces (*q.v.*) 99–142; *Kon-Tiki* expedition (*q.v.*) 145–77; *Kon-Tiki* book, films, lectures 178–95, *Plate 38*; marriage to Yvonne (*q.v.*) 186–7; academic writings and controversy 196–217, *Plate 39*, 230–1, 265–74; Galápagos expedition 218–27; Araguaia river (*q.v.*) 231–6; Tiahuanaco 236–7; Easter Island (*q.v.*) 238–64; honours 204, 206, 274–6, *Plate 43*; Colla Micheri (*q.v.*) 277–80

Works: *Aku-Aku* (*q.v.*); *American Indians in the Pacific* (*q.v.*); *Archaeological Evidence of Pre-Spanish Visits to the Galápagos Islands* 226; *Archaeology of Easter Island* (*q.v.*); *Did Polynesian Culture Originate in America?* 91; *In Search of Paradise* (*q.v.*); *Kon Tiki Expedition* (*q.v.*); *Polynesia and America* (*q.v.*); *Sea Routes to Polynesia* 281; *Turning Back Time in the South Seas* (*q.v.*)

Heyerdahl, Thor (son of TH): born 71; Bella Coola 78; hungry in Vancouver 83, 84–5; British Columbia 86, 95–6, *Plate 16*; and Peik 105–6; Easter Island 241, *Plate 46*; other refs 74, 96, 97, 99, 101, 103, 104, 110, 111, 142

Heyerdahl, Yvonne (2nd wife of TH, née Yvonne Dedekam-Simonsen): early life and marriage 186–7; assists TH's work 196–7, *Plate 39*; at congresses 209–10, 212, 213, 215, 230, 265, 271; birth of Anette and Oslo home 228; Araguaia river 231–6, *Plates 44–5*; Easter Island 241, 242, 244, *Plates 46, 51*; Colla Micheri 279, *Plate 53*; other refs 189, 195, 218, 229, 236, 238, 239, 267–8, 274, 276

Hill-Tout, Prof Charles: *Oceanic Origin of the Kwakiutl-Nootka and Salish Stocks of British Columbia* 77

Hiva Oa 60–1; Puamau valley 61

Honolulu Congress 271–4

Hörnsjö 20, 28–9, 39, 69

Hotu Matua, King 241, 244, 245

Humboldt, Friedrich von 201

Humboldt Current 161, 163, 166, 194, 219; *see also* Polynesian migration theories

I-Group: creation and training 104–6, *Plate 19*; promotion muddles 104, 111, 115, 116; in England 110–1; in Scotland, near mutiny 111–5; disbanded 116; other refs 102, 122, 142

Illa-Tici (Fire-Tici) 147

Imbelloni, Prof J. 230–1

In Search of Paradise 74, 157, 180; quoted 45–6, 49, 51, 63–4

Indians of the Northwest Coast: quoted 72

Indonesia *see* Polynesian migration theories

International Americanist Congress: 29th, New York 199, 210; 30th, Cambridge 209–11; 31st, São Paulo 230–1; 32nd, Copenhagen 265–6; 33rd, Costa Rica 227; 34th, Vienna 215–6; 37th, Argentina 231

International Congress of Anthropologists and Ethnologists: 4th, Vienna 212–5, 218, 219; 7th, Moscow 269

International Science 91

Introduction to Polynesian Anthropology, An: quoted 149

Izvestiya 269

Jacoby, Arnold: at school with TH 15, 26–7, 29–30, 31–2; fellow-students 33, *Plate 4*; discussions with TH: on Bella Coola 73, 75, on *Kon-Tiki* expedition 145–6, 150, on Easter Island 238–9; letters, etc, from TH quoted 145, 156, 228–30; with TH at Colla Micheri and Castello Romano 278–80, *Plate 56*; other refs 43, 74, 182, 186, 240–1

Japan current *see* Polynesian migration theories

Jungk, Dr Robert: quoted 193

Kallax, Sweden 137, 138, 139, 140, 142

Karsten, Prof Rafael 201–3, 212

Kazan 34–6, 39–41, *Plates 5–6*

Kirkenes *see* Finnmark campaign

Knorozov, Dr Y. V. 266, 267, 269–70

Kon-Tici (Sun-Tici) *Viracocha* 147, 148, 236, 237; *see also* Polynesian migration theories

Kon-Tiki (raft): crew *see Kon-Tiki* crew; construction 157–60, *Plates 30–1*; expert forebodings 160–1; christening 162; voyage 162–72, *Plates 32–35*; logbook 167, quoted 165, 165–6, 172; shipwreck 172–6, *Plates 36–7*; salvage 176, 177; preservation 178, 178–9, 185, *see also Kon-Tiki* Museum; imitations 192–3

Kon-Tiki crew: chosen 152, 154, 158; assembled 158, 159; voyage *see Kon-Tiki* (raft); later lives 194–5, *Plate 38*; other refs 203; *see also* under names: Danielsson, Bengt; Haugland, Knut; Hesselberg, Erik; Raaby, Torstein; Watsinger, Herman

Kon-Tiki expedition: the theory 146–9; the plan 149, 151–3; practical preparations 153–9; finances 151, 153, 155–7, 162; Washington headquarters 159, 177, 178, 179; crew *see Kon-Tiki* crew; raft and voyage *see Kon-Tiki* (raft); communications re-established 176–7; welcome to Raroia and Tahiti 177, to U.S.A. 178–80; other refs 7, 121, 145, 239; *see also* balsa rafts

Kon-Tiki Expedition, The (book): publishers offer advance 157; writing 182; publication in Norway 182, 183, Sweden 183, Great Britain 183, 184, U.S.A. 183–4, in sixty languages 184; earnings 184–5; educational use 192; reasons for success 193–4; academic condemnation 199–200, 200–1, 201–3, 207; quoted 69–70, 162, 163–4, 168–9, 169, 171, 172–6; other refs 150, 165, 214, 269, 281

Kon-Tiki Expedition, The (film 1): commercial movie version 186

Kon-Tiki Expedition, The (film 2): TH's film: first showing 179; cut to lecture film 179, 180; Explorers Club showing 180; shown on lecture tours 180, 181–2, 182–3, 187; bought and re-made by Artfilm 187–8; royal premières 188; reception 188, 191, *Plate 40*; re-sold 188–9; lawsuit 189–91; awards 191; reasons for success 193–4; other refs 194, 201, 206

Kon-Tiki lecture tours 180, 181–2, 182–3, 187

Kon-Tiki Museum: building to house raft 185–6; success 185–6; further development 194–5; royal visits 228, 229, *Plates 41–2, 52*; other refs 165, 191, 228

Koppers, Prof Wilhelm 213, 215

Kroepelien, Bjarne 37, 44, 70

Kwakiutl tribes 73, 77, 79; *see also* Polynesian migration theories

Kwatna valley, British Columbia 79–80

Larvik: TH's childhood at 7 Stengaten 15–28, 29–32, *Plate 2*; Manor Pond 18, 22, 25, 27; Kirkebukten (Church Bay) 22–3; Animal House 25–6; visits to 182, 186, 238; other refs 43, 74, 145, 219, 228

Lavachery, Prof Henri 238; quoted 208

Lehmann, Dr Walter 207

León, Cieza de 147

Lepsoe, Gunnar 86

Lepsoe, Robert: TH employed by 86; promoted by 94; friendship with Heyerdahl family 95, 96, 99; quoted on TH 94

Lesser, Sol 188–91

Lewis, Colonel R. L. 154–5

Life magazine 180, 198

Lillehammer 20, 70, 98, 135, 145

Lima 158, 159, 162

Linné, Prof S. 210

Linton, Prof Ralph 99; quoted 198, 199

Little Norway, Ontario 101–4, 113

Little Skaugum, Ontario 102, 104–6, 109–10

Living Races of Mankind 22

London: TH's visits during war 110–11, 112, 116; recalled to by Russian Embassy 127–8, 129, 134, 136; Royal Geographical Society 183, 275–6; other refs 196

Lothrop, Dr Samuel K.: believes balsa rafts will sink 148, 161; converted 211, 270–1; *Aboriginal Navigation off the West Coast of South America* 148; other refs 226, 227

Lunenburg, Nova Scotia 100–1, 102, 103

Lyng, Alison *see* Heyerdahl, Fru Alison

McDonald, Jimmy 89–90, 91, 93

Mannerfelt, Dr Carl 203–4, 218

Margaret, Princess 228–30, *Plate 42*

Marquesas collection: assembly 52–3, 59, 63; attempt to sell 84; sold 99; other refs 103, 198

Marquesas Islands 37–8, 43, 44–65
    Fatu Hiva (*q.v.*); Hiva Oa 60–1; Motane 60, 61; Tahuata 60, 61; TH's archaeological collection *see* Marquesas collection; other refs 274; *see also In Search of Paradise*; Polynesian migration theories

Martha, Crown Princess of Norway 106

Mead, Margaret 81

Means, P. A.: *Pre-Spanish Navigation off the Andean Coast* quoted 148

Meggers, Dr Betty 226; quoted 270

Menzies, T. P. O. 77

Merrill, Dr E. D. 215–6, 272

Métraux, Dr Alfred: attack on TH 206–7; confrontation 207–8; Galápagos stone head 218–9, 219–20; views on Easter Island 200, 238, 253, 266; quoted 208–9

Moose-skin Tent 79–80, *Plate 17*

Motane 60, 61

Mulloy, Dr William: on Easter Island with TH 242, 250, 257; other refs 267, 271

Mungo Park Gold Medal 206

Munthe-Kaas, Colonel Otto 154, 156, 157, 180

Murmansk, Russia: TH in 124, 130–1; convoys 122–4, 131–4, *Plate 28*; other refs 127, 129–30

'Mystery' 94–5

Mystery of Easter Island, The 241, 244, 253; quoted 241, 265

National Geographic Magazine 85, 90, 153–4, 155

National Geographic Society 154, 155, 166

'Navel of the World': mountain in Peru 237; native name for Easter Island 239

New Mexico 186–7

New York: Norwegian recruiting office 99; TH in before *Kon-Tiki* expedition 150–4, after *Kon-Tiki* expedition 179–80; before Galápagos expedition 219–20; other refs 111, 156

New York Herald Tribune quoted 184

New York Times 81, 179; quoted 201

New Zealand *see* Polynesian migration theories

Nicolaysen, Captain 102

Nissen, Gunnar 34, 39, *Plate 5*

Nordemar, Olle 187–8, 191

North American Indians of the Pacific Coast: experts on 187; *see also* Polynesian migration theories

North American Newspaper Alliance 153, 155

Northwest Coast Indians: experts on 187; *see also* Polynesian migration theories

Norway: TH in *see* Finnmark campaign, Larvik, Lillehammer, Oslo; invaded 80–81; heroic resistance recognised 98, 113, 135–6; last year of war *see* Finnmark campaign; TH's late recognition in 205–6, 274

Norwegian forces *see* Free Norwegian Forces

Norwegian Maritime Museum 185

Norwegians: unpopular in America 82, 91, no longer 96, 98

Nya Pressen, Helsinki 201, 203

Oceanic Origin of the Kwakiutl-Nootka and Salish Stocks of British Columbia 77

Olav, Crown Prince of Norway 104, 106, 239; as King *Plate 41*

Olsen, Fred 74; *see also* Fred Olsen Line

Olsen, Thomas 74–5, 85, 89, 111

Omua valley *see* Fatu Hiva

Oslo: Alison Heyerdahl and TH in 33, 34; TH's dislike of 36; TH's demobilization 142; attitude to *Kon-Tiki* expedition 180–1, and raft 185; TH and Yvonne make home in 228; *see also* *Kon-Tiki* Museum; Oslo University

Oslo University: TH student at 33–4, 36–7, 37–8, 39, 41, 69; research at 70; support by professors 205; doctorate 274

Ouia valley *see* Fatu Hiva

Owl's Creek *see* Uglevika

Pacific Islands *see* Polynesia

Pacific Science Congress, 10th, Honolulu 271–4

Papeete, Tahiti 177, 178, 189

Papeno valley, Tahiti 44–5, 177

Peik 105–6, 110, *Plate 20*

Peña, Prof Gustavo 259–60

Pentagon 154–5, 156, 157

Per (of Norwegian Air Force) 106–9

'Per' (a saboteur) 135

Peru: Spanish conquest 146–8; TH in before *Kon-Tiki* expedition 158, 159–62; TH's visit to Tiahuanaco (*q.v.*) 236–7; other refs 63, 193, 194; *see also* balsa rafts; Polynesian migration theories; Tiahuanaco

Petsamo, Finland 124, 125, 127

'Pettersen, Lt' *see* Raaby, Torstein

Pinto 259, 260, 263

Pitcairn 264

Pizarro, Francisco 146, 147

Pizarro, Pedro 146, 147

Poike ditch *see* Easter Island

Polynesia: TH's youthful interest in 18, 22, 29, *Plate 1*; plan to return to nature in 37–9, 41–3; *see also* Polynesian migration theories, and names of individual islands

Polynesia and America: written 145; manuscript of no interest in America 150–1, 156; revised as *American Indians in the Pacific* (*q.v.*) 185

Polynesian migration theories: TH's theory: conception and development 70–3, 74–5, 76–7, 79, 81, 91, 146–8; scholastic opposition to 76–7, 81, 150–1; academic disputes 197–217, 265–7, 268–74; growing recognition 203–6, 227, 274–6; *see also* balsa rafts

Prescott, William: quoted 201

Pre-Spanish Navigation off the Andean Coast quoted 148

Prix Bonaparte-Wyse 206

Puamau valley, Hiva Oa 61

Puka Puka 171

R.K.O. 179, 188, 189, 191

Raaby, Torstein: war exploits as 'Lt Pettersen' 129, 137, 138–40; joins *Kon-Tiki* crew 154, 158; on voyage 166, 167, 170, 172–3, 174–5, 175, 176, 176–7, *Plates 34–5*; later life and death 195, *Plate 38*

Ragnhild, Princess 106

Raivavae 264

Rand McNally and Company 183–4

Rano Raraku *see* Easter Island

Rapa Iti 264

Raroia 172–7, 178, 195

Rarotonga 176–7

Ray, Prof Verne 76

Reasin, Purea 189–91

Reed, Dr Erik: with TH on Galápagos Islands 220–1, 223, and in Ecuador 225–6; other refs 187

Retzius Gold Medal 204

Riiser-Larsen, Hjalmar 101

Rivet, Dr Paul 211, 213, 230, 265–6

Roggeveen, Jacob 242, 247

Rörholt, Lt Björn: with Norwegian forces in Great Britain 115, 116, 117; in Finnmark campaign 122, 124, 125, 126, *Plates 24–5*; in London and Kallax 136–8, 140; in Washington 154, 156, 158

Routledge, Katherine: *The Mystery of Easter Island* cited 241, 244, 253, quoted 241, 265; other refs 238

Royal Geographical Society, London 183, 212, 275–6

Royal Gold Medal 275–6

Royal Norwegian Academy of Science and Letters 205–6

Rulle 106–9
Russia: part in Finnmark campaign 122–5, 127, 129–31, 138; TH's academic visit 268–9
Russian Embassy, London 127–8, 129, 134
Rydén, Stig 200–1, 227

S.O.E. 117–9, 120–1, 136, *Plates 22–3*
St. Olav, Order of 206, 263–4
Samoa 177, 178; *see also* Polynesian migration theories
San Francisco 178
Santa Fé 186–7
Santiago Island 223–4
São Paulo Congress 230–1
Schjerven, Erling 151, 246
Schultz, Wilma 231–3, 236
Scientific American: quoted 267
Sea Routes to Polynesia 281
Sebastian, Father: on Easter Island traditions 246–7, 253, 254, 258; shows *Ana o Keke* caves 247–9; honoured by King Haakon 263–4; quoted 258; other refs 243, 245, 260, *Plate 50*
Second World War: outbreak 73, 75; invasion of Norway 80–1; Norway believed to have surrendered 82; Pearl harbour 97; D-Day 115–6; *see also* Finnmark campaign; Free Norwegian Forces; Norway
Selling, Prof Olof 203–4, 218, 254; quoted 204, 209; *Criticism of Kon-Tiki Criticisms* 204
Simmons, Dr R. T. 271–2
Simonsen, Yvonne Dedekam- *see* Heyerdahl, Yvonne
Skjölsvold, Arne: with TH on Galápagos 220–1, 223–4, in Ecuador 225–6, on Easter Island 241–2, 250, 257; joint author with TH of *Archaeological Evidence of Pre-Spanish Visits to the Galápagos Islands* 226; other refs 267
Skottsberg, Prof Carl 199–200; quoted 255–6
Smith, Prof Carlyle 242, 253, 257, 267, 271
Smith, Prof Kaj Birket- *see* Birket-Smith, Prof Kaj
South America *see* Polynesian migration theories; *see also* Brazil; Ecuador; Peru
South Sea islands *see* Polynesia
Southeast Asia *see* Polynesian migration theories
Spanish explorations: conquest of Peru 146–8; Galápagos Islands 218, 222
Special Operations Executive 117–9, 120–1, 136, *Plates 22–3*
Spinden, Dr Herbert 99, 150–1
Stabell, Lt Rolf: journey to Finnmark 122, 125, 126; in Finnmark 127, 136, 138–9, 141, *Plate 24*
Stamp, Prof Dudley 276
Stenersen, Björn 100–1, 102–3, 104
Stengaten *see* Larvik
Stockholms-Tidningen quoted 188
Stonehenge 119–20
Sun-Tici 147, 148
Svenska Dagbladet, Stockholm 202–3

Sweden: in Finnmark campaign 136–7, *see also* Kallax; early recognition of TH's work 182–3, 188, 203–4
Swedish Society for Anthropology and Geography 203, 204, 205, 274–5

Tahaoa beach *see* Fatu Hiva
Tahiti: TH visits 44–5; *Kon-Tiki* crew arrive at 177; in *Kon-Tiki* film 189
    Papeete 177, 178, 189; Papeno valley 44–5, 177; other refs 37, 50, 54, 60, 61, 195. *See also* Teriieroo, Chief; Reasin, Purea; Polynesian migration theories
Tahuata 60, 61
Takaroa 54–5
Takume reef 172
Tei Tetua: a cannibal 62; songs and legends 62–3 *Plate 13*, on Tiki 62, 64, 146; and modern warfare 121, 123, 279
Tereora 45–6, 54, 65
Teriieroo, Chief of Tahiti: welcomes TH to Tahiti 44–5, 177; other refs 47, 50, 55, 71, *Plate 7*
Thor I 177, 178, 179
Tiahuanaco: Spanish discoveries 147; Galápagos pottery typical of 225; TH visits 236–7; similarities of culture to Easter Island *see* Easter Island; *see also* Polynesian migration theories
Tiki: 'many gods' 52; Tei Tetua's legends of 62, 64, 146; *see also* Polynesian migration theories
Titicaca, Lake 147–8, 236–7; *see also* Tiahuanaco
Torp, Liv Coucheron *see* Heyerdahl, Liv
Trail, British Columbia: TH employed at *see* Consolidated Mining and Smelting Company; lecture at Rotary Club 90
Truman, President Harry S. 179, 184
Tuamotu Islands: Angatau 171–2; Puka Puka 171; Raroia 172–7, 178, 195; Takaroa 54–5; Takume reef 172
Tunsberg Castle 125, 126, 127, 136, 138
Turning Back Time in the South Seas 85, 90, 153
21-Club 179–80

U.S.S.R. *see* Russia
Uglevika (Owl's Creek) 20, 42, 189, 228
Ullstein Verlag 214–5
Ustaoset 20, 30

Vancouver: TH's arrival and research in 75–7; return to 81; stranded and penniless 82–5; other refs 89, 97
Vega Gold Medal 274–5, *Plate 43*
Victorin, Père 50, 54–6, 58–9
Vienna Congress: International Congress of Anthropologists and Ethnologists 212–5, 218; International Americanist Congress 215–6
Vienna Ethnographical Museum's year book 214–5
Vold, Gerd 159, 178

Washington: TH in before *Kon-Tiki* expedition 154–7, 158–9; Norwegian Embassy 96, 99, 154, 159; *Kon-Tiki* expedition's headquarters 159, 177, 178, 179

Watzinger, Herman: assists in U.S.A. with preparations for *Kon-Tiki* expedition 152, 153, 154, 154–5, 156; fells and transports balsa logs 157–8, 159, *Plates 30–1*; on voyage 165, 166, 167, 168, 170, 171, 174–5, 176, *Plate 34*; later life 194, *Plate 38*

Weckler, J. E.: quoted 148–9
Werenskiold, Prof Werner 37, 205
Wilhelm, Prof Ottmar 259
Wittmer, Heinz 221, 226
Wölfel, Prof Dominik 214
Wright, Sir Michael: quoted 275–6
Wright, Lady 228

Zambesi 131–4